DESIGN AND IMPLEMENTATION OF DATA MINING TOOLS

DESIGN AND IMPLEMENTATION OF DATA MINING TOOLS

M. Awad
Latifur Khan
Bhavani Thuraisingham
Lei Wang

CRC Press
Taylor & Francis Group
Boca Raton   London   New York

CRC Press is an imprint of the
Taylor & Francis Group, an **informa** business

AN AUERBACH BOOK

CRC Press
Taylor & Francis Group
6000 Broken Sound Parkway NW, Suite 300
Boca Raton, FL 33487-2742

First issued in paperback 2019

ISBN-13: 978-1-4200-4590-1 (hbk)
ISBN-13: 978-0-367-38555-2 (pbk)

Library of Congress Cataloging-in-Publication Data

Design and implementation of data mining tools / M. Awad ... [et al.].
    p. cm.
  Includes bibliographical references and index.
  ISBN 978-1-4200-4590-1 (hardcover : alk. paper)
  1. Data mining. I. Awad, M. (Mamoun)

QA76.9.D3D47145 2009
005.74--dc22
                                2009000519

Dedication

We dedicate this book to our respective families for
their support that enabled us to write this book

Contents

Preface

Introductory Remarks

Data mining is the process of posing queries to large quantities of data and extracting information, often previously unknown, using mathematical, statistical and machine learning techniques. Data mining has many applications in a number of areas including marketing and sales, Web and E-commerce, medicine, law, and manufacturing and, more recently, in national and cyber security. For example, using data mining one can uncover hidden dependencies between terrorist groups as well as possibly predict terrorist events based on past experience. Furthermore, one can apply data mining techniques for targeted markets to improve E-commerce. Data mining can be applied for multimedia applications including video analysis and image classification. Finally, data mining can be used in security applications such as suspicious event detection as well as detecting malicious software. This book focuses on three applications of data mining: cyber security, Web, and multimedia. In particular, we will describe the design and implementation of systems and tools for intrusion detection, Web-page surfing prediction, and for image classification.

We are writing two series of books related to data management, data mining, and data security. This book begins our second series of books, which describes techniques and tools in detail and is coauthored with faculty and students at the University of Texas at Dallas. It has evolved from the first series of books (authored by Bhavani Thuraisingham), which currently consists of eight books: Book 1 (*Data Management Systems Evolution and Interoperation*), discussing data management systems and interoperability; Book 2 (*Data Mining*), providing an overview of data mining concepts; Book 3 (*Web Data Management and E-Commerce*), discussing concepts in Web databases and E-commerce; Book 4 (*Managing and Mining Multimedia Databases*), discussing concepts in multimedia data management as well as text, image, and video mining; Book 5 (*XML, Databases, and the Semantic Web*), discussing high level concepts relating to the semantic Web; Book 6 (*Web Data Mining and Applications in Counter-Terrorism*) discussed how data mining may be applied for national security; Book 7, which is a textbook (*Database and Applications Security*) detailing data security; and Book 8, also a textbook (*Building Trustworthy Semantic Webs*), discussing how semantic Webs may be made secure. Our current book (which is the first book of Series Number Two) has evolved from Books 3, 4, 6, and 7 of Series Number One, and discusses data mining applications in intrusion detection, Web page surfing prediction, and image classification. It is based mainly on the research work carried out at the University of Texas at Dallas by Dr. Mamoun Awad for his Ph.D. thesis and Dr. Lei Wang for his Ph.D. thesis, together with their advisors, Professor Latifur Khan and Professor Bhavani Thuraisingham.

Background on Data Mining

As stated earlier, data mining is the process of posing various queries and extracting useful information, patterns, and trends, often previously unknown, from large quantities of data, possibly stored in databases. Essentially, for many organizations, the goals of data mining include improving marketing capabilities, detecting abnormal patterns, and predicting the future based on past experiences and current trends. There is clearly a need for this technology. There are large amounts of current and historical data being stored. Therefore, as databases become larger, it becomes increasingly difficult to support decision making. In addition, the data could be from multiple sources and multiple domains. There is a clear need to analyze the data to support planning and other functions of an enterprise.

Some of the data mining techniques include those based on statistical reasoning techniques, inductive logic programming, machine learning, fuzzy sets, and neural networks, among others. The data mining problems include classification (finding rules to partition data into groups), association (finding rules to make associations between data), and sequencing (finding rules to order data). Essentially, one arrives at some hypothesis, which is the information extracted from examples and patterns observed. These patterns are observed from posing a series of queries; each query may depend on the responses obtained to the previous queries posed.

Data mining is an integration of multiple technologies. These include data management such as database management, data warehousing, statistics, machine learning, decision support, and others such as visualization and parallel computing. There are a series of steps involved in data mining. These include getting the data organized for mining, determining the desired outcomes of mining, selecting tools for mining, carrying out the mining process, pruning the results so that only the useful ones are considered further, taking actions based on the mining, and evaluating the actions to determine benefits. There are various types of data mining. By this we do not mean the actual techniques used to mine the data, but what the outcomes will be. These outcomes have also been referred to as data mining tasks. These include clustering, classification anomaly detection, and forming associations.

While several developments have evolved, there are also many challenges. For example, due to the large volumes of data, how can the algorithms determine which technique to select, and what type of data mining to do? Furthermore, the data may be incomplete and/or inaccurate. At times there may be redundant information, and at times there may not be sufficient information. It is also desirable to have data mining tools that can switch to multiple techniques and support multiple outcomes. Some of the current trends in data mining include mining Web data, mining distributed and heterogeneous databases, and privacy-preserving data mining where one ensures that one can get useful results from mining and at the same time maintain the privacy of individuals.

Data Mining for Intrusion Detection

Data mining has applications in cyber security, which involves protecting the data in computers and networks. The most prominent application is in intrusion detection. For example, our computers and networks are being intruded by unauthorized individuals. Data mining techniques such as those for classification and anomaly detection are being used extensively to detect such unauthorized intrusions. For example, data about normal behavior is gathered and when something occurs out of the ordinary, it is flagged as an unauthorized intrusion. Normal behavior could be that John's computer is never used between 2 and 5 a.m. When John's computer is in use, say, at 3 a.m., then this is flagged as an unusual pattern.

Data mining is also being applied for other applications in cyber security such as auditing. Here, again, data on normal database access is gathered, and when something unusual happens, then this is flagged as a possible access violation. Data mining is also being used for biometrics. Here, pattern recognition and other machine learning techniques are being used to learn the features of a person and then to authenticate the person based on the features. In Part I of this book we will describe the design and implementation of a data mining tool for intrusion detection. In particular, we will discuss designs and performance results as well as the strengths and weaknesses of the approaches.

Data Mining for Web Page Prediction

Web page surfing prediction (which we also call WWW prediction or Web page prediction) is a key aspect of applications including E-commerce, knowledge management, and social network analysis, where Web searches need to be improved by giving advice and guidance to the Web surfer. WWW prediction is an important area upon which many applications improvements depend. These improvements include latency reduction, Web search, and personalization/recommendation systems. The applications utilize surfing prediction to improve their performance.

In Part III of the book, we study the WWW prediction problem, which is a multiclass problem, and present techniques to solve it. Such techniques are based on the generalization of binary classification. Specifically, we present one-vs-one and one-vs-all techniques.

We also introduce the problems and challenges in the WWW prediction problem. Briefly, in WWW prediction, the number of classes is very large. Hence, prediction accuracy is very low because conflicts between classifiers arise and choosing the correct label/class fails. Solutions to the WWW prediction as a multiclass problem are presented by studying a hybrid classification model to improve accuracy. Two powerful classification techniques, namely, Support Vector Machines (SVM) and the Markov model, are fused using Dempster's rule to increase the predictive accuracy. The Markov model is a powerful technique for predicting seen data; however, it cannot predict unseen data. On the other hand, SVM is a powerful technique, which can predict not only for the seen data, but also for the unseen data. In addition to the fusion mechanism, we utilize and extract domain knowledge for classifier reduction in order to reduce the conflicts among classifiers. We will introduce several classification algorithms, the multiclass problem, and hybrid models using Dempster's rule.

Data Mining for Image Classification

Data mining has been applied for multimedia data including text mining, image mining, video mining and, more recently, audio mining. Text mining may involve analyzing the documents and producing documents that have close associations. Image mining may involve analyzing the images for unusual patterns; video mining may involve analyzing video data to extract nuggets from a scene not visible in general. Audio mining may involve analyzing the audio data and determining who the speaker is.

Our work has focused on text and video as well as image mining. For example, we have analyzed surveillance videos to determine suspicious behavior. We have also analyzed documents to determine abnormal reports. Our image mining work has been fairly extensive. We have mined images to determine abnormal patterns such as new activities being carried out in the middle of a desert. Much of our research has also focused on image classification. Here we extract features from the images and determine the group to which the images belong.

In Part IV of the book we will describe the techniques that we have developed for image classification. We will describe models for image classification, approaches to image classification and annotations, and our experimental results

Organization of This Book

This book is divided into four parts. Part I, consisting of two chapters, provides some background information on data mining techniques and applications that have influenced our tools. Parts II, III, and IV describe our tools. Part II consists of four chapters and describes our tool for intrusion detection. Part III consists of three chapters and describes our tool for Web page surfing prediction. Part IV consists of four chapters and describes our tool for image classification.

Concluding Remarks

Data mining applications are exploding. Yet many of the books, including the authors' own, have discussed concepts at a high level. Some books have made the topic very theoretical. However, data mining approaches depend on nondeterministic reasoning as well as heuristics approaches. There is no book yet that shows, step by step, how data mining tools are developed. This book attempts to do just that.

We select three application areas: intrusion detection, Web page surfing prediction, and image classification. We describe step by step the systems we have developed for each of the three applications. We discuss performance results, unique contributions of the systems, and the limitations, as we see them. We believe that this is one of the few books that will help tool developers as well as technologists and managers. It describes algorithms as well as the practical aspects. For example, technologists can decide on the tools to select for a particular application. Developers can focus on alternative designs if an approach is not suitable. Managers can decide whether to proceed with a data mining project. It will be a very valuable reference guide to those in industry, government, and academia as it focuses both on concepts as well as practical techniques. Experimental results will also be given.

The book will also be used as a textbook at the University of Texas at Dallas by Dr. Khan and Dr. Thuraisingham, both of whom teach courses in data mining and data security. Dr. Awad is a professor at the University of United Arab Emirates and will be using this book in his classes. Dr. Wang is working for the Microsoft Corporation in data mining and will be teaching professional courses based on this book.

About the Authors

Mamoun Awad, Ph.D., joined the University of the United Arab Emirates in August 2006. He received his Ph.D. in software engineering at the University of Texas at Dallas in 2005 and was a postdoctoral research fellow also at the University of Texas at Dallas. His research interests are in data mining, software engineering, and information security. He has published papers in several journals and conferences including the *VLDB Journal*.

Latifur Khan, Ph.D., is an associate professor of computer science in the Erik Jonsson School of Engineering and Computer Science at the University of Texas at Dallas where he directs the data mining laboratory. He joined the university after completing his Ph.D. at the University of Southern California in 2000. His research interests are in multimedia data mining, geospatial data management, and information security. He has published over 50 papers in various journals and conferences including *IEEE Transactions on Systems, Man and Cybernetics* and the *VLDB Journal*.

Bhavani Thuraisingham, Ph.D., joined the University of Texas at Dallas (UTD) in October 2004 as a professor of computer science and director of the Cyber Security Research Center in the Erik Jonsson School of Engineering and Computer Science. She is an elected fellow of three professional organizations: the IEEE (Institute for Electrical and Electronics Engineers), the AAAS (American Association for the Advancement of Science), and the BCS (British Computer Society) for her work in data security. She received the IEEE Computer Society's prestigious 1997 Technical Achievement Award for "outstanding and innovative contributions to secure data management." Prior to joining UTD, Dr. Thuraisingham worked for the MITRE Corporation for 16 years, which included an IPA (Intergovernmental Personnel Act) at the National Science Foundation as Program Director for Data and Applications Security. Her work in information security and information management has resulted in more than 80 journal articles, more than 200 refereed conference papers, over 50 keynote addresses, and three U.S. patents. She is the author of eight books in data management, data mining, and data security.

Lei Wang, Ph.D., joined the Microsoft Corporation in January 2007 and is working in data mining. He received his Ph.D. in computer science at the University of Texas at Dallas in December 2006. His research interests are in image mining and multimedia information management. He has published papers in several journals and conferences including *Multimedia Tools* and *ACM Multimedia*.

Acknowledgments

We thank the administration of the University of Texas at Dallas for their support for our work. We also thank our colleagues for interesting discussions that have helped us in our work.

Chapter 1

Introduction

1.1 Trends

Data mining is the process of posing, querying, and extracting information that is often previously unknown from large quantities of data, using statistical and machine learning techniques. Over the past decade, tremendous progress has been made in data mining research and development, and now data mining is being taught as a mainstream subject in most universities around the world.

Although data mining techniques have improved during the past decade, advances have also taken place in building data mining tools based on a variety of techniques for numerous applications. These application areas include marketing and sales, healthcare, medical, financial, E-commerce, multimedia and, more recently, security. Data mining has evolved from multiple technologies, including data management, data warehousing, machine learning, and statistical reasoning; one of the major challenges in the development of data mining tools is to eliminate false positives and false negatives.

Our previous books have discussed various data mining technologies, techniques, tools, and trends. In our current book, however, our main focus is to explain the design and development as well as results obtained for the three tools that we have developed. These tools include one for intrusion detection, one for Web page surfing prediction, and one for image classification. They fall under the application areas of information security, Web, and multimedia. We are also developing numerous other data mining tools for cyber security and national security, including for malicious code detection, buffer overflow detection, fault detection, and surveillance. These tools will be discussed in forthcoming papers and books.

The organization of this chapter is as follows. First, we give an overview of data mining in Section 1.2. The tools that we will discuss in this book are briefly described in Sections 1.3, 1.4, and 1.5. These tools are used in data mining for intrusion detection, Web page surfing prediction, and image classification. The contents of this book will be summarized in Section 1.6. Next steps will be discussed in Section 1.7.

1.2 Data Mining Techniques and Applications

As stated in Section 1.1, development of data mining techniques has exploded over the past decade, and we now have tools and products for a variety of applications. In Part I of this book, we will discuss the data mining techniques that we will describe in this book and provide an overview of the applications we will discuss.

Data mining techniques include those based on machine learning, statistical reasoning, and mathematics. Some of the popular techniques include association rule mining, decision trees, and K-means clustering. Figure 1.1 illustrates the various data mining techniques.

Data mining has been used for numerous applications in several fields, including in healthcare, E-commerce, and security. We will focus on three applications: data mining for cyber security applications, Web, and multimedia.

1.3 Data Mining for Cyber Security: Intrusion Detection

As discussed earlier, data mining has many applications in the fields of national security and cyber security. For example, data mining techniques could be used

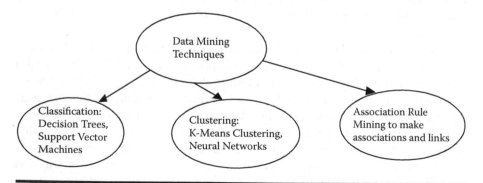

Figure 1.1 Data mining techniques.

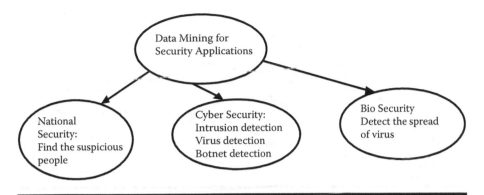

Figure 1.2   Data mining for security applications.

to determine suspicious behavior of individuals as well as to determine whether a computer system has been broken into or whether it has been infected by a virus. Figure 1.2 illustrates data mining applications in security.

We are developing several tools that apply data mining techniques to intrusion detection as well as malicious code detection. We are also applying data mining techniques to suspicious event detection. In this book, we will describe the design and development of one such tool, applying data mining for intrusion detection. Our tool will be described in Part II of the book.

1.4   Data Mining for Web: Web Page Surfing Prediction

Data mining has many applications in Web technologies, including E-commerce, knowledge management, and social networking. For example, data mining is being applied in targeted markets to predict behaviors of members of social groups. One key aspect of these applications is predicting the Web pages a user would traverse in order to give guidance to others, such as service providers. Figure 1.3 illustrates data mining applications in Web information management.

We are developing a number of data mining tools for Web applications, including social networking and knowledge management. These include developing tools for analyzing the interactions between users of a social group to determine if they are involved in any suspicious activity. In this book, we will describe one such tool, Web page surfing prediction. In particular, we use data mining techniques to determine the Web pages that a user is likely to traverse based on his or her past Web search patterns. Our tool will be described in detail in Part III of this book.

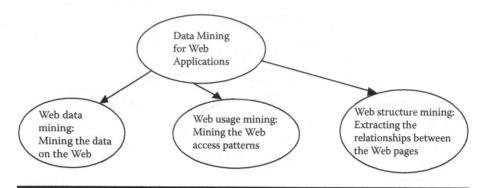

Figure 1.3 Data mining for Web applications.

1.5 Data Mining for Multimedia: Image Classification

Data mining has many applications in multimedia technologies, including mining text, images, voice, and video. For example, an agency may have to mine multimedia data to determine associations between words, images, or video clips. Much of the data on the Web is unstructured, including text, images, audios, and video. There is an urgent need to mine this data and make it more understandable to the user. Figure 1.4 illustrates data mining for multimedia applications.

We are developing a number of data mining tools for multimedia applications, including mining images, video, and text data. For example, we are mining reports describing software faults to determine whether one can extract patterns. We are also mining video data to determine suspicious behavior.

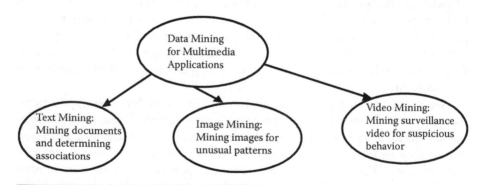

Figure 1.4 Data mining for multimedia applications.

We are mining images to determine whether there is any unusual activity. In this book, we will describe one such tool we have developed for image mining. One key aspect of image mining is classifying images. Our tool will classify images and carry out automatic annotations. This tool will be described in Part IV of this book.

1.6 Organization of This Book

This book is divided into four parts. Part I consists of two chapters, 2 and 3, and provides some background information in the data mining techniques and applications that have influenced our research and tools. Parts II, III, and IV describe our tools. Part II consists of four chapters, 4, 5, 6, and 7, and describes our tool for intrusion detection. In Chapter 4, we provide an overview of data mining for security applications. Our novel algorithms are discussed in Chapter 5. Data reduction techniques are discussed in Chapter 6. Performance results and analysis are given in Chapter 7.

Part III consists of four chapters, 8–11. It describes our tool for Web page surfing prediction. Chapter 8 describes Web data management and mining. Our hybrid model for Web page prediction is discussed in Chapter 9. Chapter 10 describes our algorithms. Chapter 11 describes our results. Part IV consists of five chapters, 12–16. Chapter 12 describes multimedia data management and mining. Chapter 13 describes models for classification. Chapter 14 describes models for image annotation. Chapter 15 describes subspace clustering algorithms, which are an aspect of image classification. Chapter 16 describes performance analysis.

The book concludes with Chapter 17. Appendix A provides an overview of data management and describes the relationship between our books. We have essentially developed a three-layer framework to explain the concepts in this book. This framework is illustrated in Figure 1.5. Layer 1 is the data mining techniques layer, Layer 2 is our tools layer, and Layer 3 is the applications layer. Figure 1.6 illustrates how Chapters 2–16 in this book are placed in the framework.

1.7 Next Steps

This chapter has provided an introduction to the book. We first provided a brief overview of data mining and then discussed the data mining techniques and applications we will discuss in this book. In particular, Chapters 2 and 3 discuss these techniques and applications. Then we provided a summary of the tools that we discuss in Parts II, III, and IV of this book. Finally, we described the organization of this book.

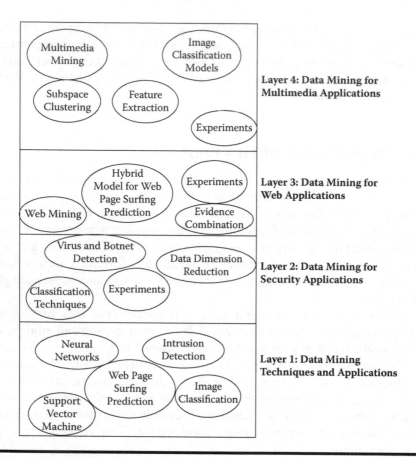

Figure 1.5   Framework for data mining tools.

This book enables a reader to become familiar with data mining concepts and understand how the techniques are applied step by step in real-world applications. One of the chief objectives of this book is to raise awareness of the importance of data mining for a variety of applications. This book could be used as a guide to building data mining tools.

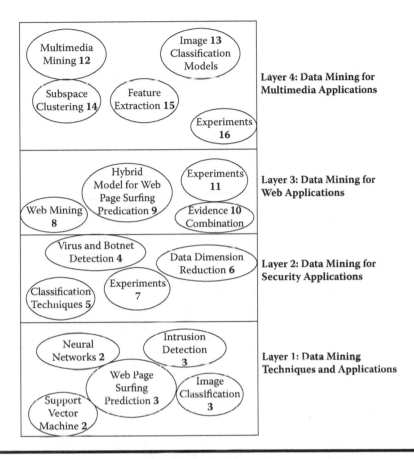

Figure 1.6   Contents of the book with respect to the framework.

We provide several references that can help the reader to understand the subtleties of the problems we investigate. Our advice to the reader is to keep up with the developments in data mining, become familiar with the tools and products, and apply them to a variety of applications. Then the reader will have a better understanding of the limitation of the tools and will be able to determine when new tools have to be developed.

Figure 1.5 Layout of the book with respect to the framework.

DATA MINING TECHNIQUES AND APPLICATIONS

Introduction to Part I

In this part of the book, we introduce some well-known techniques that are commonly used in data mining. Specifically, we present the Markov model, support vector machines, artificial neural networks, association rule mining, and the problem of multiclassification. These techniques were used in developing our tools, which will be described in Parts II, III, and IV. We have particularly utilized hybrid models to improve the prediction accuracy of data mining algorithms in three important applications, namely, intrusion detection, World Wide Web (WWW) prediction, and image classification.

Part 1 consists of Chapters 2 and 3. In Chapter 2, we discuss the various data mining techniques utilized in the development of our tools. In Chapter 3, we discuss the three application areas with which our data mining tools are concerned: intrusion detection, Web page surfing predictions, and image classification. The applications of these techniques will be our major focus in Parts II, III, and IV.

DATA MINING TECHNIQUES AND APPLICATIONS

Introduction to Part I

Chapter 2

Data Mining Techniques

2.1 Introduction

Data mining outcomes (also called *tasks*) include classification, clustering, forming associations, and detecting anomalies. Our tools have mainly focused on classification as the outcome, and we have developed classification tools. The classification problem is also referred to as *supervised learning*, in which a set of labeled examples is learned by a model, and then a new example with an unknown label is presented to the model for prediction.

There are many prediction models that have been used, such as the Markov model, decision trees, artificial neural networks (ANNs), support vector machines (SVMs), association rule mining (ARM), and many others. Each of these models has its strengths and weaknesses. However, there is a common weakness among all of these techniques, which is the inability to suit all applications. The reason that there is no such ideal or perfect classifier is that each of these techniques is initially designed to solve specific problems under certain assumptions.

In this chapter, we discuss the data mining techniques utilized in the development of our tools. Specifically, we present the Markov model, SVMs, ANNs, ARM, the problem of multiclassification, and image classification, which is an aspect of image mining. These techniques are also used in developing and comparing results in Parts II, III, and IV. In our research and development, we propose hybrid models to improve the predictive accuracy of data mining algorithms in various applications, namely, intrusion detection, WWW prediction, and image classification.

The organization of this chapter is as follows. In Section 2.2, we provide an overview of various data mining tasks and techniques. The techniques that are relevant to the contents of this book are discussed in Sections 2.2 through 2.6. In particular, neural networks, SVMs, Markov models, and ARM as well as some other classification techniques will be described. The chapter is summarized in Section 2.7.

2.2 Overview of Data Mining Tasks and Techniques

Before we discuss data mining techniques, we provide an overview of some of the data mining tasks (also known as *data mining outcomes*). Then we will discuss the techniques. In general, data mining tasks can be grouped into two categories: predictive and descriptive. Predictive tasks essentially predict whether an item belongs to a class or not. Descriptive tasks, in general, extract patterns from the examples. One of the most prominent predictive tasks is classification. In some cases, other tasks such as anomaly detection can be reduced to a predictive task such as whether a particular situation is an anomaly or not. Descriptive tasks, in general, include making associations and forming clusters. Therefore, classification, anomaly detection, making associations, and forming clusters are also thought to be data mining tasks.

Next, the data mining techniques can either be predictive, or descriptive, or both. For example, neural networks can perform classification as well as clustering. Classification techniques include decisions trees, SVMs, and memory-based reasoning. ARM techniques are used, in general, to make associations. Link analysis can also make associations between links and predict new links. Clustering techniques include *K*-means clustering. An overview of the data mining tasks (i.e., the outcomes of data mining) is illustrated in Figure 2.1. The techniques to be discussed in this book (e.g., neural networks, SVMs) are illustrated in Figure 2.2.

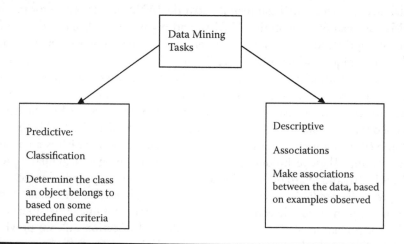

Figure 2.1 Data mining tasks.

Data Mining Techniques Utilized

Support Vector Machine

Neural Networks

Association Rule Mining

Decision Trees

Figure 2.2   Data mining techniques utilized in the tools.

2.3 Artificial Neural Networks

Artificial neural network (ANN) is a very well-known, powerful, and robust classification technique that has been used to approximate real-, discrete-, and vector-valued functions from examples [1]. It has been used in many areas such as interpreting visual scenes, speech recognition, and learning robot control strategies. An ANN simulates the human nervous system, which is composed of a large number of highly interconnected processing units (neurons) working together to produce our emotions and reactions. ANNs, similar to people, learn by example. The learning process in the human brain involves adjustments to the synaptic connections between neurons. Similarly, the learning process of ANNs involves adjustments to the node weights. Figure 2.3 presents a simple neuron unit, which is called a *perceptron*. The perceptron input, x, is a vector- or real-valued input, and w is the weight vector, in which its value is determined after training. The perceptron computes a linear combination of an input vector x as follows (Equation 2.1):

$$o(x_1,...,x_n) = \begin{cases} 1 \text{ if } w_0 + w_1 x_1 + \cdots + w_n x_n > 0 \\ -1 \text{ otherwise} \end{cases}$$ (2.1)

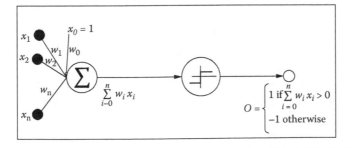

Figure 2.3   The perceptron.

Notice that w_i corresponds to the contribution of the input vector component x_i of the perceptron output. Also, in order for the perceptron to output a1, the weighted combination of the inputs ($\sum_{i=1}^{n} w_i x_i$) must be greater than the threshold w_0.

Learning the perceptron involves choosing values for the weights $w_0 + w_1 x_1 + \cdots + w_n x_n$. Initially, random weight values are given to the perceptron. Then, the perceptron is applied to each training example, updating the weights of the perceptron whenever an example is misclassified. This process is repeated many times until all training examples are correctly classified. The weights are updated according to the following rule (Equation 2.2):

$$\begin{cases} w_i = w_i + \delta w_i \\ \delta w_i = \eta(t - o)x_i \end{cases}$$
(2.2)

where η is a learning constant, o is the output computed by the perceptron, and t is the target output for the current training example.

The computational power of a single perceptron is limited to linear decisions. However, the perceptron can be used as a building block to construct powerful multilayer networks. In this case, a more complicated updating rule is needed to train the network weights. In this work, we employ an ANN consisting of two layers; each layer is composed of three building blocks (see Figure 2.4). We use the back-propagation algorithm for learning the weights. The back-propagation algorithm attempts to minimize the squared error function.

A typical training example in WWW prediction is $\langle [k_{t-\tau+1}, \ldots, k_{t-1}, k_t]^T, d \rangle$, where $[k_{t-\tau+1}, \ldots, k_{t-1}, k_t]^T$ is the input to the ANN, and d is the target Web page. Note that the input units of the ANN in Figure 2.5 are τ previous pages that the user has recently visited, where k is a Web page ID. The output of the network is a Boolean value, not a probability. We will see later how to approximate the probability of the output by fitting a sigmoid function after an ANN output.

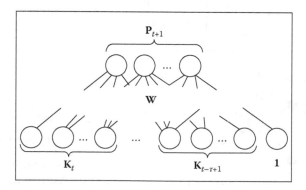

Figure 2.4　Artificial neural network.

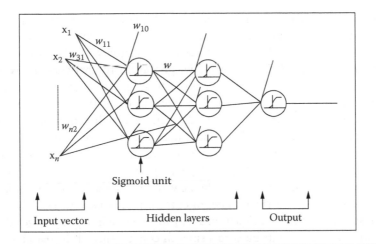

Figure 2.5   The design of ANN used in our implementation.

The approximated probabilistic output becomes $o' = f(o(I)) = p_{t+1}$, where I is an input session and $p_{t+1} = p(d \mid k_{t-\tau+1}, \ldots, k_t)$. We choose the sigmoid function (Equation 2.3) as a transfer function so that the ANN can handle nonlinearly separable dataset [1]. Note that in our ANN design (Figure 2.5), we use a sigmoid transfer function (Equation 2.3) in each building block. In Equation 2.3, I is the input to the network, O is the output of the network, W is the matrix of weights, and σ is the sigmoid function.

$$\begin{cases} o = \sigma\ (w \cdot I) \\ \sigma(y) = \dfrac{1}{1 + e^{-y}} \end{cases} \tag{2.3}$$

$$E(W) = \frac{1}{2} \sum_{k \in D} \sum_{i \in\ ouputs} (t_{ik} - o_{ik})^2 \tag{2.4}$$

$$\begin{cases} w_{ji} = w_{ji} + \delta w_{ji} \\ \delta w_{ji} = -\eta \dfrac{\partial E_d}{\partial w_{ji}} \end{cases} \tag{2.5}$$

$$\delta w_{ji}(n) = -\eta \frac{\partial E_d}{\partial w_{ji}} + \alpha \delta w_{ji}(n-1) \tag{2.6}$$

We implement the back-propagation algorithm for training the weights. It employs gradient descent to attempt to minimize the squared error between the network output values and the target values of these outputs. The sum of the error over all of the network output units is defined in Equation 2.4. In this equation, the *outputs* is the set of output units in the network, D is the training set, and t_{ik} and o_{ik} are the target and the output values associated with the *i*-th output unit and training example k. For a specific weight w_{ji} in the network, w_{ji} is updated for each training example as in Equation 2.5, where η is the learning rate and w_{ji} is the weight associated with the *i*-th input to the network unit j (for details, see [1]). As we can see from Equation 2.5, the search direction δw is computed using the gradient descent, which guarantees convergence toward a local minimum. To mitigate that, we add a momentum to the weight update rule such that the weight update direction $\delta w_{ji}(n)$ depends partially on the update direction in the previous iteration $\delta w_{ji}(n-1)$. The new weight update direction is shown in Equation 2.6, where n is the number of current iterations, and α is the momentum constant. Note that in Equation 2.6, the step size is slightly larger than that in Equation 2.5. This contributes to a smooth convergence of the search in regions where the gradient is unchanging [1].

In our implementation, we set the step size η dynamically based on the distribution of the classes in the dataset. Specifically, we set the step size to large values when updating the training examples that belong to low-distribution classes and vice versa. This is because when the distribution of the classes in the dataset varies widely (for example, a dataset might have 5% positive examples and 95% negative examples), the network weights converge toward the examples from the class of larger distribution, which causes a slow convergence. Furthermore, we adjust the learning rates slightly by applying the momentum constant, Equation 2.6, to speed up the convergence of the network [2].

2.4 Support Vector Machines

Support vector machines (SVMs) are learning systems that use a hypothesis space of linear functions in a high-dimensional feature space, trained with a learning algorithm from optimization theory. This learning strategy, introduced by Vapnik et al. [3], is a very powerful method that has been applied in a wide variety of applications. The basic concept in SVM is the hyperplane classifier, or linear separability. To achieve linear separability, SVM applies two basic ideas: margin maximization and kernels, that is, mapping input space to a higher-dimension space, feature space.

For binary classification, the SVM problem can be formalized as in Equation 2.7. Suppose we have N training data points $\{(x_1, y_1), (x_2, y_2), \dots, (x_N, y_N)\}$, where $x_i \in R^d$ and $y_i \in \{+1, -1\}$. We would like to find a linear separating hyperplane classifier as in Equation 2.8. Furthermore, we want this hyperplane to have the maximum separating margin with respect to the two classes (see Figure 2.6). The functional margin, or the margin for short, is defined geometrically as the Euclidean distance of the closest point from the decision boundary to the input space. Figure 2.7 gives

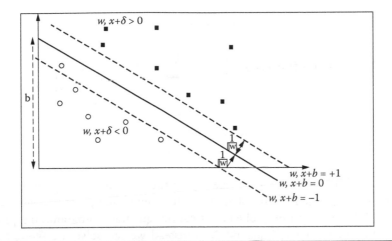

Figure 2.6 Linear separation in SVM.

an intuitive explanation of why margin maximization gives the best solution of separation. In Part A of Figure 2.7, we can find an infinite number of separators for a specific dataset. There is no specific or clear reason to prefer one separator over another. In Part B, we see that maximizing the margin provides only one thick separator. Such a solution proves to achieve the best generalization accuracy, that is, prediction for the unseen data [3–5].

$$\begin{cases} \text{minimize}_{(w,b)} \dfrac{1}{2} w^T w \\ \text{subject to } y_i(w \cdot x_i - b) \geq 1 \end{cases} \tag{2.7}$$

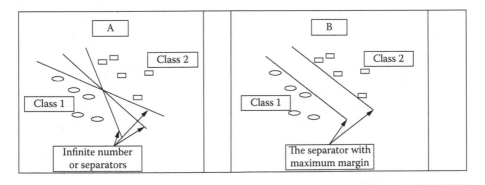

Figure 2.7 The SVM separator that causes the maximum margin.

$$f(x) = sign(w \cdot x - b) \tag{2.8}$$

$$\text{maximize } L(w, b, \alpha) = \frac{1}{2} w^T w - \sum_{i=1}^{N} \alpha_i y_i (w \cdot x_i - b) + \sum_{i=1}^{N} \alpha_i \tag{2.9}$$

$$f(x) = sign(wx - b) = sign\left(\sum_{i=1}^{N} \alpha_i y_i (x \cdot x_i - b)\right) \tag{2.10}$$

Note that Equation 2.8 computes the sign of the functional margin of point x in addition to the prediction label of x, that is, functional margin of x equals $wx - b$.

The SVM optimization problem is a convex quadratic programming problem (in w, b) in a convex set (Equation 2.7). Instead we can solve the Wolfe dual as in Equation 2.9 with respect to α, subject to the constraints that the gradient of $L(w, b, \alpha)$ with respect to the primal variables w and b vanish, and $\alpha_i \geq 0$. The primal variables are eliminated from $L(w, b, \alpha)$ (see [2] for more details). When we solve α_i, we can get $w = \sum_{i=1}^{N} \alpha_i y_i x_i$, and we can classify a new object x using Equation 2.10. Note that the training vectors occur only in the form of a dot product, and that there is a Lagrangian multiplier α_i for each training point, which reflects the importance of the data point. When the maximal margin hyperplane is found, only points that lie closest to it will have $\alpha_i > 0$, and these points are called *support vectors*. All other points will have $\alpha_i = 0$ (see Figure 2.8A). This means that only those points that lie closest to the hyperplane give the representation of the hypothesis or classifier. These most important data points serve as support vectors.

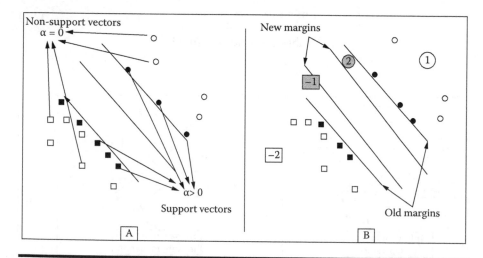

Figure 2.8 **(A) The values of support vectors and nonsupport vectors; (B) The effect of adding new data points on the margins.**

Their values can also be used to give an independent boundary with respect to the reliability of the hypothesis or classifier [6].

Figure 2.8A shows two classes and their boundaries (i.e., margins). The support vectors are represented by solid objects, whereas the empty objects are nonsupport vectors. Note that the margins are only affected by support vectors, that is, if we remove or add empty objects, the margins will not change. Meanwhile, any change in the solid objects, by either adding or removing objects, could change the margins. Figure 2.8B shows the effects of adding objects in the margin area. As we can see, adding or removing objects far from the margins, for example, data point 1 or −2, does not change the margins. However, adding or removing objects near the margins, for example, data point 2 and/or −1, has created new margins.

2.5 Markov Model

Some recent and advanced predictive methods for Web surfing have been developed using Markov models [7, 8]. For these predictive models, the sequences of Web pages visited by surfers are typically considered as Markov chains, which are then fed as input. The basic concept of the Markov model is that it predicts the next action depending on the result of previous action or actions. Actions can mean different things for different applications. For the purpose of illustration, we will consider actions specific to the WWW prediction application. In WWW prediction, the next action corresponds to prediction of the next page to be traversed. The previous actions correspond to the previous Web pages to be considered. Based on the number of previous actions considered, a Markov model can have different orders.

$$pr(P_k) = pr(S_k) \tag{2.11}$$

$$pr(P_2 \mid P_1) = pr(S_2 = P_2 \mid S_1 = P_1) \tag{2.12}$$

$$pr(P_N \mid P_{N-1}, ..., P_{N-k}) = pr(S_N = P_N \mid S_{N-1} = P_{N-1}, ..., S_{N-k} = P_{N-k}) \tag{2.13}$$

The zeroth-order Markov model is defined as the unconditional probability of the state (or Web page), Equation 2.11. In this equation, P_k is a Web page, and S_k is the corresponding state. The first-order Markov model, Equation 2.12, can be computed by taking page-to-page transitional probabilities or the n-gram probabilities of $\{P_1, P_2\}, \{P_2, P_3\}, \dots, \{P_{k-1}, P_k\}$.

In the following, we present an illustrative example of different orders of the Markov model, and how it can make predictions.

Example

Imagine a Web site consisting of six Web pages: P1, P2, P3, P4, P5, and P6. Suppose we have user sessions as in Table 2.1. Table 2.1 depicts the navigation of

Table 2.1 Collection of user sessions and their frequencies

Session	Frequency
P1,P2,P4	5
P1,P2,P6	1
P5,P2,P6	6
P5,P2,P3	3

many users of that Web site. Figure 2.9 shows the first-order Markov model, where the next action is predicted only on the basis of the last action performed, that is, last page traversed, by the user. States S and F correspond to the initial and final states, respectively. The probability of each transition is estimated by the ratio of the number of times the sequence of states was traversed and the number of times the anchor state was visited. Next to each arch in Figure 2.8, the first number is the frequency of that transition, and the second number is the transition probability. For example, the transition probability of the transition (P2–P3) is 0.2 because the number of times users traverse from page 2 to page 3 is 3, and the number of times page 2 is visited is 15 (i.e., 0.2 = 3/15).

Note that the transition probability is used to resolve prediction. For example, given that a user has already visited P2, the most probable page he or she visits next is P6. That is because the transition probability from P2 to P6 is the highest.

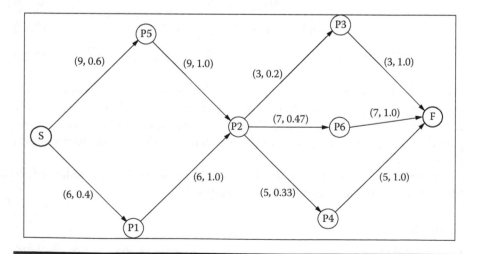

Figure 2.9   First-order Markov model.

Note that the transition probability might not be available for some pages. For example, the transition probability from P2 to P5 is not available because no user has visited P5 after P2. Hence, these transition probabilities are set to zero. Similarly, the k-th order Markov model is where the prediction is computed after considering the last k-th action performed by the users (Equation 2.13). In WWW prediction, the k-th-order Markov model is the probability of user visit to the P_k-th page given its previous $k - 1$ page visits.

Figure 2.10 shows the second-order Markov model that corresponds to Table 2.1. In the second-order model, we consider the last two pages. The transition probability is computed in a similar fashion. For example, the transition probability of the transition (P1, P2) to (P2, P6) is $0.16 = 1 \times 1/6$ because the number of times users traverse from state (P1, P2) to state (P2, P6) is 1, and the number of times pages (P1, P2) is visited is 6 (i.e., $0.16 = 1/6$). It is used for prediction. For example, given that a user has visited P1 and P2, he or she most probably visits P4 because the transition probability from state (P1, P2) to state (P2, P4) is greater than the transition probability from state (P1, P2) to state (P2, P6).

The order of the Markov model is related to the sliding window. The k-th order Markov model corresponds to a sliding window of size $K - 1$.

Note that there is another concept that is similar to the sliding window concept, which is number of hops. In this thesis, we use number of hops and sliding window interchangeably.

In WWW prediction, Markov models are built based on the concept of n-gram. The n-gram can be represented as a tuple of the form $\langle x_1, x_2, \ldots, x_n \rangle$ to depict sequences of page clicks by a population of users surfing a Web site. Each component of the n-gram takes a specific page ID value that reflects the surfing path of

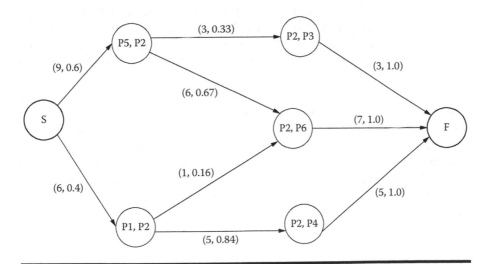

Figure 2.10   Second-order Markov model.

a specific user surfing a Web page. For example, the *n*-gram $\langle P_{10}, P_{21}, P_4, P_{12} \rangle$ for some user U states that the user U has visited the pages 10, 21, 4 and, finally, page 12 in a sequence.

2.6 Association Rule Mining (ARM)

Association rule is a data mining technique that has been applied successfully to discover related transactions. ARM finds the relationships among itemsets based on their co-occurrence in the transactions. Specifically, ARM discovers the frequent patterns (regularities) among those itemsets. For example, what are the items purchased together in a super store. In the following, we briefly introduce ARM. For more details, see [9, 10].

Assume we have *m* items in our database; define $I = \{i_1, i_2, \ldots, i_m\}$ as the set of all items. A transaction T is a set of items such that $T \subseteq I$. Let D be the set of all transactions in the database. A transaction T contains X if $X \subseteq T$ and $X \subseteq I$. An association rule is an implication of the form $X \rightarrow Y$, where $X \subset I$, $Y \subset I$, and $X \cap Y = \phi$. There are two parameters to consider a rule: confidence and support. A rule $R = X \rightarrow Y$ holds with confidence c if $c\%$ of the transactions of D that contain X also contain Y (i.e., $c = pr(Y \mid X)$). The rule R holds with support s if $s\%$ of the transactions in D contain X and Y (i.e., $s = pr(X, Y)$). The problem of mining association rules is defined as follows: Given a set of transactions D, we would like to generate all rules that satisfy a confidence and a support greater than a minimum confidence (σ), *minconf*, and minimum support (ϑ), *minsup*. Several efficient algorithms have been proposed to find association rules, such as AIS algorithm [9, 10], SETM algorithm [11], and AprioriTid [10].

In the case of Web transactions, we use association rules to discover navigational patterns among users. This would help to cache a page in advance and reduce the loading time of a page. Also, discovering a pattern of navigation helps in personalization. Transactions are captured from the clickstream data captured in Web server logs.

In many applications, the primary problem in using ARM concerns using global minimum support (*minsup*). Rare hits, that is, Web pages that are rarely visited, will not be included in the frequent sets because it will not achieve enough support. One solution is to have a very small support threshold; however, we will end up with a very large number of frequent itemsets, which is computationally hard to handle. Liu et al. [12] propose a mining technique that uses different support thresholds for different items. Specifying multiple thresholds allows rare transactions, which might be very important, to be included in the frequent itemsets. Other issues might arise, depending on the application itself. For example, in the case of WWW prediction, a session is recorded for each user. The session might have tens of clickstreams (and sometimes hundreds, depending on the duration of the session). Using each session as a transaction will not work because it is rare to find two sessions that are frequently repeated (i.e., identical); hence, it will not achieve even a very high support threshold, *minsup*. There is a need to break each session into many subsequences. One common method is to use a sliding window of size *w*. For example, suppose we use a sliding window $w = 3$ to break the session $S = \langle A, B, C, D, E, E, F \rangle$, then we will end up with the subsequences $S' = \{ \langle A, B, C \rangle, \langle B, C, D \rangle, \langle C, D, E \rangle, \langle D, E, F \rangle \}$. The total number of subsequences of a session S using window *w* is $length(S) - w$. To predict the next page in an active user session, we use a sliding window of the active session and ignore the previous pages. For example, if the current session is $\langle A, B, C \rangle$ and the user references page D, then the new active session becomes $\langle B, C, D \rangle$, using a sliding window 3. Note that page A is dropped, and $\langle B, C, D \rangle$ will be used for prediction. The rationale behind this is that because most users go back and forth while surfing the Web trying to find the desired information, it may be most appropriate to use the recent portions of the user history to generate recommendations or predictions [13].

Mobasher et al. [13] propose a recommendation engine that matches an active user session with the frequent itemsets in the database and predicts the next page the user most probably visits. The engine works as follows. Given an active session of size *w*, the engine finds all the frequent itemsets of length $w + 1$, satisfying some minimum support *minsup* and containing the current active session. Prediction for the active session A is based on the confidence (ψ) of the corresponding association rule. The confidence (ψ) of an association rule $X \rightarrow z$ is defined as $\psi(X \rightarrow z) = \sigma(X \cup z)/\sigma(X)$, where the length of z is 1. Page p is recommended or predicted for an active session A, iff

$$\forall V, R \text{ in the frequent itemsets,}$$

$$length(R) = length(V) = length(A) + 1 \wedge$$

$$R = A \cup \{p\} \wedge$$

$$V = A \cup \{q\} \wedge$$

$$\psi(A \rightarrow p) > \psi(A \rightarrow q)$$

The engine uses a cyclic graph called *frequent itemset graph*. The graph is an extension of the lexicographic tree used in the tree projection algorithm of [14]. The graph is organized in levels. The nodes in level *l* have itemsets of size of *l*. For example, the sizes of the nodes (i.e., the size of the itemsets corresponding to these nodes) in level 1 and 2 are 1 and 2, respectively. The root of the graph, level 0, is an empty node corresponding to an empty itemset. A node X in level *l* is linked to a node Y in level $l + 1$ if $X \subset Y$. To further explain the process, suppose we have the following sample Web transactions involving pages 1, 2, 3, 4, and 5 as in Table 2.2. The Apriori algorithm produces the itemsets as in Table 2.3, using a *minsup* = 0.49. The frequent itemset graph is shown in Figure 2.11.

Table 2.2   Sample Web transaction

Transaction ID	Items
T1	1,2,4,5
T2	1,2,5,3,4
T3	1,2,5,3
T4	2,5,2,1,3
T5	4,1,2,5,3
T6	1,2,3,4
T7	4,5
T8	4,5,3,1

Suppose we are using a sliding window of size 2, the current active session $A = \langle 2, 3 \rangle$. To predict/recommend the next page, we first start at level 2 in the frequent itemset graph and extract all the itemsets in level 3 linked to A. From Figure 2.11, the node {2, 3} is linked to {1, 2, 3} and {2, 3, 5} nodes with confidence,

$$\psi(\{2, 3\} \to 1) = \sigma(\{1, 2, 3\}/\sigma(\{2, 3\}) = 5/5 = 1.0$$

$$\psi(\{2, 3\} \to 5) = \sigma(\{2, 3, 5\}/\sigma(\{2, 3\}) = 4/5 = 0.8$$

and the recommended page is 1 because its confidence is larger. Note that, in recommendation engines, the order of the clickstream is not considered; that is, there is no distinction between a session $\langle 1, 2, 4 \rangle$ and $\langle 1, 4, 2 \rangle$. This is a disadvantage of

Table 2.3   Frequent itemsets generated by the Apriori algorithm

Size 1	Size 2	Size 3	Size 4
{2}(6)	{2,3}(5)	{2,3,1}(5)	{2,3,1,5}(4)
{3}(6)	{2,4}(4)	{2,3,5}(4)	
{4}(6)	{2,1}(6)	{2,4,1}(4)	
{1}(7)	{2,5}(5)	{2,1,5}(5)	
{5}(7)	{3,4}(4)	{3,4,1}(4)	
	{3,1}(6)	{3,1,5}(5)	
	{3,5}(5)	{4,1,5}(4)	
	{4,1}(5)		
	{4,5}(5)		
	{1,5}(6)		

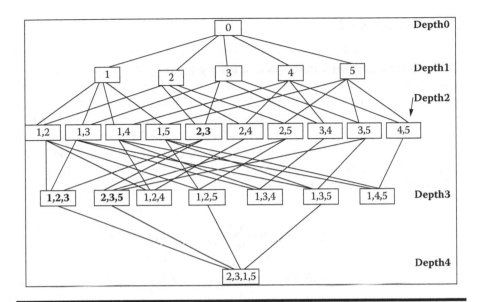

Figure 2.11 Frequent itemsets graph.

such systems because the order of pages visited might contain important information about the navigational patterns of users.

2.7 Multiclass Problem

Most classification techniques solve the binary classification problem. Binary classifiers are accumulated to generalize for the multiclass problem. There are two basic schemes for this generalization, namely, one-vs-one and one-vs-all. To avoid redundancy, we will present this generalization only for SVM.

2.7.1 One-vs-One

This approach creates a classifier for each pair of classes. The training set for each pair classifier (i, j) includes only those instances that belong to either class i or j. A new instance, x, belongs to the class upon which most pair classifiers agree. The prediction decision is quoted from the majority vote technique. There are $n(n-1)/2$ classifiers to be computed, where n is the number of classes in the dataset. It is evident that the disadvantage of this scheme is that we need to generate a large number of classifiers, especially if there are a large number of classes in the training set. For example, if we have a training set of 1,000 classes, we need 499,500 classifiers. On the other hand, the size of the training set for each classifier is small because we exclude all instances that do not belong to that pair of classes.

2.7.2 One-vs-All

It creates a classifier for each class in the dataset. The training set is preprocessed such that, for a classifier j, instances that belong to class j are marked as class (+1) and instances that do not belong to class j are marked as class (−1). In the one-vs-all scheme, we compute n classifiers, where n is the number of pages that users have visited (at the end of each session). A new instance, x, is predicted by assigning it to the class that its classifier outputs the largest positive value (i.e., maximal marginal) as in Equation 2.15. We can compute the margin of point x as in Equation 2.14. Note that the recommended or predicted page is the sign of the margin value of that page (see Equation 2.10).

$$f(x) = wx - b = \sum_{i}^{N} \alpha_i y_i (x \cdot x_i - b) \tag{2.14}$$

$$prediction(x) = \arg\max_{1 \le c \le M} f_c(x) \tag{2.15}$$

In Equation 2.15, M is the number of classes, $x = \langle x_1, x_2, \ldots, x_n \rangle$ is the user session, and f_i is the classifier that separates class i from the rest of the classes. The prediction decision in Equation 2.15 resolves to the classifier f_c that is the most distant from the testing example x. This might be explained as follows: f_c has the most separating power, among all other classifiers, of separating x from the rest of the classes.

The advantage of this scheme (one-vs-all), compared to the one-vs-one scheme, is that it has fewer classifiers. On the other hand, the size of the training set is larger for one-vs-all than for a one-vs-one scheme because we use the whole original training set to compute each classifier.

2.8 Image Mining

Along with the development of digital images and computer storage technologies, huge amounts of digital images are generated and saved every day. Applications of digital image have rapidly penetrated many domains and markets, including commercial and news media photo libraries, scientific and nonphotographic image databases, and medical image databases. As a consequence, we face the daunting problem of organizing and accessing these huge amounts of available images. An efficient image retrieval system is a prerequisite to finding images of specific entities from a database. The system expected can manage a huge collection of images efficiently, respond to users' queries with high speed, and deliver a minimum of irrelevant information (high precision), as well as ensuring that relevant information is not overlooked (high recall).

To generate such types of systems, people tried many different approaches. In the early 1990s, because of the emergence of large image collections, content-based image retrieval (CBIR) was proposed. CBIR computes relevance based on the similarity of visual content/low-level image features such as color histograms, textures, shapes, and spatial layout. However, the problem is that visual similarity is not semantic similarity. There is a gap between low-level visual features and semantic meanings. The so-called semantic gap is the major problem that needs to be solved for most CBIR approaches. For example, a CBIR system may answer a query request for a "red ball" with an image of a "red rose." If we undertake the annotation of images with keywords, a typical way to publish an image data repository is to create a keyword-based query interface addressed to an image database. If all images came with a detailed and accurate description, image retrieval would be convenient with current, powerful, pure text search techniques. These search techniques would retrieve the images if their descriptions/annotations contained some combination of the keywords specified by the user. However, the major problem is that most of the images are not annotated. It is a laborious, error-prone, and subjective process to manually annotate a large collection of images. Many images contain the desired semantic information, even though they do not contain the user-specified keywords. Furthermore, keyword-based search is useful especially to a user who knows what keywords are used to index the images and who can therefore easily formulate queries. This approach is problematic, however, when the user does not have a clear goal in mind, does not know what is in the database, and does not know what kind of semantic concepts are involved in the domain.

Image mining is a more challenging research problem than retrieving relevant images in CBIR systems. The goal of image mining is to find an image pattern that is significant for a given set of images and helpful in understanding the relationships between high-level semantic concepts/descriptions and low-level visual features. Our focus is on aspects such as feature selection and image classification.

2.8.1 Feature Selection

Usually, data saved in databases is with well-defined semantics such as numbers or structured data entries. In comparison, data with ill-defined semantics is unstructured data. For example, images, audio, and video are data with ill-defined semantics. In the domain of image processing, images are represented by derived data or features such as color, texture, and shape. Many of these features have multiple values (e.g., color histogram, moment description). When people generate these derived data or features, they usually generate as many features as possible because they are not aware which feature is more relevant. Therefore, the dimensionality of derived image data is usually very high. Actually, some of the selected features might be duplicated or may not even be relevant to the problem. Including irrelevant or duplicated information is referred to as *noise*. Problems that involve mining datasets that contain a large number of features suffer from the so-called *curse of dimensionality*. Feature selection is the research topic for finding an optimal subset of features. In this dissertation, we will discuss this problem and feature selection in detail.

We developed a wrapper-based simultaneous feature-weighting and clustering algorithm. A clustering algorithm will bundle similar image segments together and generate a finite set of visual symbols (i.e., blob token). Based on histogram analysis and chi-square value, we assign features of image segments different weights instead of removing some of them. Feature weight evaluation is wrapped in a clustering algorithm. In each iteration of the algorithm, feature weights of image segments are reevaluated on the basis of the clustering result. The reevaluated feature weights will affect the clustering results in the next iteration.

2.8.2 Automatic Image Annotation

Automatic Image Annotation is research concerned with object recognition, which is aimed at recognizing objects in an image and generating descriptions for it according to the semantics of the objects. If it is possible to produce accurate and complete semantic descriptions for an image, we can store descriptions in an image database. Based on a textual description, more functionality (e.g., browse, search, and query) of an image DBMS could be implemented easily and efficiently by applying many existing text-based search techniques. Unfortunately, the automatic image annotation problem has not been solved in general, and perhaps this problem is impossible to solve.

However, in certain subdomains, it is still possible to obtain some interesting results. Many statistical models have been published for image annotation. Some of these models took feature dimensionality into account and applied singular value decomposition (SVD) or principle component analysis (PCA) to reduce dimension. However, none of them considered feature selection or feature weight. We proposed a new framework for image annotation based on a translation model (TM). In our approach, we applied our weighted feature selection algorithm and embedded it in an image annotation framework. Our weighted feature selection algorithm improves the quality of visual tokens and generates better image annotations.

2.8.3 Image Classification

Image Classification is an important area, especially in the medical domain, because it helps manage large medical image databases and has great potential for diagnostic aid in a real-world clinical setting. We describe our experiments for the image CLEF (Cross Language Evalvation Forum) medical image retrieval task. Sizes of classes of CLEF medical image dataset are not balanced, which is a really serious problem for all classification algorithms. To solve this problem, we resample data by generating subwindows. K-nearest-neighbor (KNN) algorithm, distance-weighted KNN, fuzzy KNN, nearest-prototype classifier, and evidence-theory-based KNN are implemented and studied. Results show that evidence-based KNN has the best performance based on classification accuracy.

2.9 Summary

In this chapter, we first provided an overview of the various data mining tasks and techniques, and then discussed some of the techniques that we will utilize in this book. These include neural networks, SVMs, and ARM.

Numerous data mining techniques have been designed and developed, and many of them are being utilized in commercial tools. Several of these techniques are variations of some of the basic classification, clustering, and ARM techniques. One of the major challenges today is to determine the appropriate techniques for various applications. We still need more benchmarks and performance studies. In addition, the techniques should result in fewer false positives and negatives. Although there is still much to be done, the progress achieved over the last decade is extremely promising.

References

1. Mitchell, T.M., *Machine Learning*, McGraw Hill, New York, 1997, Chap. 4.
2. Cristianini, N. and Shawe-Taylor, J., *Introduction to Support Vector Machines*, 1st ed., Cambridge University Press, Cambridge, 2000, pp. 93–122.
3. Vapnik, V.N., *The Nature of Statistical Learning Theory*, 1st ed., Springer-Verlag, New York, 1995.
4. Vapnik, V.N., *Statistical Learning Theory*, Wiley, New York, 1998.
5. Vapnik, V.N., *The Nature of Statistical Learning Theory*, 2nd ed., Springer-Verlag, New York, 1999.
6. Bartlett, P. and Shawe-Taylor, J., Generalization performance of support vector machines and other pattern classifiers, *Advances in Kernel Methods—Support Vector Learning*, MIT Press, Cambridge, MA, 1999, pp. 43–54.
7. Yang, Q., Zhang, H., and Li, T., Mining Web logs for prediction models in WWW caching and prefetching, in *The 7th ACM SIGKDD International Conference on Knowledge Discovery and Data Mining KDD*, San Francisco, CA, August 26–29, 2001, pp. 473–478.
8. Pirolli, P., Pitkow, J., and Rao, R., Silk from a sow's ear: Extracting usable structures from the Web, in *Proceedings of the 1996 Conference on Human Factors in Computing Systems (CHI-96)*, Vancouver, British Columbia, Canada, 1996, pp. 118–125.
9. Agrawal, R., Imielinski, T., and Swami, A., Mining Association rules between sets of items in large database, in *Proceedings of the ACM SIGMOD Conference on Management of Data*, Washington, DC., May 1993, pp. 207–216.
10. Agrawal, R. and Srikant, R., Fast algorithms for mining association rules in large database, in *Proceedings of the 20th International Conference on Very Large Data Bases*, San Francisco, CA, 1994, pp. 487–499.
11. Houtsma, M. and Swanu, A., Set-oriented mining of association rules in Relational Databases, in *Proceedings of the 11th International Conference on Data Engineering*, Washington, D.C., 1995, pp. 25–33.
12. Liu, B., Hsu, W., and Ma, Y., Association rules with multiple minimum supports, in *Proceedings of the 5th ACM SIGKDD International Conference on Knowledge Discovery and Data Mining*, San Diego, CA, 1999, pp. 337–341.

13. Mobasher, B., Dai, H., Luo, T., and Nakagawa, M., Effective personalization based on association rule discovery from Web usage data, in *Proceedings of the ACM Workshop on Web Information and Data Management (WIDM01)*, 2001, pp. 9–15.
14. Agrawal, R., Aggarawal, C., and Prasad, V., A tree projection algorithm for generation of frequent item sets, *Journal of Parallel and Distributed Computing archive*, Vol. 61, Issue 3, 350–371, 2001, Orlando, FL.

Chapter 3

Data Mining Applications

3.1 Introduction

Data mining is an important technology that has been integrated in many industrial, governmental, and academic applications. It is defined as the process of analyzing and summarizing data in order to uncover new knowledge. Data mining maturity depends on other areas such as data management, artificial intelligence, statistics, and machine learning.

In this book, we concentrate mainly on the classification problem. We apply classification in three critical applications, namely, intrusion detection, World Wide Web (WWW) prediction, and image classification. Specifically, we strive to improve performance (time and accuracy) by incorporating multiple (two or more) learning models. In intrusion detection, we try to improve the training time, whereas in WWW prediction, we study hybrid models to improve the prediction accuracy. The classification problem is also sometimes referred to as *supervised learning*, in which a set of labeled examples is learned by a model, and then a new example with unknown labels is presented to the model for prediction.

Many prediction models have been used, such as the Markov model, decision trees, artificial neural networks (ANNs), support vector machines (SVMs), association rule mining (ARM), and many others. Each of these models has its strengths and weaknesses. However, they have a common weakness, which is the inability to suit all applications. There is no such ideal or perfect classifier because each of these techniques was initially designed to solve specific problems under certain assumptions.

There are two considerations in designing data mining techniques: model complexity and performance. In model complexity, new data structures, training-set reduction techniques, or small numbers of adaptable parameters are proposed in order to simplify computations during learning without compromising the prediction accuracy. In model performance, the goal is to improve the prediction accuracy with some complication of the design or model. It is evident that there is a trade-off between the performance complexity and the model complexity. In this book, we present studies of hybrid models to improve the prediction accuracy of data mining algorithms in two important applications, namely, intrusion detection and WWW prediction.

Intrusion detection involves processing and learning a large number of examples in order to detect intrusions. Such a process becomes computationally costly and impractical when the number of records to train against grows dramatically. Eventually, this limits our choice of which data mining technique to apply. Powerful techniques, such as SVM, will be avoided because of the algorithm's complexity. We propose a hybrid model based on SVM and clustering analysis to overcome this problem. The idea is to apply a reduction technique using clustering analysis to approximate support vectors in order to speed up the training process of SVM. We propose a method, namely, *clustering-trees-based SVM* (CT-SVM), to reduce the training set and approximate the support vectors. We exploit clustering analysis to generate support vectors to improve the accuracy of the classifier.

Surfing prediction is another important research area on which many application improvements depend. Applications such as latency reduction, Web search, and recommendation systems utilize surfing prediction to improve their performance. There are several challenges to be met in this area. They include low accuracy rate [1], sparsity of the data [2, 3], large number of labels that makes it a complex multiclass problem [4], and not fully utilizing the domain knowledge. Our goal is to improve predictive accuracy by combining several powerful classification techniques, namely, SVMs, ANNs, and Markov model. Markov model is a powerful technique for predicting seen data; however, it cannot predict unseen data. On the other hand, techniques such as SVM and ANN are powerful predictors and can predict not only the seen data but also the unseen data. However, when dealing with a large number of classes/labels or when there is a possibility that one instance may belong to many classes, predictive power may decrease. We use Dempster's rule to fuse the prediction outcomes of these models. Such fusion combines the best of different models and achieves the best accuracy over the individual models.

In this chapter, we discuss the three applications we have considered in our book, as illustrated in Figure 3.1. In Section 3.2, we discuss intrusion detection. WWW surfing prediction is discussed in Section 3.3. Image classification is discussed in Section 3.4. More details about broader applications of data mining such as data mining for security applications, Web data mining, and image or multimedia data mining will be discussed in Chapters 4, 8, and 12, respectively.

Data Mining Applications

Intrusion detection
Web usage analysis
Image analysis
Customer relationship management
Detecting abnormal behavior
Targeted marketing

Figure 3.1   Data mining applications.

3.2   Intrusion Detection

Security and defense networks, proprietary research, intellectual property, and data-based market mechanisms, which depend on untrammeled access, can all be severely compromised by intrusions. We need to find the best way to protect such systems.

An intrusion can be defined [5, 6] as "any set of actions that attempts to compromise the integrity, confidentiality, or availability of a resource." User authentication (e.g., using passwords or biometrics), avoidance of programming errors, and information protection (e.g., encryption) have all been used to protect computer systems. As systems become more complex, there arise weaknesses due to design and programming errors that can be exploited through the use of various "socially engineered" penetration techniques. For example, exploitable "buffer overflow" still exists in some recent system software because of programming errors. Elements central to intrusion detection are resources to be protected in a target system, that is, user accounts, file systems, and system kernels; models that characterize the normal or legitimate behavior of these resources; and techniques that compare the actual system activities with the established models, identifying those that are abnormal or intrusive. In pursuit of a secure system, different measures of system behavior have been proposed, based on an ad hoc presumption that normalcy and anomaly (or illegitimacy) will be accurately manifested in the chosen set of system features.

Intrusion detection attempts to detect computer attacks by examining various data records observed through processes on the same network. Such attacks are split into two categories: host-based attacks [5, 7, 8] and network-based attacks [9–11]. Host-based attacks target a machine and try to gain access to privileged services or resources on that machine. Host-based detection usually uses routines that obtain system call data from an audit process, which tracks all system calls made on behalf of each user.

Network-based attacks make it difficult for legitimate users to access various network services by deliberately occupying or sabotaging network resources and services. This can be done by sending large amounts of network traffic, exploiting well-known faults in networking services, and overloading network hosts.

Network-based attack detection uses network traffic data (i.e., tcpdump) to look at traffic addressed to the machines being monitored. Intrusion detection systems are split into two groups: anomaly detection systems and misuse detection systems. Anomaly detection is the attempt to identify malicious traffic based on deviations from established normal network traffic patterns [11, 12]. Misuse detection is the ability to identify intrusions based on a known pattern for malicious activity [9, 10]. Such known patterns are referred to as *signatures*. Anomaly detection is capable of catching new attacks. However, new legitimate behavior can also be falsely identified as an attack, resulting in a false positive. Our research focuses on network-level systems. A significant challenge in data mining is to reduce false negative and false positive rates. However, we also need to develop a realistic intrusion detection system.

SVM is one of the most successful classification algorithms in the data mining area, but its long training time limits its use. Many applications, such as data mining for bioinformatics and geoinformatics, require the processing of huge datasets. The training time of SVM is a serious obstacle in the processing of such datasets. According to [13], it would take years to train SVM on a dataset consisting of 1 million records. Many proposals have been submitted to enhance SVM to increase its training performance [14, 15], either through random selection or approximation of the marginal classifier [16]. However, such approaches are still not feasible with large datasets, where even multiple scans of the entire dataset are too expensive to perform or result in the loss, through oversimplification, of any benefit to be gained through the use of SVM [13].

In Part II of this book, we propose a new approach for enhancing the training process of SVM when dealing with large training datasets. It is based on a combination of SVM and clustering analysis. The idea is as follows: SVM computes the maximal margin separating data points; hence, only those patterns closest to the margin can affect the computations of that margin, whereas other points can be discarded without affecting the final result. Those points lying close to the margin are called *support vectors* (see Chapter 2 for more details). We try to approximate these points by applying clustering analysis.

In general, using hierarchical clustering analysis based on a dynamically growing self-organizing tree (DGSOT) involves expensive computations, especially if the set of training data is large. However, in our approach, we control the growth of the hierarchical tree by allowing tree nodes (support vector nodes) close to the marginal area to grow, while halting the distant ones. Therefore, the computations involved in SVM and further clustering analysis will be reduced dramatically. Also, to avoid the cost of computations involved in clustering analysis, we train SVM on the nodes of the tree after each phase or iteration, in which few nodes are added to the tree. Each iteration involves growing the hierarchical tree by adding new child nodes to the tree. This could cause a degradation in the accuracy of the resulting classifier. However, we use the support vector set as a priori knowledge to instruct the clustering algorithm to grow support vector nodes and to stop growing nonsupport vector nodes. Thus, the accuracy of the classifier improves, and the size of the training set is kept to a minimum.

We report results here using one benchmark dataset—the 1998 DARPA dataset [17]. Also, we compare our approach with Rocchio bundling algorithm, proposed for classifying documents by reducing the number of data points [18]. Note that the Rocchio bundling method reduces the number of data points before feeding them as support vectors to SVM for training. On the other hand, our clustering approach is intertwined with SVM. We have observed that our approach outperforms pure SVM and the Rocchio bundling technique in terms of accuracy, FP rate, FN rate, and processing time.

Our contributions to intrusion detection are as follows:

1. We propose a new support vector selection technique using clustering analysis to reduce the training time of SVM. Here, we combine clustering analysis and SVM training phases.
2. We show analytically the degree to which our approach is asymptotically quicker than pure SVM, and validate this claim with experimental results.
3. We compare our approach with random selection and Rocchio bundling on a benchmark dataset, and demonstrate impressive results in terms of training time, FP rate, FN rate, and accuracy.

3.3 Web Page Surfing Prediction

Surfing prediction is an important research area on which many application improvements depend. Applications such as latency reduction, Web search, and personalization systems utilize surfing prediction to improve their performance. Latency of viewing with regard to Web documents is an early application of surfing prediction. Web caching and prefetching methods are developed to prefetch multiple pages for improving the performance of WWW systems. The fundamental concept behind all these caching algorithms is the ordering of various Web documents using some ranking factors, such as the popularity and size of the document according to existing knowledge. Prefetching the highest-ranking documents results in a significant reduction of latency during document viewing [19–23].

Improvements in Web search engines can also be achieved using predictive models. Surfers can be viewed as having traversed the entire WWW link structure. The distribution of visits over all WWW pages is computed and used for reweighting and reranking results. Surfer path information is considered more important than the text keywords entered by the surfers; hence, the more accurate the predictive models, the better the search results [24].

In recommendation systems, collaborative filtering (CF) has been applied successfully to find the k top users having the same tastes or interests based on a given target user's records [3]. The *k*-nearest-neighbor (KNN) approach is used to compare a user's historical profile and records with the profiles of other users to find the top *k* similar users. Using ARM, Mobasher et al. [25] propose a method that matches an active user session with frequent itemsets and predicts the next page the user is likely to visit. These CF-based techniques suffer from very well-known limitations, including scalability and efficiency [25, 26]. Pitkow and Pirolli [1] explore pattern extraction and pattern matching based on a Markov model that predicts future surfing paths. Longest repeating subsequences (LRS) is proposed to reduce the model complexity (not predictive accuracy) by focusing on significant surfing patterns.

There are several problems with the current state-of-the-art solutions. First, the predictive accuracy using a proposed solution such as a Markov model is low; for example, the maximum training accuracy is 41% [1]. Second, prediction using ARM and LRS pattern extraction is done based on choosing the path with highest probability in the training set; hence, any new surfing path is misclassified because the probability of such a path occurring in the training set is zero. Third, the sparse nature of user sessions used in training can result in unreliable predictors [2, 3]. Finally, many of the previous methods have ignored domain knowledge as a means of improving prediction. Domain knowledge plays a key role in improving the predictive accuracy because it can be used to eliminate irrelevant classifiers during prediction or reduce their effectiveness by assigning them lower weights.

WWW prediction is a multiclass problem, and prediction can resolve into many classes. Most multiclass techniques, such as one-vs-one and one-vs-all, are based on binary classification. Prediction is required to check any new instance against all classes. In WWW prediction, the number of classes is very high (11,700 classes in our experiments). Hence, prediction accuracy is very low [4] because the method fails to choose the right class. For a given instance, domain knowledge can be used to eliminate irrelevant classes.

We use several classification techniques, namely, SVM, ANN, ARM, and Markov model, in WWW prediction. We propose a hybrid prediction model by combining two or more of them using Dempster's rule. The Markov model is a powerful technique for predicting seen data; however, it cannot predict unseen data. On the other hand, SVM is a powerful technique that can predict not only the seen data but also the unseen data. However, when dealing with too many classes or when there is a possibility that one instance may belong to many classes (e.g., a user after visiting the Web pages p1, p2, and p3 might go to page 10, whereas another might go to page 100), SVM predictive power may decrease because such examples confound the training process. To overcome these drawbacks with SVM, we extract domain knowledge from the training set and incorporate this knowledge in the testing set to improve prediction accuracy of SVM by reducing the number of classifiers during prediction.

ANN is also a powerful technique, which can predict not only the seen data but also the unseen data. Nonetheless, ANN has similar shortcomings as SVM when dealing with too many classes or when there is a possibility that one instance may belong to many classes. Furthermore, the design of ANN becomes complex with a large number of input and output nodes. To overcome these drawbacks with ANN, we employ domain knowledge from the training set and incorporate this knowledge in the testing set by reducing the number of classifiers consulted during prediction. This improves the prediction accuracy and reduces the prediction time.

Our contributions to WWW prediction are as follows:

1. We overcome the drawbacks of SVM and ANN in WWW prediction by extracting and incorporating domain knowledge in prediction to improve accuracy and prediction time.
2. We propose a hybrid approach for prediction in WWW. Our approach integrates different combinations of prediction techniques, namely, SVM, ANN, and Markov model, using Dempster's rule [27] to improve accuracy.
3. We compare our hybrid model with different approaches, namely, Markov model, ARM, ANN, and SVM on a standard benchmark dataset, and demonstrate the superiority of our method.

3.4 Image Classification

Image classification is about determining the class an image belongs to. It is an aspect of image data mining. Other image data mining outcomes include determining anomalies in images in the form of change detection as well as clustering images. In some situations, making links between images may also be useful. One key aspect of image classification is *image annotation*. Here, the system understands thaw images and automatically annotates them. The annotation is essentially a description of the images.

Our contributions to image classification include the following:

1. We present a new framework of automatic image annotation.
2. We propose a dynamic feature weighting algorithm based on histogram analysis and chi-square distribution.
3. We present an image resampling method to solve the imbalanced data problem.
4. We present a modified KNN algorithm based on evidence theory.

In our approach, we first annotate images automatically. In particular, we utilize K-means clustering algorithms to cluster image blobs, and then make a correlation between the blobs and words. This will result in annotating images. Our research has also focused on classifying images using ontologies for geospatial data. Here, we classify images using a region-growing algorithm and then use high-level concepts in the form of homologies to classify the regions.

3.5 Summary

In this chapter, we have discussed three applications that we will consider in this book. We have developed data mining tools for these three applications. They are intrusion detection, Web page surfing prediction, and image classification, which are part of the broader classes of applications: cyber security, Web information management, and multimedia or image information management, respectively. These broader classes of applications will be discussed in future chapters. Each part of this book will focus on one application. Part II will describe our data mining tool for intrusion detection. Part III will describe our data mining tool for Web page surfing prediction. Part IV will describe our data mining tool for image classification.

Future directions will focus on two aspects. One direction is enhancing the data mining algorithms to address limitations such as reducing false positives and negatives as well as reasons for uncertainty. Another direction of research is to apply our new techniques in data mining to broader classes of applications such as search engines and medicine data sets.

References

1. Pitkow, J. and Pirolli, P., Mining longest repeating subsequences to predict World Wide Web surfing, in *Proceedings of the 2nd USENIX Symposium on Internet Technologies and Systems (USITS'99)*, Boulder, CO, October 1999, pp. 139–150.
2. Grcar, M., Fortuna, B., Mladenic, D., *k*NN versus SVM in the collaborative filtering framework, *WebKDD '05*, August 21, Chicago, IL.
3. Burke, R., Hybrid Recommender systems: Survey and experiments, *User Modeling and User-Adapted Interaction*, Vol. 12, No. 4, 331–370, 2002.
4. Chung, V., Li, C.H., and Kwok, J., Dissimilarity learning for nominal data, *Pattern Recognition*, Vol. 37, No. 7, 1471–1477, 2004.
5. Axelsson, S., Research in Intrusion Detection Systems: A Survey, Technical Report TR 98-17 (revised in 1999), Chalmers University of Technology, Goteborg, Sweden, 1999.
6. Debar, H., Dacier, M., and Wespi, A., A Revised taxonomy for intrusion detection systems, *Annales des Telecommunications*, Vol. 55, No. 7–8, 361–378, 2000.
7. Anderson, D., Frivold, T., and Valdes, A., Next-generation intrusion detection expert system (NIDES): A summary, Technical Report SRI-CSL-95-07, Computer Science Laboratory, SRI International, Menlo Park, CA, May 1995.
8. Freeman, S., Bivens, A., Branch, J., and Szymanski, B., Host-based intrusion detection using user signatures, in *Proceedings of the Research Conference*, RPI, Troy, NY, October 2002.
9. Ilgun, K., Kemmerer, R.A., and Porras, P.A., State transition analysis: A rule-based intrusion detection approach, *IEEE Transactions on Software Engineering*, Vol. 21, No. 3, 181–199, 1995.

10. Marchette, D., A statistical method for profiling network traffic, *First {USENIX} Workshop on Intrusion Detection and Network Monitoring*, Santa Clara, CA, 1999, pp. 119–128.
11. McCanne, S., Leres, C., and Jacobson, V., libcap, available via anonymous ftp at ftp:// ftp.ee.lbl.gov/, 1989.
12. Mukkamala, S., Janoski, G., and Sung, A., Intrusion detection: support vector machines and neural networks, in *Proceedings of IEEE International Joint Conference on Neural Networks (ANNIE)*, St. Louis, MO, 2002, pp. 1702–1707.
13. Yu, H., Yang, J., and Han, J., Classifying large data sets using SVM with hierarchical clusters, *SIGKDD 2003*, August 24–27, 2003, Washington, D.C., pp. 306–315.
14. Agarwal, D.K., Shrinkage estimator generalizations of proximal support vector machines, in *Proceedings of the 8th International Conference Knowledge Discovery and Data Mining*, Edmonton, Canada, 2002, pp. 173–182.
15. Cauwenberghs, G. and Poggio, T. Incremental and decremental support vector machine learning, in *Proceedings of Advances in Neural Information Processing Systems*. Vancouver, Canada, 2000, pp. 409–415.
16. Feng, G. and Mangasarian, O.L., Semi-supervised support vector machines for unlabeled data classification, *Optimization Methods and Software*, Vol. 15, 2001, pp. 29–44.
17. Lippmann, R.P., Graf, I., Wyschogrod, D., Webster, S.E., Weber, D.J., and Gorton, S., The 1998 DARPA/AFRL Off-line intrusion detection evaluation, *First International Workshop on Recent Advances in Intrusion Detection (RAID)*, Louvain-la-Neuve, Belgium, 1998.
18. Shih, L., Rennie, Y.D.M, Chang, Y., and Karger, D.R, Text bundling: Statistics-based data Reduction, *Proceedings of the 20th International Conference on Machine Learning (ICML)*, 2003, Washington, D.C., pp. 696–703.
19. Yang, Q., Zhang, H., and Li, T., Mining Web logs for prediction models in WWW caching and prefetching, in *The 7th ACM SIGKDD International Conference on Knowledge Discovery and Data Mining KDD*, August 26–29, 2001, pp. 473–478.
20. Teng, W.-G., Chang, C.-Y., and Chen, M.-S., Integrating Web caching and Web prefetching in client-side proxies, *IEEE Transaction on Parallel and Distributed Systems*, Vol. 16, No. 5, 444–455, May 2005.
21. Chinen, K. and Yamaguchi, S., An interactive prefetching proxy server for improvement of WWW latency, in *Proceedings of the 7th Annual Conference of the Internet Society (INEt'97)*, Kuala Lumpur, June 1997.
22. Duchamp, D., Prefetching hyperlinks, in *Proceedings of the 2nd USENIX Symposium on Internet Technologies and Systems (USITS)*, Boulder, CO, 1999, pp. 127–138.
23. Griffioen, J. and Appleton, R., Reducing file system latency using a predictive approach, in *Proceedings of the 1994 Summer USENIX Technical Conference*, Cambridge, MA.
24. Brin, S. and Page, L., The anatomy of a large-scale hypertextual web search engine, in *Proceedings of the 7th International WWW Conference*, Brisbane, Australia, 1998, pp. 107–117.
25. Mobasher, B., Dai, H., Luo, T., and Nakagawa, M., Effective personalization based on association rule discovery from web usage data, in *Proceedings of the ACM Workshop on Web Information and Data Management (WIDM01)*, 2001, pp. 9–15.

26. Sarwar, B. M., Karypis, G., Konstan, J., and Riedl, J., Analysis of recommender algorithms for e-commerce, in *Proceedings of the 2nd ACM E-Commerce Conference (EC'00)*, October 2000, Minneapolis, MN, pp. 158–167.
27. Lalmas, M., Dempster-Shafer's Theory of Evidence applied to Structured Documents: Modelling Uncertainty, in *Proceedings of the 20th Annual International ACM SIGIR*, Philadelphia, PA, 1997, pp. 110–118.

Conclusion to Part I

In Part I, we discussed data mining techniques and applications. There are many prediction models that we have considered in our work. Each of these models has its strengths and weaknesses. However, there is a common weakness for all these techniques, which is their inability to suit all applications. The reason there is no ideal or perfect classifier is that each of these techniques was designed initially to solve specific problems under certain assumptions. To concentrate on a specific problem in a specific application, one should target either decreasing the model complexity or increasing the performance. With regard to model complexity, new data structures, training-set reduction techniques, or small numbers of adaptable parameters are proposed to simplify computations during learning without compromising the prediction accuracy. Regarding model performance, the goal is to improve the prediction accuracy with some complication of the design or model. It is evident that there is a trade-off between the performance complexity and the model complexity.

Data mining has many applications in numerous domains, of which we have considered cyber security (intrusion detection), Web information management (Web page surfing prediction), and multimedia information management (image classification). Our tools for these applications will be described in Parts II, III, and IV.

DATA MINING TOOL ▐ II

FOR INTRUSION

DETECTION

Introduction to Part II

Now that we have described data mining techniques and applications, we are ready to discuss the tools that we have developed. In this part, we will describe our tool for intrusion detection, which is a key aspect of cyber security. We consider two types of defenses: anomaly detection and misuse detection. Anomaly detection is the attempt to identify malicious traffic based on deviations from established normal network traffic patterns. Misuse detection is the ability to identify intrusions based on a known pattern for the malicious activity.

Part II consists of four chapters. Chapter 4 provides an overview of data mining for cyber security. In Chapter 5, we discuss a novel algorithm we have developed that will enhance data mining techniques. Data reduction, as well as our approach, is discussed in Chapter 6. The performance results of our algorithm are presented in Chapter 7.

11 DATA MINING TOOL FOR INTRUSION DETECTION

Introduction to Part II

Chapter 4

Data Mining for Security Applications

4.1 Overview

Ensuring the integrity of computer networks, both in relation to security and with regard to the institutional life of the nation in general, is a growing concern. Security and defense networks, proprietary research, intellectual property, data-based market mechanisms that depend on untrammeled access can all be severely compromised by malicious intrusions. We need to find the best way to protect these systems. In addition, we need techniques to detect security breaches. Data mining has many applications in security, including in national security (e.g., surveillance) as well as in cyber security (e.g., virus detection). The threats to national security include attacking buildings and destroying critical infrastructures such as power grids and telecommunication systems. Data mining techniques are being investigated to find out who the suspicious people are and who is capable of carrying out terrorist activities. Cyber security is concerned with protecting the computer and network systems against corruption due to Trojan horses and viruses. Data mining is also being applied to provide solutions such as intrusion detection and auditing. In this chapter, we will focus mainly on data mining for cyber security applications.

To understand the mechanisms to be applied to safeguard the nation and its computers and networks, we need to understand the types of threats. In [1] we described real-time threats as well as non-real-time threats. A real-time threat is a

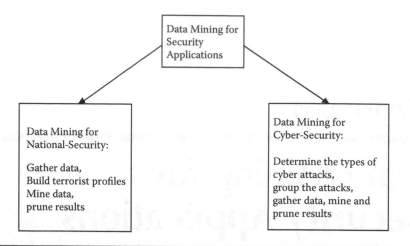

Figure 4.1 Data mining applications in security.

threat that must be acted upon within a certain time to prevent some catastrophic situation. Note that a non-real-time threat could become a real-time threat over time. For example, one could suspect that a group of terrorists will eventually perform some act of terrorism. However, when we set time bounds, such as a threat will likely occur say before July 1, 2004, then it becomes a real-time threat and we have to take action immediately. If the time bounds are tighter, such as a two-day time frame, then we cannot afford to make any mistakes in our response.

A lot of work has been done on applying data mining to both national security and cyber security. Much of the focus of our previous book was on applying data mining to national security [1]. In this part of the book, we will discuss data mining for cyber security. In Section 4.2, we will discuss data mining for cyber security applications. In particular, we will discuss the threats to computers and networks and describe the applications of data mining that detect such threats and attacks. Some of our current research at the University of Texas at Dallas will be discussed in Section 4.3. The chapter is summarized in Section 4.4. Figure 4.1 illustrates data mining applications in security.

4.2 Data Mining for Cyber Security

4.2.1 Overview

This section discusses information-related terrorism. By information-related terrorism we mean cyber terrorism as well as security violations through access control and other means. Trojan horses as well as viruses are also information-related security violations, which we group into information-related terrorism activities.

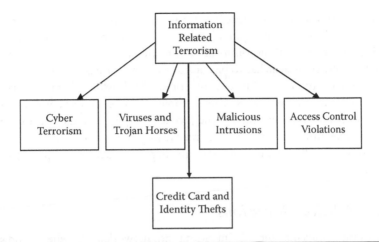

Figure 4.2 Cyber security threats.

In the next few subsections, we discuss various information-related terrorist attacks. In Section 4.2.2, we give an overview of cyber terrorism and then discuss insider threats and external attacks. Malicious intrusions are the subject of Section 4.2.3. Credit card and identity theft are discussed in Section 4.2.4. Attacks on critical infrastructures will be discussed in Section 4.2.5 Data mining for cyber security will be discussed in Section 4.2.6. Figure 4.2 illustrates cyber security threats.

4.2.2 Cyber Terrorism, Insider Threats, and External Attacks

Cyber terrorism is one of the major terrorist threats posed to our nation today. As we have mentioned earlier, there is now so much information available electronically and on the Web. Attacks on our computers as well as networks, databases, and the Internet could be devastating to businesses. It is estimated that cyber terrorism could cause billions of dollars of losses to businesses. For example, consider a banking information system. If terrorists attack such a system and siphon off funds from accounts, then the bank could lose millions and perhaps billions of dollars. By crippling the computer system, millions of hours of productivity could be lost, and that equates to money in the end. Even a simple power outage at work through some accident could cause several hours of productivity loss and result in a major financial loss. Therefore, it is critical that our information systems be secure. We discuss various types of cyber terrorist attacks. One is spreading viruses and Trojan horses that can wipe away files and other important documents; another is intruding into computer networks.

Note that threats can arise from outside or from inside an organization. Outside attacks are attacks on computers from someone outside the organization. We hear of hackers breaking into computer systems and causing havoc within an organization.

There are hackers who start spreading viruses, and these viruses cause great damage to the files in various computer systems. However, a more sinister problem is the insider threat. As with non-information-related attacks, the insider threat with information-related attacks has to be considered. There are people inside an organization who have studied the business practices and develop schemes to cripple the organization's information assets. These people could be regular employees or even those working at computer centers. The problem is quite serious, because someone may be masquerading as someone else and causing all kinds of damage. In the next few sections, we will examine how data mining could detect and perhaps prevent such attacks.

4.2.3 Malicious Intrusions

Malicious intrusions may include intruding into networks, Web clients and servers, databases, and operating systems. Many cyber terrorism attacks are due to malicious intrusions. We hear much about network intrusions. What happens is that intruders try to tap into the networks and get the information that is being transmitted. These intruders may be human intruders or Trojan horses set up by humans. Intrusions could also happen on files. For example, one can masquerade as someone else and log into someone else's computer system and access the files. Intrusions can also occur on databases. Intruders posing as legitimate users can pose SQL queries, for example, and access data that they are not authorized to know.

Essentially, cyber terrorism includes malicious intrusions as well as sabotage through malicious intrusions or other means. Cyber security consists of security mechanisms that attempt to provide solutions to cyber attacks or cyber terrorism. When we discuss malicious intrusions or cyber attacks, we may need to think about attacks in the noncyber world, that is, non-information-related terrorism, and then draw analogies to attacks on computers and networks. For example, a thief could enter a building through a trapdoor. In the same way, a computer intruder could enter the computer or network through some sort of a trapdoor that has been intentionally built by a malicious insider and left unattended, perhaps through careless design. Another example is a thief entering the bank with a mask and stealing money. The analogy here is an intruder masquerading as someone else, legitimately entering the system, and taking all the information assets. Money in the real world would translate to information assets in the cyber world. That is, there are many parallels between non-information-related attacks and information-related attacks. We can proceed to develop countermeasures for both types of attacks.

4.2.4 Credit Card Fraud and Identity Theft

We are hearing a lot these days about credit card fraud and identity theft. In the case of credit card fraud, others get hold of a person's credit card number and make all kinds of purchases, and by the time the owner of the card finds out, it may be too late.

The thief may have left the country by then. A similar problem occurs with telephone calling cards. In fact, this type of attack has happened to me once. Perhaps while I was making phone calls using my calling card at airports, someone must have noticed, say, the dial tones and used my calling card. This was my company calling card. Fortunately, our telephone company detected the problem and informed my company. The problem was dealt with immediately.

A more serious theft is identity theft. Here one assumes the identity of another person, say, by getting hold of the Social Security number and essentially carrying out all transactions under the other person's name. This could even be selling houses and depositing the income in a fraudulent bank account. By the time the owner finds out, it will be far too late. It is possible that the owner may have lost millions of dollars due to the identity theft.

We will explore the use of data mining both for credit card fraud detection as well as for identity theft. Some efforts have been put into detecting credit card fraud (see [2]). We need to start working actively on detecting and preventing identity thefts.

4.2.5 Attacks on Critical Infrastructures

Attacks on critical infrastructures could cripple a nation and its economy. Infrastructure attacks include attacking telecommunication lines, electronic equipment, power, gas and water reservoirs and supplies, food supplies, and other basic necessities that are critical for the operation of a nation.

Attacks on critical infrastructures could occur during any type of attack, whether they are non-information-related, information-related, or bioterrorism attacks. For example, one could attack the software used by telecommunications industry and close down all the telecommunications lines. Similarly, software that runs the power and gas supplies could be attacked. Attacks could also occur through bombs and explosives; that is, telecommunication lines could be attacked through bombs. Attacks on transportation lines such as highways and railway tracks are also attacks on infrastructures.

Infrastructures could also be attacked by natural disasters such as hurricanes and earthquakes. Our main interest here is the attacks on infrastructures through malicious attacks, both information-related and non-information-related. Our goal is to examine data mining and related data management technologies to detect and prevent such infrastructure attacks. Figure 4.3 illustrates attacks on critical infrastructures.

4.2.6 Data Mining for Cyber Security

Data mining is being applied to problems such as intrusion detection and auditing. For example, anomaly detection techniques could be used to detect unusual patterns and behaviors. Link analysis may be used to trace the viruses to the perpetrators. Classification may be used to group various cyber attacks and then

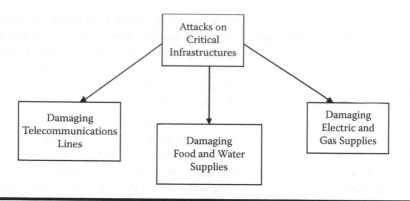

Figure 4.3 Attacks on critical infrastructures.

use the profiles to detect an attack when it occurs. Prediction may be used to determine potential future attacks, depending in a way on information learned about terrorists through e-mail and phone conversations. Also, for some threats, non–real-time data mining may suffice, whereas for certain other threats such as network intrusions, we may need real-time data mining. Many researchers are investigating the use of data mining for intrusion detection. Although we need some form of real-time data mining, that is, the results have to be generated in real-time, we also need to build models in real-time. For example, credit card fraud detection is a form of real-time processing. However, here models are usually built ahead of time. Building models in real time remains a challenge. Data mining can also be used for analyzing Web logs as well as analyzing audit trails. On the basis of the results of the data mining tool, one can determine whether any unauthorized intrusions have occurred or whether any unauthorized queries have been posed.

Other applications of data mining for cyber security include analyzing audit data. One could build a repository or a warehouse containing the audit data and then conduct an analysis using various data mining tools to see if there are potential anomalies. For example, there could be a situation where a certain user group may access the database between 3 and 5 am in the morning. It could be that this group is working the night shift, in which case there may be a valid explanation. However, if this group is working between, say, 9 am and 5 pm, then this is an unusual occurrence. Another example is when a person always accesses the databases between 1 pm and 2 pm, but for the last 2 days has been accessing the database between 1 am and 2 am. This could then be flagged as an unusual pattern requiring further investigation.

Analysis of an insider threat is also a problem from both a national security as well as from a cyber security perspective. That is, those working in a corporation who are considered to be trusted could commit espionage. Similarly, those with proper access to the computer system could plant Trojan horses and viruses. Catching such terrorists is far more difficult than catching terrorists outside of an organization.

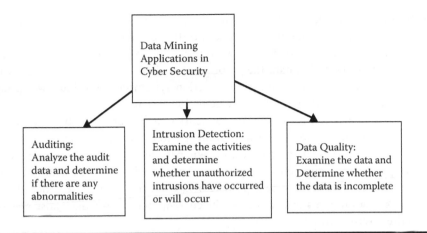

Figure 4.4 Data mining for cyber security.

One may need to monitor the access patterns of all the individuals of a corporation, even if they are system administrators, to see whether they are carrying out cyber terrorism activities. There is some research now on applying data mining for such applications by various groups including Kumar et al. at the University of Minnesota [3].

Although data mining can be used to detect and prevent cyber attacks, data mining also exacerbates some security problems, such as the inference and privacy problems. With data mining techniques, one could infer sensitive associations from the legitimate responses. We will address privacy concerns in the next chapter. Figure 4.4 illustrates data mining for cyber security. For more details on a high-level overview, we refer the reader to [4] and [5].

4.3 Current Research and Development

We are developing a number of tools on data mining for cyber security applications at the University of Texas at Dallas. In Chapters 5, 6, and 7 we will discuss in detail one such tool for intrusion detection. An intrusion can be defined as any set of actions that attempts to compromise the integrity, confidentiality, or availability of a resource. As systems become more complex, weaknesses due to design and programming errors arise that can be exploited through the use of various "socially engineered" penetration techniques. Computer attacks are split into two categories, host-based attacks and network-based attacks. Host-based attacks target a machine and try to gain access to privileged services or resources on that machine. Host-based detection usually uses routines that obtain system call data from an audit process that tracks all system calls made on behalf of each user. Network-based attacks make it difficult for legitimate users to access various network services, by deliberately occupying or sabotaging network resources and services. This can be done by sending large amounts of network traffic, exploiting well-known faults in networking services, overloading network hosts, etc. Network-based attack detection uses network traffic data (i.e., tcpdump) to look at traffic addressed to the machines being monitored. Intrusion detection systems are split into two groups: anomaly detection systems and misuse detection systems.

Anomaly detection is the attempt to identify malicious traffic based on deviations from established normal network traffic patterns. Misuse detection is the ability to identify intrusions based on a known pattern of malicious activity. These known patterns are referred to as signatures. Anomaly detection is capable of catching new attacks. However, new legitimate behavior can also be falsely identified as an attack, resulting in a false positive. The current focus is to reduce false negative and false positive rates.

Chapters 5, 6, and 7 will describe in detail our work on data mining for intrusion detection. We have used multiple models such as SVM. However, we have improved SVM a great deal by combining it with a novel algorithm that we have developed. We will describe this novel algorithm as well as our approach to combining it with SVM. In addition, we will also discuss our experimental results.

Our other tools include those for e-mail worm detection, malicious code detection, buffer overflow detection, and botnet detection, as well as analyzing firewall policy rules. Figure 4.5 illustrates the various tools we have developed. These tools have been described in technical reports of the University of Texas at Dallas. We will briefly discuss these tools in this section.

For e-mail worm detection, we examine e-mails and extract features such as "number of attachments" and train a data mining tool with techniques such as SVM (support vector machine) Naïve Bayesian classifiers and develop a model. Then we test the model and determine whether the e-mail has a virus/worm or not. We use training and testing datasets posted on various Web sites. Similarly, for malicious code detection, we extract n-gram features both with assembly code and binary code. We train the data mining tool with SVM-based classification techniques.

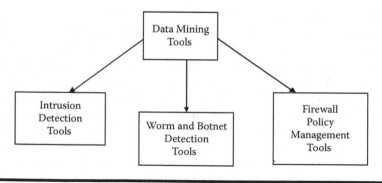

Figure 4.5   Data mining tools at the University of Texas at Dallas.

The classifier will determine whether the code is malicious or not. For buffer over-flow detection, we assume that malicious messages contain code while normal messages contain data. We train SVM and then test to see if the message contains code or data. For firewall policy rule analysis, we use association rule mining techniques to determine whether there are any conflicts with the policy rule set.

Our research on botnet detection is based essentially on stream data mining. We are developing novel ensemble-based stream mining techniques.

4.4 Summary and Directions

This chapter has discussed data mining for security applications. We first started with a discussion of data mining for cyber security applications and then provided a brief overview of the tools we have developed. One such tool will be described in detail in the next three chapters,

Data mining for national security as well as for cyber security is a very active research area. Various data mining techniques including link analysis and association rule mining are being explored to detect abnormal patterns. Because of data mining, users can now make all kinds of correlations. This also raises privacy concerns. More details on privacy can be obtained in [6].

References

1. Thuraisingham, B., *Web Data Mining Technologies and Their Applications in Business Intelligence and Counter-Terrorism*, CRC Press, Boca Raton, FL, 2003.
2. Chan, P. et al., Distributed data mining in credit card fraud detection, *IEEE Intelligent Systems*, Vol. 14, No. 6, 1999.
3. Lazarevic, A. et al., Data mining for computer security applications, *Tutorial Proceedings of the IEEE Data Mining Conference*, 2003.
4. Thuraisingham, B., *Managing Threats to Web Databases and Cyber Systems, Issues, Solutions and Challenges*, Eds. V. Kumar et al., Reading, MA, 2004.
5. Thuraisingham, B., *Database and Applications Security*, CRC Press, Boca Raton, FL, 2005.
6. Thuraisingham, B., Data mining, national security, privacy and civil liberties, *ACM SIGKDD Explorations*, Vol. 4, No. 2, 2002.

Chapter 5

Dynamic Growing
Self-Organizing
Tree Algorithm

5.1 Overview

We have described data mining for intrusion detection at a high level in both Chapters 3 and 4. In particular, we discussed both anomaly detection and misuse detection, and described how data mining could be applied to detect intrusions. In Chapters 5, 6, and 7, we will discuss the data mining tool that we have developed for intrusion detection.

Our tool is based on support vector machine (SVM), but overcomes some of its limitations. The SVM is one of the more successful classification algorithms in the data mining area, but its long training time limits its use. Many applications, such as data mining for bioinformatics and geoinformatics, require the processing of huge datasets. The training time of SVM is a serious obstacle in the processing of such datasets.

In this chapter, we describe our novel approach to enhancing the training process of SVM when dealing with large training datasets. It is based on a combination of SVM and clustering analysis. The idea is as follows: SVM computes the maximal margin separating data points; hence, only those patterns closest to the margin can affect the computations of that margin, whereas other points can be discarded without affecting the final result. Those points lying close to the margin are called *support vectors*. We try to approximate these points by applying clustering analysis. The novelty of our approach lies in the algorithm that we have developed, called the *Dynamically Growing Self-Organizing Tree* (DGSOT). We will see that this algorithm facilitates hierarchy construction. In this chapter, we will describe DGSOT, and in Chapter 6, we will discuss how it is applied to intrusion detection.

The organization of this chapter is as follows: Our overall approach is discussed in Section 5.2. Details of DGSOT are given in Section 5.3. We state some observations in Section 5.4. The chapter is summarized in Section 5.5.

5.2 Our Approach

In clustering analysis, we would like to organize a set of data or records into a number of clusters in which a cluster may contain more than one record. Furthermore, we would like to extend our hierarchy to several levels. For this, several existing techniques are available, such as the hierarchical agglomerative clustering (HAC) algorithm [1], the self-organizing map (SOM) [2], the self-organizing tree algorithm (SOTA) [3], and so on. In this research, we will exploit a new algorithm, the hierarchical DGSOT algorithm, to construct a hierarchy from top to bottom rather than from bottom up, as in HAC. We have observed that this algorithm constructs a hierarchy with better precision and recall than an HAC algorithm [4, 5]. Hence, we believe that there will be fewer false positives and false negatives (similar to precision and recall area in information retrieval) using our new algorithm as compared to HAC. Furthermore, it works in a top-down fashion. We can stop growing the tree earlier, and it can be entirely mixed with an SVM classifier.

The DGSOT is a tree-structured self-organizing neural network. It is designed to discover the correct hierarchical structure in an underlying dataset. The DGSOT grows in two directions: vertical and horizontal. In the direction of vertical growth, the DGSOT adds descendants. In the vertical growth of a node (*x*), only two children are added to the node. The need is to determine whether these two children, added to node *x*, are adequate to represent the proper hierarchical structure of that node. In horizontal growth, we strive to determine the number of siblings of these two children needed to represent the data associated with *x*. Thus, the DGSOT chooses the right number of children (subclusters) of each node at each hierarchical level during the tree construction process. During each vertical and horizontal growth, a learning process is invoked in which data will be distributed among newly created children of node *x*. The pseudocode of DGSOT is shown in Figure 5.1.

In Figure 5.1, at lines 1–4, initialization is done with only one node—the root node (see Figure 5.2A). All input data belong to the root node, and its reference vector is initialized with the centroid of the data. At lines 5–29, the vertical growing strategy is invoked. For this, first we select a victim leaf for expansion based on heterogeneity. Because we have only one node that is both leaf and root, two children

```
1 /*Initialization*/
2          Create a tree has only one root node. The reference vector of the root node is
3          initialized with the centroid of the entire data and all data will be associated with
4          the root. The time parameter t is initialized to 1.
5 /*Vertical Growing*/
6 Do
7          For any leaf x which is heterogeneous (see Section 5.3.2)
8          Changes the leaf x to a node and create two descendent leaves. The reference
9          vector of a new leaf is initialized with x reference vector
10         /*Learning*/
11             Do
12                     For each input data of node, x
13                     Find winner (using KLD, see Section 5.3.5), and update
14                     reference vectors of winner and its neighborhood
15             While the relative error of the entire tree is less than error threshold (Є)
16         /*Horizontal Growing*/
17         Do
18             If the horizontal growing stop rule (see Section 5.3.4) is unsatisfied
19                 Add a child leaf to this node, x
20                 /*Learning*/
21                 Do
22                         For each input data of node, x
23                         Find winner (using KLD, see Section 5.3.5), and update
24                         reference vectors of winner and its neighborhood
25                 While the relative error of the entire tree is less than Є.
26             Else
27                 Delete a child leaf to this node, x
28         While the node, x is unsatisfied with the horizontal growing stop rule
29 While there are more level necessary in the hierarchy
```

Figure 5.1   DGSOT algorithm.

will be added (at lines 7–9). In clustering-trees-based SVM (CT-SVM) case, at line 7, we need to perform additional checks. Recall that support vector nodes will be candidates for vertical expansion. The reference vector of each of these children will be initialized to the root's reference vector. Now, all input data associated with the root will be distributed between these children by invoking a learning strategy (see Section 5.3.2). The tree at this stage will be as shown in Figure 5.2B. Now, we need to determine the right number of children for the root by investigating horizontal growth (see Section 5.3.3; lines 16–28).

At line 19 in Figure 5.1, we check whether the horizontal growing stop rule has been reached (see Section 5.3.4). If it has, we remove the last child and exit from the horizontal growth loop at line 28. If the stop rule has not been reached, we add one more child to the root, and the learning strategy is invoked to distribute the data of the root among all the children. After adding two children (i.e., a total of four children) to the root one by one, we notice that the horizontal stop rule has been reached, and then we delete the last child from the root (at line 27).

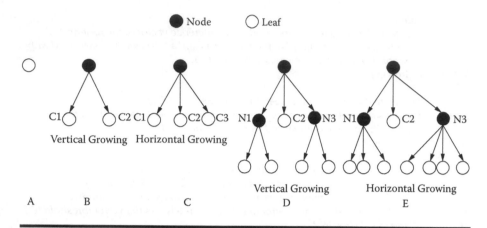

Figure 5.2   Illustration of DGSOT algorithm.

At this point, the tree will be as shown in Figure 5.2C. After this, at line 29, we check whether or not we need to expand to another level. If the answer is yes, a vertical growing strategy is invoked. In addition, in the CT-SVM case, to incorporate intrusion detection facility with SVM, the stopping criterion will be checked (see Section 5.3.1). For this, first, we determine the heterogeneous leaf node (leaf node N3 in Figure 5.2D) at line 7; add two children to this node; and distribute the data of N3 within its children using learning strategy. Next, horizontal growth is undertaken for N3, and so on (see Figure 5.2E).

5.3   DGSOT

5.3.1   *Vertical Growing*

In DGSOT, a process of nongreedy vertical growth is used to determine the victim leaf node for further expansion in the vertical direction. During vertical growth, any leaf whose heterogeneity is greater than a given threshold will change itself to a node and create two descendant leaves. The reference vectors of these leaves will be initialized by the parent. There are several ways to determine the heterogeneity of a leaf. One simple way is to use the number of data items associated with a leaf to determine heterogeneity, which we call *profile heterogeneity*, T_P (for symbol description and details, see Table 5.1). This simple approach controls the number of data that appear in each leaf node. Here, data will be evenly distributed among the leaves. This may generate too many tiny, fragmented clusters in which data points are densely placed. Hence, the alternative is based on the radius of clusters, which we call *radius heterogeneity*. In this case, if a cluster radius exceeds a threshold T_R, we split the node. Hence, it is possible that data for a cluster may be sparsely distributed.

Table 5.1   Symbols used in this chapter

Symbols	Description
$\eta(t)$	Learning rate function
α	Learning constant
$\varphi(t)$	Learning function
n_i	Reference vector of leaf node i
$d(x_j, n_i)$	Distance between data x_j and leaf node i
ε	Threshold for average distortion
e_i	Average error of node i
T_R	Radius heterogeneity
T_P	Profile heterogeneity

In our implementation, we combine both approaches. We choose a node to split whose profile heterogeneity and radius heterogeneity exceed their thresholds simultaneously. Thus, we guarantee that clusters will be compact, while at the same time, on average, they will have similar shapes. It is also possible that a node with too few points that are sparsely distributed may not be selected for expansion.

5.3.2   Learning Process

In DGSOT, the learning process consists of a series of procedures to distribute all the data to leaves and update the reference vectors. Each procedure is called a *cycle*. Each cycle contains a series of *epochs*. Each epoch consists of a presentation of input data, with each presentation having two steps: finding the best matching node and updating the reference vector.

The input data is only compared to the leaf nodes bounded by a subtree based on the K-level up distribution (KLD) mechanism (see Section 5.3.5) in order to find the best matching node, which is known as the *winner*. The leaf node c, which has the minimum distance to the input data x, is the best matching node (i.e., the winner; Equation 5.1):

$$c : \| x - n_c \| = \min\{\| x - n_i \|\} \tag{5.1}$$

$$\Delta n_i = \phi(t) \times (x - n_i) \tag{5.2}$$

$$\phi(t) = \alpha \times \eta(t), \ 0 < \eta(t)1 \tag{5.3}$$

After a winner c is found, the reference vectors of the winner and its neighborhood will be updated using Equation 5.2. The term $\phi(t)$ in Equation 5.2 is the neighborhood function, and it is defined as in Equation 5.3, where $\eta(t)$ is the learning rate function, α is the learning constant, and t is the time parameter. The convergence of the algorithm depends on a proper choice of α and $\eta(t)$. We want to make sure that the reference vector of the winner will be updated quickly, compared to the reference vector of the sibling. For this, the $\eta(t)$ value of the winner will be larger compared to that of the siblings. We define a Gaussian neighborhood function in such a manner that for a sibling node j, $\eta(t)$ will be calculated as follows:

$$\eta(t) = \exp(-\frac{\| h(i,j) \|^2}{2\sigma^2(t)} \qquad (5.4)$$

where σ gives the width of the Gaussian kernel function, and $h(i, j)$ is the number of hops between the winner i and node j. Here, the number of hops represents the length of the shortest acyclic path that connects two sibling nodes. Figure 5.3 shows the path that connects two sibling nodes, assuming that node 4 is the winner. It also shows the distance between each sibling. Here, two siblings are any two nodes that have a common parent. Note that from Equation 5.4, the learning rate to update node 9 is less than that to update node 8 because the length of the path from the winner node 4 to node 8 is shorter. Therefore, the closest sibling of a winner will receive a higher value of $\eta(t)$ compared to the most distant sibling node.

The *Error* of the tree, which is defined as the summation of the distance of each input data to the corresponding winner, is used to monitor the convergence of the learning process. A learning process has converged when the relative increase of *Error* of the tree falls below a given threshold for average distortion,

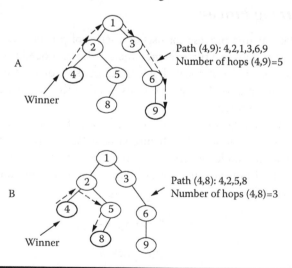

Figure 5.3 The hop distance between siblings.

as in Equation 5.5. It is easier to avoid overtraining the tree in the early stages by controlling the value of the threshold during training.

$$\left| \frac{Error_{t+1} - Error_t}{Error_t} \right| < \varepsilon \tag{5.5}$$

5.3.3 Horizontal Growing

In each stage of vertical growth, only two leaves are created for a growing node. In each stage of horizontal growth, the DGSOT tries to find an optimal number of leaf nodes (subcluster) of a node to represent the clusters in each node's expansion phase. Therefore, DGSOT adopts a dynamically growing scheme in the horizontal growing stage. Recall that in vertical growing, a leaf that is the most heterogeneous among all the leaves will be determined, and two children will be created for this heterogeneous node. Now, in horizontal growth, a new child (subcluster) is added to the existing children of this heterogeneous node. This process continues until a certain stopping rule is reached. Once the stopping rule (see Section 5.3.4) is reached, the number of child nodes is optimized. After each addition or deletion of a node, a process of learning takes place (see Section 5.3.1).

5.3.4 Stopping Rule for Horizontal Growing

To stop the horizontal growth of a node, we need to know the total number of clusters/children of that node. For this, we can apply the cluster validation approach. Because the DGSOT algorithm tries to optimize the number of clusters for a node in each expansion phase, cluster validation is used heavily. Therefore, the validation algorithms used in DGSOT must have a low computational cost and must be easily evaluated. A simple method is suggested for the DGSOT here, the measures of average distortion. However, the cluster scattering measure [6] can be used to minimize the intracluster distance and maximize the intercluster distance.

Average distortion (AD) is used to minimize intracluster distance. The AD of a subtree with j children is defined as in Equation 5.6:

$$AD_j = \frac{1}{N} \sum_1^N \left| d(x_i, n_k) \right|^2 \tag{5.6}$$

$$\left| \frac{AD_{j+1} - AD_j}{AD_j} \right| < \varepsilon \tag{5.7}$$

where N is the total number of input data assigned in the subtree, and n_k is the reference vector of the winner of input data x_i. AD_j is the average distance between an input data item and its winner.

During DGSOT learning, the total distortion is already calculated, and the AD measure is easily computed after the learning process is finished. If AD vs. the number of clusters is plotted, the curve will be monotonically decreasing. There will be a much smaller drop after the number of clusters exceeds the "true" number of clusters, because once we have crossed this point we will simply be adding more clusters to partitions within a cluster rather than between true clusters. Thus, the AD can be used as a criterion for choosing the optimal number of clusters. In the horizontal growth phase, if the relative value of AD after adding a new sibling is less than a threshold ε (Equation 5.7), then the new sibling will be deleted and horizontal growth will stop. In Equation 5.7, j is the number of children in a subtree, and ε is a small value, generally less than 0.1.

5.3.5   K-Level Up Distribution (KLD)

Clustering in a self-organizing neural network is distortion-based competitive learning. The nearest-neighbor rule is used to make the clustering decision. In SOTA, data associated with the parent node will only be distributed between its children. If data points are incorrectly clustered in the early stages, these errors cannot be corrected in the later learning process. To improve the clustering result, a new distribution approach called *K-level up distribution* (KLD) is proposed [4]. In the KLD strategy, a data point associated with a parent node will be distributed not only to its child leaves but also to its neighboring leaves. The following is the KLD strategy:

1. For a selected node x, compute the K-level ancestor node y.
2. Compute the subtree s rooted by the ancestor node y.
3. Redistribute the data points that are assigned to the selected node x among all leaves of the subtree s.

For example, Figure 5.4 shows the scope of $K = 1$. Now, the data associated with node M needs to be distributed to the newly created leaves. For $K = 1$, the immediate ancestor

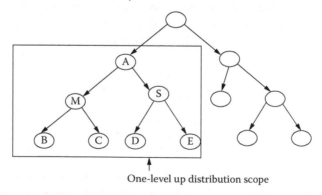

One-level up distribution scope

Figure 5.4   One-level up distribution scope ($K = 1$).

of M will be determined, which is node A. The data associated with node M will be distributed to leaves B, C, D, and E of the subtree rooted by A. For each data value, the winning leaf will be determined among B, C, D, and E by using Equation 5.1. Note that if $K = 0$, the data of node M will be distributed between leaves B and C.

Note that vertical growing is a nongreedy expansion. Therefore, in vertical growing, if the heterogeneities of two leaves are greater than ε, then both will be victims and will be expanded simultaneously.

5.4 Discussion

In intrusion detection, we have applied reduction techniques using clustering analysis to approximate support vectors in order to speed up the training process of SVM. We have proposed a method, namely, CT-SVM, to reduce the training set and approximate the support vectors. We exploit clustering analysis to generate support vectors to improve the accuracy of the classifier. Note that careful analysis and study should be devoted to choosing the models. That is because we cannot just combine any two models and expect an improvement in the results. Instead, a very thorough study and analysis should be conducted before combining two different models.

Our techniques worked well and outperformed all other methods in terms of accuracy, false positive rate, and false negative rate. In the case of Rocchio bundling, the partitions produced were not good representatives, as support vectors, of the whole dataset; hence, the results demonstrated only fair accuracy. Therefore, we observe that our approach outperforms the Rocchio bundling algorithm on a standard benchmark data, namely, the 1998 DARPA data originated at the MIT Lincoln Lab. More details of our approach as well as the results obtained are given in Chapters 6 and 7.

5.5 Summary and Directions

Intrusion detection is a significant research area in cyber security, and now we have many data mining tools employed in it. Furthermore, data mining is being applied extensively in intrusion detection. Such tools give false positives and false negatives. Furthermore, it takes time to train them. In this chapter, we have proposed a particular technique called DGSOT that when combined with SVM will significantly improve the training time as well as reduce false positives and false negatives. More details are given in Chapters 6 and 7.

Although we believe that DGSOT provides a significant enhancement to SVM, we see that the tool still gives some false positives and false negatives. Therefore, as we progress with data mining and understand the nature of attacks, we need to incorporate more knowledge into the tools to reduce the false positives and false negatives and improve accuracy. We believe that although tools are being developed to support humans in decision making and detecting intrusions, unless we can eliminate the false positives and false negatives, such tools cannot be automated one hundred percent. Therefore, much research is still needed in this area.

References

1. Voorhees, E.M., Implementing agglomerative hierarchic clustering algorithms for use in document retrieval, *Information Processing and Management*, Vol. 22, No. 6, 465–476, 1986.
2. Kohonen, T., *Self-Organizing Maps*, Springer Series, Springer-Verlag, Berlin, 1995.
3. Dopazo, J. and Carazo, J.M., Phylogenetic reconstruction using an unsupervised growing neural network that adopts the topology of a phylogenetic tree, *Journal of Molecular Evolution*, Vol. 44, 226–233, 1997.
4. Khan, L. and Luo, F., Hierarchical clustering for complex data, *International Journal on Artificial Intelligence Tools*, Vol. 14, No. 5, 791–810, 2005.
5. Luo, F., Khan, L., Bastani, F.B., Yen, I., and Zhou, J., A dynamically growing self-organizing tree (DGSOT) for hierarchical clustering gene expression profiles, *Bioinformatics*, Vol. 20, No. 16, 2605–2617, 2004.
6. Ray, S. and Turi, R.H., Determination of number of clusters in K-means clustering and application in color image segmentation, in *Proceedings of the 4th International Conference on Advances in Pattern Recognition and Digital Techniques (ICAPRDT '99)*, Calcutta, India, 1999, pp. 137–143.

Chapter 6

Data Reduction Using Hierarchical Clustering and Rocchio Bundling

6.1 Overview

One of the challenges in data mining is handling large volumes of multidimensional data. Techniques have been proposed to reduce the amount of data as well as its dimensions before applying data mining. That is, data reduction techniques have become popular for data mining. In this chapter, we present how clustering can be used as a data reduction technique to find support vectors. In particular, we will show how our algorithm Dynamically Growing Self-Organizing Tree (DGSOT) combined with clustering will enhance support vector machine (SVM). Specifically, we will present our approach to dataset reduction and support vector approximation as well as a complexity analysis of our approach.

To compare the results of our approach with others, we will describe the Rocchio bundling algorithm. It has been used for data reduction and classification [1], and uses the Rocchio classifier, which selects a decision boundary (plane) that is perpendicular to a vector connecting two class centroids. We first present the notion of Rocchio decision boundary and then describe the algorithm. The comparison of our results with those obtained by using Rocchio bundling is discussed in Chapter 7.

The organization of this chapter is as follows: Our approach to data reduction is given in Section 6.2. Essentially, we will enhance the training process of SVM with the DGSOT algorithm that was described in Chapter 5 (see also [2]). Complexity analysis is given in Section 6.3. The Rocchio decision boundary concept is discussed in Section 6.4. The Rocchio bundling technique is discussed in Section 6.5, and the chapter is summarized in Section 6.6.

6.2 Our Approach

6.2.1 Enhancing the Training Process of SVM

Our approach to enhancing the training process of SVM is based on the combination of clustering and SVM to find relevant support vectors. For this, we present an approach, namely, clustering-tree-based SVM (CT-SVM).

In this approach, we build a hierarchical clustering tree for each class in the dataset (for simplicity and without loss of generality, we assume binary classification) using the DGSOT algorithm. The DGSOT algorithm works in a top-down fashion. It builds the hierarchical tree iteratively in several epochs. After each epoch, new nodes are added to the tree based on a learning process. To avoid the computational overhead of building the tree, we do not build the entire hierarchical tree. Instead, after each epoch, we train SVM on the nodes of both trees. We use the support vectors of the classifier as prior knowledge for the succeeding epoch in order to control the growth of the tree. Specifically, support vectors are allowed to grow, whereas nonsupport vectors are stopped from growing. This has the impact of adding nodes in the boundary areas between the two classes, while eliminating distant nodes from the boundaries. Figure 6.1 outlines the steps of this approach. First, assuming binary classification, we generate a hierarchical tree

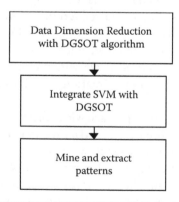

Figure 6.1 Our approach.

for each class in the dataset. Initially, we allow the two trees to grow until a certain size is reached. Basically, we want to start with a reasonable number of nodes. First, if a tree exhibits convergence earlier (i.e., fewer number of nodes), one option is to train SVM with these existing nodes. If the result is unsatisfactory, we will adjust the threshold (profile and radius thresholds) (see the discussion in Chapter 2). Reducing thresholds may increase the number of clusters and nodes. Second, we will train SVM on the nodes of the trees and compute the support vectors. Third, based on stopping criteria, we either stop the algorithm or continue growing the hierarchical trees. In the case of growing the tree, we use prior knowledge, which consists of the computed support vector nodes, to instruct the DGSOT algorithm to grow support vector nodes, whereas nonsupport vector nodes are not allowed to grow. What is meant by growing a node in the DGSOT algorithm is the creation of two child nodes for each support vector node [2]. Such grown nodes imply prior knowledge will be used in the next iteration of our algorithm, especially to direct the growth of the hierarchical trees. This process has the impact of growing the tree only in the boundary area between the two classes, while stopping the tree from growing in other areas. Hence, we save extensive computations that would have been carried out without any purpose or utility.

6.2.2 Stopping Criteria

There are several ways to set the stopping criteria. For example, we can stop at a certain size or level of the tree, upon reaching a certain number of nodes/support vectors, and/or when a certain accuracy level is attained. To ensure this accuracy level, we can stop the algorithm if the generalization accuracy over a validation set exceeds a specific value (say 98%). For this accuracy estimation, support vectors will be tested with the existing training set based on proximity. In our implementation, we adopt the second strategy (i.e., a certain number of support vectors) so that we can compare our approach with the Rocchio bundling algorithm, which reduces the dataset to a specific size.

One subtlety of using clustering analysis is that clustering might take a long time to complete, which nullifies any benefits from improvements in SVM. Our strategy here is that we do not wait until DGSOT finishes. Instead, after each epoch or iteration of the DGSOT algorithm, we train the SVM on the generated nodes. After each training process, we can control the growth of the hierarchical tree from top to bottom because nonsupport vector nodes will be stopped from growing, and only support vector nodes will be allowed to grow. Figure 6.2 shows the growth of one of the hierarchical trees during this approach. The bold nodes represent the support vector nodes. Note that nodes 1, 2, 3, 5, 6, and 9 are allowed to expand because they are support vector nodes. Meanwhile, we stop nodes 4, 8, 7, and 10 from growing because they are non-support vector nodes.

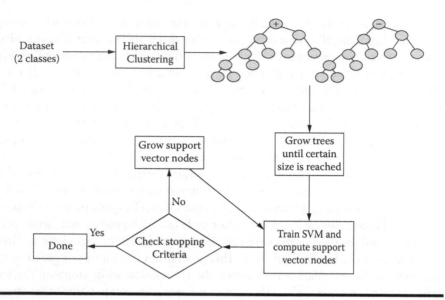

Figure 6.2 Two-tree clustering-based SVM diagram.

Growing the tree is very important to increase the number of points in the dataset so as to obtain a more accurate classifier. Figure 6.3 shows an illustrative example of growing the tree up to a certain size or level in which we have the training set (+3, +4, +5, +6, +7, −3, −4, −5, −6, −7). The dashed nodes represent the clusters' references, which are not support vectors. The bold nodes represent the support vector references. Hence, we add the children of the support vector, nodes +4 and +7, to the training set. The same applies to the support vector nodes −5 and −7. The new dataset now is (+3, +11, +12, +5, +6, +14, +15, −3, −4, −10, −11, −6, −12, −13). Note that expanded nodes, such as +4 and +7, are excluded because their child nodes are added to the training set. Part A of

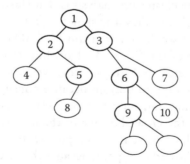

Figure 6.3 Allowing only support vectors to grow.

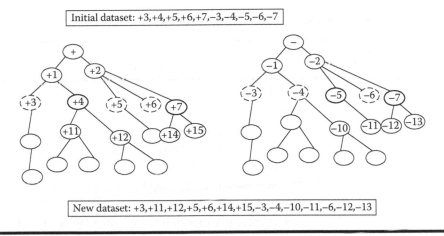

Figure 6.4 shows the layout of those clusters around the boundaries, and Part B of Figure 6.4 shows the effect of growing the trees in the boundary areas. Note that adding new nodes in the boundary area of the old classifier, represented by dashed lines, is corrected, and the new classifier, solid lines, is more accurate now than the old one. By doing so, the classifier is adjusted accordingly, creating a more accurate classifier.

6.3 Complexity and Analysis

In this section, we present an analysis of the running time for the CT-SVM algorithm. Building the hierarchical tree is the most expensive computation in CT-SVM. However, we try to reduce this cost by growing the tree only in the marginal area. In this analysis, we consider the worst-case scenario for building the hierarchical tree and the overhead of training SVM. Specifically, the time complexity of building the DGSOT tree is $O(\log_d M \times J \times N)$, where d is the branch factor of the DGSOT, J is the average number of learning iterations needed to expand the tree one more level, N is the size of the dataset, and M is the number of nodes in the tree. Note that, in the worst-case scenario, M is close to the number of data points in the dataset N; hence, $O(\log_d M \times J \times N) \approx O(\log_d N \times J \times N)$ (see Table 6.1 for symbols and definitions).

The key factor in determining the complexity of SVM is the size of the training set. In the following, we try to approximate the size of the tree in iteration i, approximate the running time of iteration i, and compute the running time of the CT-SVM algorithm.

Table 6.1 Symbols used in this chapter

Complexity and analysis symbols	Description
N	The size of the dataset
M	The number of nodes in the tree
J	The average number of learning iterations needed to expand the tree to one more level
D	The branch factor for the DGSOT
r	The average rate of the number of support entries among the training entries
B	The average number of training entries in each node
$t(\Psi)$	Training time of algorithm Ψ
s	The average number of support vector entries among the training entries
N_i	The number of nodes for iteration i.

Let us assume $t(SVM) = O(N^2)$, where $t(\Psi)$ is the training time of algorithm Ψ (note that t(SVM) is known to be at least quadratic to N and linear to the number of dimensions). Let support entries be the support vectors when the training data are entries in some nodes. Assume that r is the average rate of the number of support entries among the training entries; namely, $r = s/b$, where b is the average number of training entries, and s is the average number of support vector entries among the training entries, for example, $r = 0.01$ for $s = 10$ and $b = 1000$. Normally, $s \ll b$ and $0 < r \ll 1$ for standard SVM with large datasets [3]. For simplicity, we will consider the size of only one hierarchical tree. Therefore, at iteration i, the number of nodes is given as follows:

$$
\begin{aligned}
N_i &= b - s + bs - s^2 + \cdots + bs^{i-2} - s^{i-1} + bs^{i-1} \\
&= (b - s)(1 + s + s^2 + s^3 + \cdots + s^{i-2} + s^{i-1}) \\
&= (b - s)\frac{s^{i-1} - 1}{s - 1} + bs^{i-1}
\end{aligned}
\tag{6.1}
$$

Here, b is the average number of data points in a node, and s is the number of support vectors among the data. Figure 6.5 illustrates the computation of N_i for iterations 1, 2, 3, and 4. The size of the training set is b at the beginning (at iteration 1).

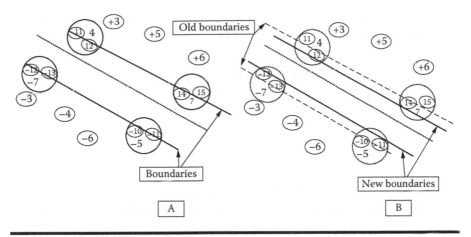

Figure 6.5 Adjusting the classifiers as a result of growing the support vector nodes.

In iteration 2, we will have s support vectors after training SVM for each node in b; hence, we expand the support vector nodes s and add bs nodes to the training set. We exclude from the training set the nodes we expand, because we have s support nodes expanded, we subtract s. In iteration 3, we expand s^2 support vectors, add bs^2 nodes, and subtract s^2. The left column of Figure 6.6 shows that the number of support vectors after each iteration increases by the factor of s; hence, the number of children added also increases by the factor of s. Now, to approximate the running time of an iteration i, we not only compute the running time of the DGSOT algorithm iteration i but also compute the running time of training SVM in that iteration.

SVs	Children of SVs	N_i	
		b	Iteration 1
$-s$	$+ bs$	$b - s + bs$	Iteration 2
$-s^2$	$+ bs^2$	$b - s + bs - s^2 + bs^2$	Iteration 3
$-s^3$	$+ bs^3$	$b - s + bs - s^2 + bs^2 - s^3 + bs^3$	Iteration 4
$-s^{i+1}$	$+ bs^{i+1}$	$b + bs^{i+2} - s^{i-1} + bs^{i+1}$	Iteration 1

Figure 6.6 Illustrative example of computing N_i for iterations 1, 2, 3, and 4.

If we assume $t(SVM) = O(N^2)$, by approximating $s - 1 \approx s$ in the denominator, Equation 6.1 becomes

$$N_i' = b\left(\frac{s^{i-1}-1}{s-1}\right) - s\left(\frac{s^{i-1}-1}{s-1}\right) + bs^{i-1}$$

$$= \frac{bs^{i-1}-b}{s} - \frac{ss^{i-1}-s}{s} + bs^{i-1}$$

$$= bs^{i-2} + 1 - \frac{b}{s} - s^{i-1} + bs^{i-1}$$

The approximate running time for an iteration $i\,(t_i(CT-SVM))$ is

$$t_i(CT-SVM) = \textit{running time of SVM for the } i\text{-th } \textit{iteration}$$
$$+ \textit{the running time for the DGSOT for the } i\text{-th } \textit{iteration}$$

$$t_i(CT-SVM) = O\left(\left[bs^{i-2} + 1 - \frac{b}{s} - s^{i-1} + bs^{i-1}\right]^2\right.$$

$$+ j\log_d\left[bs^{i-2} + 1 - \frac{b}{s} - s^{i-1} + bs^{i-1}\right]\right)$$

$$= O\left([bs^{i-1}]^2 + j\log_d(bs^{i-1})\right)$$

If we accumulate the running time of all iterations,

$$t_i(CT-SVM) = O\left(\sum_{i=1}^{h}([bs^{i-1}]^2 + j\log_d[bs^{i-1}])\right)$$

$$= O\left(\sum_{i=1}^{h}[bs^{i-1}]^2) + h \cdot j\log_d[bs^{h-1}]\right)$$

$$= O\left(b^2\sum_{i=0}^{h-1}s^{2i} + h \cdot j\log_d[bs^{h-1}]\right)$$

$$= O\left(\frac{b^2(s^{2h}-1)}{s^2-1} + h \cdot j \cdot \log_d[bs^{h-1}]\right)$$

Note that, for simplicity, we assume that the running time for creating each level of the tree is the same, and the total running time of creating the whole tree is $h \cdot j\log_d[bs^{h-1}]$. Also, we have assumed that $s - 1 \approx s$. If we replace s with rb, because

$r = s/b$, and only focus on the training time of SVM, the training time of our approach will be related to pure SVM as follows:

$$t(CT - SVM) = O([b^h r^{h-1}]^2) = O(b^{2h} r^{2h-2})$$

Therefore, the $t(CT\text{-}SVM)$ approach trains asymptotically $1/r^{2h-2}$ times faster than $t(SVM)$, Equation 6.2, which is $O(b^{2h})$ for $N = b^h$

$$\frac{t(CT - SVM)}{t(SVM)} = O(r^{2h-2}) \tag{6.2}$$

6.4 Rocchio Decision Boundary

Consider a binary classification problem. Simply put, Rocchio selects a decision boundary (plane) that is perpendicular to a vector connecting two class centroids. Let $\{x_{11}, \ldots, x_{1n}\}$ and $\{x_{21}, \ldots, x_{2n}\}$ be sets of training data for positive and negative classes, respectively. Let $c_1 = 1/n \sum_i x_{1i}$ and $c_2 = 1/m \sum_i x_{2i}$ be the centroids for the positive and negative classes, respectively. Then, we define the Rocchio score of an example x as in Equation 6.1. One selects a threshold value, b, which may be used to make the decision boundary closer to the positive or negative class centroid. Then, an example is labeled according to the sign of the score minus the threshold value as in Equation 6.2. Figure 6.7 explains the idea of the Rocchio classification

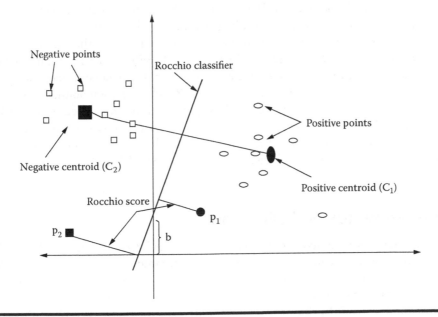

Figure 6.7   Rocchio classifier.

boundary in the binary classification case. Positive and negative points are presented in oval and square objects, respectively. The points C_1 and C_2 represent the centroids of positive and negative classes, respectively. The bold line is the Rocchio classifier, which is clearly the line perpendicular to the line connecting the two class centroids. The Rocchio score represents the distance of a point from the classifier (bold line); for example, point p_1 has Rocchio score equals to the length of the line connecting it to the Rocchio classifier (bold line).

$$\text{Rocchio Score}(x_i) = x_i(c_1 - c_2) \tag{6.1}$$

$$l(x) = sign(\text{Rocchio Score}(x) - b) \tag{6.2}$$

6.5 Rocchio Bundling Technique

The Rocchio bundling algorithm is a data reduction technique. Rocchio bundling preserves a set of k user-chosen statistics, $s = (s_1, \ldots, s_k)$, where s_i is a function that maps a set of data to a single value. It works as follows: We assume that there is a set of training examples for each class. Bundling is applied separately to each class, so we will only discuss what needs to be done for a single class. We need to select a statistic to preserve, and in our experiments we choose to preserve the mean statistic for each feature. Then, we partition the full dataset D into m equal-size partitions $P_1, \ldots, P_m$. Each partition becomes a single data point in the bundled dataset $D' = \{D'_1, \ldots, D'_m\}$. Each element D'_i is a vector of the mean of the data in partition P_i.

Now, we will discuss how bundling works. For this, first, we calculate the Rocchio score, which reflects the distance of each point from the Rocchio decision boundary created, as described in Section 6.1. Second, after computing the Rocchio score for each data point in the class, we sort the data points according to their scores. This means that points close to the Rocchio decision boundary will be placed close to one another in the list. Third, we partition this sorted list into n/m partitions. Fourth, we compute the mean of each partition as a representative of that partition. Finally, the reduced dataset will be the list of all representatives or means of all partitions and will be used for training SVM (see also [4–8]).

6.6 Summary and Directions

In Chapter 5, we discussed our novel algorithm DGSOT, which is a clustering technique for data reduction. We combine this technique with SVM to enhance the training time of SVM. We compare the results obtained with those obtained by employing an alternative technique called *Rocchio bundling*. This comparison is given in Chapter 7. In the current chapter, we explained how DGSOT enhances SVM; we also present the Rocchio bundling technique.

As we have stated in Chapter 5, although the current generation of data mining tools are a significant improvement over the tools that were developed a decade ago, there is still a need for reducing false positives and negatives as well as the training times. Our research has made a contribution toward this improvement. However, the ultimate goal of the data mining community is to virtually eliminate the current shortcomings of the tools. Only then can we confidently use these tools without the human in the loop or with very little human intervention.

References

1. Shih, L., Rennie, Y.D.M., Chang, Y., and Karger, D.R., Text bundling: Statistics-based data reduction, *Proceedings of the 20th International Conference on Machine Learning (ICML)*, 2003, Washington, D.C., pp. 696–703.
2. Luo, F., Khan, L., Bastani, F.B., Yen, I., and Zhou, J., A dynamically growing self-organizing tree (DGSOT) for hierarchical clustering gene expression profiles, *Bioinformatics*, Vol. 20, No. 16, 2605–2617, 2004.
3. Yu, H., Yang, J., and Han, J., Classifying large data sets using SVM with hierarchical clusters, *SIGKDD 2003*, August 24–27, 2003, Washington, D.C., pp. 306–315.
4. Voorhees, E.M., Implementing agglomerative hierarchic clustering algorithms for use in document retrieval, *Information Processing and Management*, Vol. 22, No. 6, 465–476, 1986.
5. Kohonen, T., *Self-Organizing Maps*, Springer Series, Springer-Verlag, Berlin, 1995.
6. Dopazo, J. and Carazo, J.M., Phylogenetic reconstruction using an unsupervised growing neural network that adopts the topology of a phylogenetic tree, *Journal of Molecular Evolution*, Vol. 44, 226–233, 1997.
7. Khan, L. and Luo, F., Hierarchical clustering for complex data, *International Journal on Artificial Intelligence Tools*, Vol. 14, 771–790, 2005.
8. Ray, S. and Turi, R.H., Determination of number of clusters in K-means clustering and application in color image segmentation, in *Proc. of the 4th International Conference on Advances in Pattern Recognition and Digital Techniques (ICAPRDT'99)*, Calcutta, India, 1999, pp. 137–143.

Chapter 7

Intrusion Detection Results

7.1 Overview

In Chapter 4, we discussed data mining for security applications. In Chapters 5 and 6, we described the design of the tool that we have developed for intrusion detection. In particular, in Chapter 5 we discussed our dynamically growing self-organizing tree (DGSOT) algorithm, and in Chapter 6, we discussed how DGSOT could be used to enhance support vector machine (SVM). We also described the Rocchio bundling algorithm, with which we have compared our results.

In this chapter, we present the experimental results of combining SVM and DGSOT to reduce the training time of SVM. We compare the results with pure SVM, Rocchio bundling, and random selection SVM. We also present a complexity analysis of our approach (SVM and DGSOT). Furthermore, we discuss and explain the results. However, first, we present our experimental setup, algorithm parameter values, and the dataset used in these experiments.

The organization of this chapter is as follows. The dataset we have used is discussed in Section 7.2. Results are discussed in Section 7.3. Complexity analysis is given in Section 7.4. Discussion of the results is provided in Section 7.5. The chapter is summarized in Section 7.6.

7.2 Dataset

Our system focuses on network-based anomaly detection. We have applied our algorithm to a set of standard benchmark data, namely, the 1998 DARPA data [1] that originated from the MIT Lincoln Laboratory. Network traffic can be captured using packet-capturing utilities (e.g., libpcap [2]) or operating system utilities at the system-call level (e.g., BSM), and then stored as a collection of records in the audit file.

Each data point represents either an attack or a normal connection. There are four categories of attacks: denial-of-service (DoS), surveillance (Probe), remote-to-local (R2L), and user-to-root (U2R). Therefore, overall training and testing data will be categorized into these five classes, that is, one normal and four attack categories. As a training set, we have a total of 1,132,365 data points; distribution of data among these normal, DoS, U2R, R2L, and Probe classes are as follows: 830405, 287088, 22, 999, and 13851, respectively. Note that the U2R and R2L classes do not have sufficient training examples compared to others. Distribution of test data is as follows: normal, DoS, U2R, R2L, and Probe classes, each with 47913, 21720, 17, 2328, and 1269 data points, respectively. Note that we ensure that the test data is not from the same probability distribution as the training data. In other words, the testing set also includes novel attacks that are variants of known attacks.

Each data point is described by 41 features. Each record is represented by a vector. Note that some attributes are continuous, and some are nominal. Because the clustering and classification algorithms require continuous values, these nominal values will be first converted into continuous values. We have used a bit vector to represent each nominal value.

We use the LIBSVM for SVSM implementation; more specifically, we use the $v - SVM$ with RBF kernel. In our experiments, we set v very low (0.001). As we address the problem of multiclass classification (i.e., five classes), we implement the "one-vs-one" scheme owing to its reduction of training time over "one-vs-all" classification.

With regard to setting parameters for the DGSOT, ε is set to 0.08, with α set to 0.01. K, T_R, and T_P are set to 3, 100, and 300, respectively. The parameter settings are purely based on observation. A higher value of K produces a good-quality cluster in relation to the cost of running time. Hence, we choose a moderate value for K. A larger value of ε causes quick convergence for learning. Hence, we set a lower value of ε to achieve smooth convergence. T_R and T_P are set in such a way as to produce densely populated uniform clusters.

7.3 Results

Random selection has been used in many applications to reduce the size of the dataset. For this purpose, we randomly select 14% from the overall training data set. Here, we report the results by applying a random selection technique to reduce the training set of SVM (see Table 7.1). In this table along with Tables 7.2, 7.3, and

Table 7.1   Results of random selection

	Normal	DOS	U2R	R2L	Probe	Accuracy (%)	FP(%)	FN(%)
Normal	47137	86	2	6	682	98	5	2
DOS	303	8491	0	0	12926	39	1	61
U2R	13	0	4	0	0	23	100	76
R2L	1955	2	1	368	0	15	2	84
Probe	148	1	0	0	1120	88	92	12

Table 7.2   Results of pure SVM

	Normal	DOS	U2R	R2L	Probe	Accuracy (%)	FP(%)	FN(%)
Normal	47180	138	4	7	584	98	7	2
DOS	1510	18437	0	0	1773	84	1	15
U2R	16	0	0	1	0	0	100	100
R2L	1888	0	8	431	1	18	2	81
Probe	144	3	0	0	1122	88	68	12

Table 7.3   Results of SVM + Rocchio bundling

	Normal	DOS	U2R	R2L	Probe	Accuracy (%)	FP(%)	FN(%)
Normal	47044	67	3	130	669	98	9	2
DOS	2896	7530	0	34	11260	34	1	65
U2R	14	0	2	1	0	11	100	88
R2L	1685	2	0	640	1	27	20	73
Probe	148	0	0	0	1121	88	91	12

7.4, diagonal values represent the numbers that are correctly classified. For example, out of 47913 data points, 47137, 86, 2, 6, and 682 data points are classified as normal, DoS, U2R, R2L, and Probe, respectively. In Tables 7.3 and 7.4, the last two columns represent the false positive (FP) rate and the false negative (FN) rate, respectively. Accuracy rates for normal, DoS, U2R, R2L, and Probe are 98, 39, 23, 15, and 88%, respectively. The FP rate is 5, 1, 100, 2, and 92%, respectively. Note that the accuracy rate is low for U2R and R2L classes. This is due to a shortage of training set for these classes. In Table 7.5, we report results based on accuracy.

Table 7.4   Results of SVM + DGSOT

	Normal	DOS	U2R	R2L	Probe	Accuracy (%)	FP(%)	FN(%)
Normal	45616	541	92	267	1397	95	3	5
DOS	316	21145	0	48	211	97	2	3
U2R	4	0	4	9	0	23	100	76
R2L	793	0	408	1024	103	43	24	56
Probe	112	1	0	0	1156	91	60	9

Table 7.5   Training time, average accuracy, FP, and FN rates of various methods

Method	Average accuracy (%)	Training time (Hours)	Average FP (%)	Average FN (%)
Random selection	52	.44	40	47
Pure SVM	57.6	17.34	35.5	42
SVM + Rocchio	51.6	26.7	44.2	48
CT-SVM	**69.8**	**13.18**	**37.8**	**29.8**

In Table 7.5, we observe that random selection, pure SVM, SVM + Rocchio bundling, and SVM + DGSOT give 52, 57.6, 51.6, and 69.8% accuracy, respectively. Note that the total training time is higher for pure SVM (17.34 hours) and SVM + Rocchio bundling (26.7 hours). Although SVM + Rocchio bundling reduces the dataset first, it incurs significant training time due to preprocessing of dataset. On the other hand, the average training time of SVM + DGSOT (13.18 hours) is lower than pure SVM with improved accuracy. This is the lowest training time compared to other methods, except random selection. Furthermore, SVM + DGSOT time includes clustering time and SVM training time.

7.4   Complexity Validation

We notice that 99.8% of the total training time was used for DGSOT, and 0.2% time (2.14 minute) was used for training SVM. Recall that DGSOT deals with the entire training dataset; however, for later SVM training, we only use a smaller subset of data from this dataset. In experimental results, we gathered parameters *b*, *s*, and *h* for time complexity analysis. In particular, for a dominating normal class, we got $b = 209.33$, $s = 11.953$, and $h = 28$. On the other hand, for a DOS class, we obtained $b = 604.39$, $s = 8.89$, and $h = 13$. After taking the average, we have $b = 406.86$, $s = 10.4215$, and $h = 20.5$, and using these values in Equation 6.2 (Chapter 6), $t(\text{CT-SVM})$ is asymptotically 1.1749×10^{62} times faster than $t(\text{SVM})$. With our experimental results, we observed $t(\text{CT-SVM})$ is 361 times faster than $t(\text{SVM})$, and this validates our claim that, with complexity analysis, training rate over pure SVM is increased. It is obvious from Table 7.5 that, for SVM + DGSOT, accuracy rate is the highest, FN rate is the lowest, and the FP rate is as good as pure SVM. This demonstrates that SVM + DGSOT can be deployed as a real-time modality for intrusion detection.

7.5 Discussion

Random selection proves at times to be a successful technique to save training time. However, in general, this may not hold. This is because the distribution of the training data is different from the testing data results. Furthermore, some intrusion experts believe that most novel attacks are variants of known attacks, and the "signature" of known attacks can be sufficient to catch novel variants. This is precisely what happens with SVM + DGSOT. We note that the accuracy rate of our SVM + DGSOT is the best, and it is better than pure SVM. It is possible that pure SVM training accuracy for a testing set may be good, but the generalization accuracy may not be as good as the accuracy of SVM + DGSOT. DGSOT provides a set of supporting vectors, and using SVM, we generate a hyperplane that would be more accurate for the testing set compared to the hyperplane generated by pure SVM from the entire training dataset. Furthermore, FN is lowest for SVM + DGSOT, and the FP rate is as low as pure SVM. Performance of Rocchio bundling is the worst in terms of training time, FP, and FN rate. Therefore, from the previous discussion, we note that our SVM + DGSOT method is superior to other methods.

In the intrusion detection area, we have applied reduction techniques using clustering analysis to approximate support vectors in order to speed up the training process of SVM. We have proposed a method, namely, clustering-trees-based SVM (CT-SVM), to reduce the training set and approximate support vectors. We exploit clustering analysis to generate support vectors to improve the accuracy of the classifier.

It should be noted that careful attention (analysis and study) is required before choosing the models. That is because we cannot just combine any two models and expect improvement in the results. Instead, a very thorough study and analysis should be done before combining two different models.

Our techniques proved to work well and to outperform all other methods in terms of accuracy, false positive rate, and false negative rate. In the case of Rocchio bundling, the partitions produced were not good representatives, as support vectors, of the whole dataset; hence, the results demonstrated only fair accuracy. Therefore, we observe that our approach outperforms the Rocchio bundling algorithm on standard benchmark data, namely, the 1998 DARPA, data originated at the MIT Lincoln Laboratory.

7.6 Summary and Directions

In this chapter, we have described the dataset used and presented our experimental results. We have observed that SVM together with DGSOT has outperformed the other approaches, on average, in terms of training time, false positives, false negatives, and accuracy. We have used the same environment to test all the algorithms. It should be noted that our dataset is the MIT Lincoln dataset that was obtained in 1998.

There are several areas for improvements. One is that our approach is not perfect and results in false positives and negatives, and therefore, we need to continue with research and development on various data mining techniques for intrusion detection. On the basis of research we have carried out, we believe that combinations of approaches have significant benefits as they incorporate the advantages of the individual approaches. However, we have to be careful to reduce the disadvantages of the individual approaches. Another possibility is to test the algorithms with more recent datasets. Therefore, one of the significant challenges is to obtain viable and realistic datasets.

References

1. Lippmann, R.P., Graf, I., Wyschogrod, D., Webster, S.E., Weber, D.J., and Gorton, S., The 1998 DARPA/AFRL off-line intrusion detection evaluation, *First International Workshop on Recent Advances in Intrusion Detection (RAID)*, Louvain-la-Neuve, Belgium, 1998.
2. McCanne, S., Leres, C., and Jacobson, V., libpcap, available via anonymous ftp at ftp://ftp.ee.lbl.gov/, 1989.

Conclusion to Part II

Our data mining tool for intrusion detection was discussed in Part II. In particular, we provided an overview of data mining for cyber security applications and also discussed the design and development of our tool for intrusion detection. We also presented our performance results. We have observed that SVM together with DGSOT has outperformed the other approaches, on average, in terms of training time, false positives, false negatives, and accuracy. Our current research in data mining for cyber security includes virus detection, botnet detection, and firewall policy analysis.

DATA MINING TOOL III
FOR WEB PAGE
SURFING PREDICTION

Introduction to Part III

In this part of this book, we use several classification techniques, namely, support vector machines (SVMs), artificial neural networks (ANNs), association rule mining (ARM), and the Markov model in World Wide Web (WWW) prediction. We propose a hybrid prediction model by combining two or more of them using Dempster's rule. The Markov model is a powerful technique for predicting seen data; however, it cannot predict unseen data.

The organization of this part is as follows. In Chapter 8, we discuss Web data management and mining. In Chapter 9, we present a new hybrid model for prediction. In Chapter 10, we present the feature extraction process in mining and explain the importance of domain knowledge in classifier reduction. We also introduce a multiple evidence combination approach for WWW prediction. In Chapter 11, we show some of the experimental results and analysis.

DATA MINING TOOL FOR WEB PAGE SURFING PREDICTION

Introduction to Part III.

Chapter 8

Web Data Management and Mining

8.1 Overview

In Part I we discussed supporting technologies for the data mining tools we have developed, and in Part II we discussed our data mining tool for intrusion detection. In this part we will describe our data mining tool for Web page surfing prediction. The application we are considering is, in effect, an aspect of Web data mining. Our Web page prediction tool that utilizes data mining techniques will be described in Chapters 9, 10, and 11. In this chapter, we will provide a broad overview of Web data management and mining, which essentially encompasses Web page surfing prediction. We need efficient Web data management and mining techniques for Web page surfing prediction.

There is a lot of data on the Web, and this data has to be managed and mined so that the relevant nuggets of information can be extracted. In addition, the Web usage patterns have to be mined so that one can identify who is browsing the Web. Finally, the Web structure has to be mined so that Web searches can be made more efficient. Lots of technologies have to work together to support Web data mining. First, we need to index and retrieve the data; that is, we need to efficiently manage the digital libraries hosted on the Web. Next, we need support for E-commerce technologies. Third, we need to develop semantic Web technologies to understand the Web pages. This chapter describes all these aspects of Web data management and mining, as illustrated in Figure 8.1.

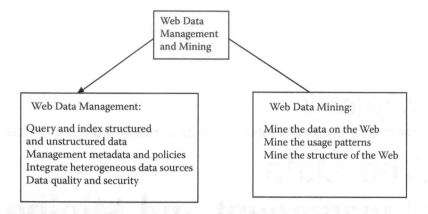

Figure 8.1 Web data management and mining.

The organization of this chapter is as follows. In Section 8.2, we discuss digital libraries. E-commerce technologies that make use of digital libraries are discussed in Section 8.3. Semantic Web technologies that enable machine untreatable Web pages are discussed in Section 8.4. Web data mining will be discussed in Section 8.5. It should be noted that our Web page prediction tool utilizes Web data mining technologies. Finally, the chapter is summarized in Section 8.6.

8.2 Digital Libraries

8.2.1 Overview

Digital libraries gained prominence with the initial effort by the National Science Foundation (NSF), the Defense Advanced Research Projects Agency (DARPA), and the National Aeronautics and Space Administration (NASA). NSF continued to fund special projects in this area, and as a result, the field has grown very rapidly. The idea behind digital libraries is to digitize all types of documents and provide efficient access to these digitized documents.

Several technologies have to work together to make digital libraries a reality. These include Web data management, search engines, and question-answering systems. This section will review the various developments in some of the digital libraries technologies. Figure 8.2 illustrates the various components.

The organization of this section is as follows. We discuss Web data management in Section 8.2.2. Search engines will be discussed in Section 8.2.3. A note on question-answering systems will be provided in Section 8.2.4.

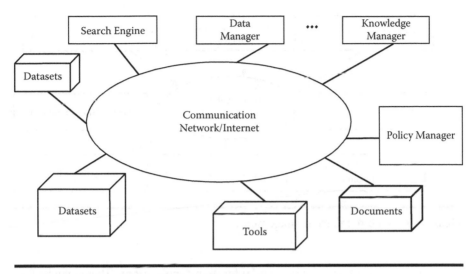

Figure 8.2   Components of digital libraries.

8.2.2   Web Database Management

This section discusses the core concepts in Web data management. A major challenge confronting Web data management researchers and practitioners is to come up with an appropriate data representation scheme. The question is, is there a need for a standard data model for Web database systems? Is it at all possible to develop such a standard? If so, what are the relationships between the standard and the individual models used by the databases on the Web?

Database management functions for the Web include query processing, metadata management, security, and integrity. In [1], we have examined various database management system functions and discussed the impact of Web database access on these functions. Some of the issues are discussed here. Figure 8.3 illustrates the functions. Querying and browsing are two of the key functions. First of all, an appropriate query language is needed. As Structure Query Language (SQL) is a popular language, appropriate extensions to SQL may be desired. XML-QL, which has evolved from XML (eXtensible Markup Language) and SQL, is moving in this direction. Query processing involves developing a cost model. Are there special cost models for Web database management? With respect to browsing, the query processing techniques have to be integrated with techniques for following links.

Updating Web databases could mean different things. One could create a new Web site, place servers at that site, and update the data managed by the servers. A question to consider is, can a user of the library send information to update the data at a Web site? An issue here concerns security privileges. If the user has write privileges, then he or she could update the databases that he or she is authorized to modify. Agents and mediators could be used to locate the databases and process the update.

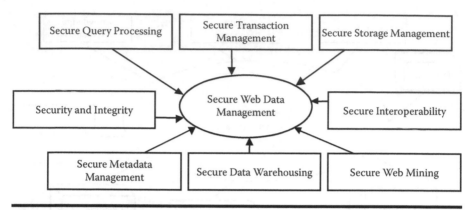

Figure 8.3   Web database management.

Transaction management is essential for many applications. There may be new kinds of transactions on the Web. For example, various items may be sold through the Web. In this case, the item should not be locked immediately when a potential buyer makes a bid. It has to be left open until several bids are received and the item is sold; that is, special transaction models are needed. Appropriate concurrency control and recovery techniques have to be developed for the transaction models.

Metadata management is a major concern for Web data management. What is metadata? It describes all of the information pertaining to the library. This could include the various Web sites, the types of users, access control issues, and the policies enforced. Where should the metadata be located? Should each participating site maintain its own metadata? Should the metadata be replicated or should there be a centralized metadata repository? Metadata in such an environment could be very dynamic, especially because the users and the Web sites may be changing continuously.

Storage management for Web database access is a complex function. Appropriate index strategies and access methods for handling multimedia data are needed. In addition, due to the large volumes of data, techniques for integrating database management technology with mass storage technology are also needed. Other data management functions include integrating heterogeneous databases, managing multimedia data, and mining. Security cuts across all these functions.

8.2.3   Search Engines

Since the early 1990s, numerous search engines have been developed. They have their origins in the information retrieval systems developed in the 1960s and beyond. Typically, when we invoke a browser such as Netscape or Microsoft's Explorer, we have access to several search engines. Some of the early search engines were AltaVista, Yahoo, Infoseek, and Lycos. These systems were developed around 1995 and were fairly effective for their times. They are much improved now.

Since around 1999, one of the popular search engines has been Google. It started off as a Stanford University research project funded by organizations such as the National Science Foundation and the Central Intelligence Agency as well as the industry, and was later commercialized. Systems such as Google, as well as some of the other search engines, provide intelligent searches. However, they still have a long way to go before users can get exact answers to their queries.

Search engines are accessed via browsers. When you click on the search engines, you will get a window requesting what you want to search for. Then the keywords and the various Web pages are listed. How does a search engine find the Web pages? It essentially uses information retrieval on the Web.

The rating of a search engine is determined by the speed with which it produces results, and more importantly the accuracy with which it produces the results. That is, does the search engine list the relevant Web pages for the query? For example, when you type a query called "lung cancer," does it provide the relevant information you are looking for with respect to lung cancer? It can, for example, list resources about lung cancer or list information about who has had lung cancer. Usually, people want to get resources about lung cancer. If they want to find out who has lung cancer, then they could type in "people with lung cancer."

The problem with many searches, although extremely useful, is that they often provide a lot of irrelevant information. To get timely results, they have to build sophisticated indexing techniques. They also may cache information from Web servers for frequently posed queries. Some typical modules of a search engine are illustrated in Figure 8.4. The search engines have a directory about the various Web servers they have to search. This directory is updated as new servers are registered. Then the search engines build indices for various keywords. When a user poses a

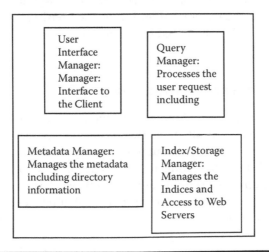

Figure 8.4   Modules of the search engines.

query, the search engine will consult its knowledge base, which consists of information about the Web servers and various indices. It also examines the caches if it has any, and will then search the Web servers for information. All functions have to be carried out in real-time.

Web mining enables one to mine the user log and build profiles for the various users so that the search can be made more efficient. Note that there are millions of users, so building profiles is not straightforward. We need to mine the Web logs and find out what the preferences of the users are. Then we list those Web pages for the user. Furthermore, if a user is searching for some information, from time to time the search engines can list Web pages that could be relevant to the user's request. That is, search engines will have to dynamically carry out searches, depending on what the user wants.

8.2.4 Question-Answering Systems

Question-answering systems are the early information retrieval systems and were developed in the late 1960s. They would typically give yes or no answers. Since then, there have been many advances in information retrieval systems, including text, image, and video systems. However, with the advent of the Web, the question-answering systems have received much prominence. They are not just limited to a yes or no answer. They give answers to various complex queries such as "what is the weather forecast today in Chicago?" or "retrieve the flight schedules from London to Tokyo that make, at most, one stop."

The various search engines, such as Google, are capable of performing complex searches. However, they are yet to answer complex queries. The research on question-answering systems is just beginning, and we can expect search engines to have this capability. Question-answering systems integrate many technologies, including natural language processing, information retrieval, search engines, and data management. This is illustrated in Figure 8.5.

8.3 E-Commerce Technologies

Various models, architectures, and technologies are being developed. Business-to-business E-commerce is all about two businesses conducting transactions on the Web. We give some examples. Suppose corporation A is an automobile manufacturer and needs microprocessors to be installed in its automobiles. It will then purchase the microprocessors from corporation B, which manufactures the microprocessors. Another example is when an individual purchases some goods such as toys from a toy manufacturer. This manufacturer then contacts a packaging company via the Web to deliver the toys to the individual. The transaction between the manufacturer and the packaging company is a business-to-business transaction. Business-to-business E-commerce also involves one business purchasing a unit of

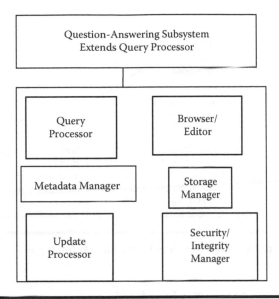

Figure 8.5 Question answering and text retrieval.

another business or two businesses merging. The main point is that such transactions have to be carried out on the Web. Business-to-consumer E-commerce is when a consumer such as a member of the mass population makes purchases on the Web. In the toy manufacturer example, the purchase transaction between the individual and the toy manufacturer is a business-to-consumer transaction.

The modules of the E-commerce server may include modules for managing the data and Web pages, mining customer information, security enforcement, and transaction management. E-commerce client functions may include presentation management, user interface, as well as caching data and hosting browsers. There could also be a middle tier that may implement the business objects to carry out the business functions of E-commerce. These business functions may include brokering, mediation, negotiations, purchasing, sales, marketing, and other E-commerce functions. The E-commerce server functions are impacted by the information management technologies for the Web. In addition to the data management functions and the business functions, the E-commerce functions also include those for managing distribution, heterogeneity, and federations.

E-commerce also includes nontechnological aspects such as policies, laws, social impacts, and psychological impacts. We are now doing business in an entirely different way, and therefore we need a paradigm shift. We cannot do successful E-commerce if we still want the traditional way of buying and selling products. We have to be more efficient and rely on the technologies a lot more to gain a competitive edge. Some key points of E-commerce are illustrated in Figure 8.6.

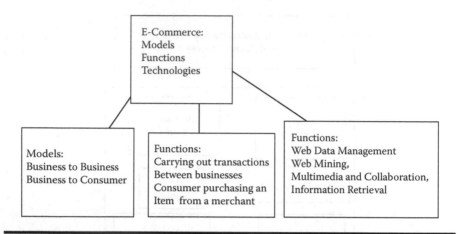

Figure 8.6 E-commerce models, functions, and technologies.

8.4 Semantic Web Technologies

The semantic Web essentially is about machine-understandable Web pages. Tim Berners Lee has specified various layers for the semantic Web (see Figure 8.7). At the lowest level, one has the protocols for communication including TCP/IP (Transmission Control Protocol/Internet protocol), HTTP (Hypertext Transfer Protocol), and SSL (Secure Socket Layer). The next level is the XML (eXtensible Markup Language) layer, which also includes XML schemas. The next level is the RDF (Resource Description Framework) layer. Next comes the Ontologies layer. This is followed by the Query and Rules layer. Finally, at the highest level one has the Trust Management layer. Each of the layers is discussed in the following text.

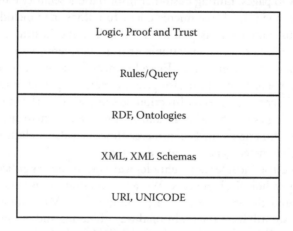

Figure 8.7 Layers for the semantic Web.

TCP/IP, SSL, and HTTP are the protocols for data transmission. They are built on top of more basic communication layers. With these protocols, one can transmit Web pages over the Internet. At this level, one does not deal with the syntax or the semantics of the documents. Then come the XML and XML Schemas layer. XML is the standard representation language for document exchange. For example, if a document is not marked up, then each machine may display the document in its own way. This makes document exchange extremely difficult. XML is a markup language that follows certain rules, and if all documents are marked up using XML, then there is uniform representation and presentation of documents. This is one of the significant developments of the WWW. Without some form of common representation of documents, it is impossible to have any sort of meaningful communication on the Web. XML schemas essentially describe the structure of XML documents. Both XML and XML schemas are the invention of Tim Berners Lee and the W3C (see [2, 3]).

Now, XML focuses only on the syntax of the document. A document could have different interpretations at different sites. This is a major issue for integrating information seamlessly across the Web. To overcome this significant limitation, W3C started discussions on a language called *RDF* in the late 1990s. RDF essentially uses XML syntax but can express semantics. One needs to use RDF to integrate and exchange information in a meaningful way on the Web. Although XML has received widespread acceptance, RDF is only now beginning to get acceptance.

The next layer is the Ontologies and Interoperability layer. Now, RDF is only a specification language for expressing syntax and semantics. The question is, what entities do we need to specify? How can the community accept common definitions? To solve this issue, various communities, such as the medical, financial, defense, and even the entertainment community, have come up with what are called *ontologies*. One could use ontologies to describe the various wines of the world or the different types of aircraft used by the U.S. Air Force. Ontologies can also be used to specify various diseases or financial entities. Once a community has developed ontologies, it has to publish these ontologies on the Web. The idea is for anyone interested in the ontologies developed by a community to use those ontologies. Now, within a community, there could be different interest groups and each such group could come up with its own ontologies. For example, the American Medical Association could come up with its ontologies for diseases, whereas the British Medical Association could come up with its own ontologies. This poses a challenge as the system, and in this case, the semantic Web has to examine the ontologies and decide how to develop some common ontologies. Although the goal is for the British and American communities to agree and come up with common ontologies, in the real world, differences do exist. The next question is, what do ontologies do for the Web? Now, using these ontologies, different groups can communicate information; that is, ontologies facilitate information exchange and integration. Ontologies are used by Web services so that the Web can provide semantic Web services to the humans. They may be specified using RDF syntax.

The Query and Rules layer is responsible for querying the Web resources and using the Web rules language to support various policies. The final layer is logic, proof, and trust. The issue here is, how do you trust the information on the Web? Obviously, it depends on whom it comes from. How do you carry out trust negotiation? That is, interested parties have to communicate with each other and determine how to trust each other and how to trust the information obtained on the Web. Closely related to trust issues is security, which will be discussed later on. Logic-based approaches and proof theories are being examined for enforcing trust on the semantic Web.

8.5 Web Data Mining

Web data mining is a key aspect of Web information management. There are three types of Web data mining, as illustrated in Figure 8.8. One is to mine the data on the Web and extract the nuggets. The data may be in Web databases or Web information sources. The second is mining Web logs and Web usage patterns. This is the most common type of Web data mining. For example, several Web sites mine the usage patterns to get a competitive advantage. Furthermore, various E-commerce transactions are mined so that a Web site may offer advice

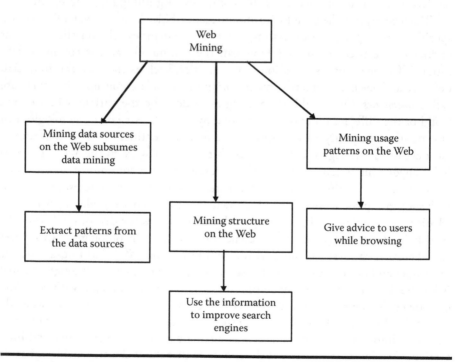

Figure 8.8 Web data mining.

to a customer to purchase a new item. The third type is managing the Web structure so that the organization and relationship the various Web pages share can be extracted.

The tool that we will describe in the next three chapters is on Web page surfing prediction. One can view this as a form of Web usage mining. Here, we collect information about the Web pages users have visited and use this information to give advice to the user regarding future Web pages to visit. This will also give the Web site administrator some idea of the Web pages that the user visits so that he or she can develop profiles of the users to give them future advice or to determine whether the user is visiting certain Web sites that he or she should not be visiting. For more details of Web data mining, we refer to [4].

8.6 Summary and Directions

This chapter has essentially provided a broad overview of Web data management and mining. In particular, we discussed digital libraries, including Web data management and search engine technologies, E-commerce technologies, semantic Web technologies, and aspects of Web data mining. As we have stated, Web data mining includes mining the databases on the Web as well as Web usage mining and Web structure mining. Our Web page surfing prediction tool is an example of a Web usage mining tool.

The next three chapters will describe our Web page surfing prediction tool. In particular, the data mining techniques that we have utilized, the description of our tool, and the experimental results will be given. Web page surfing prediction is an important aspect of Web mining whereby we learn the usage patterns of a user and give him or her advice to traverse the Web.

References

1. Thuraisingham, B., *Web Data Management and Electronic Commerce*, CRC Press, Boca Raton, FL, 2000.
2. St. Laurent, S., *XML: A Primer*, M&T Book, New York, 2001.
3. Lee, T.B, *Weaving the Web*, HarperOne, New York, 1999.
4. Thuraisingham, B., *Web Data Mining and Applications to Business Intelligence and Counter-Terrorism*, CRC Press, Boca Raton, FL, 2003.

Chapter 9

Effective Web Page Prediction Using Hybrid Model

9.1 Overview

As we have stated in Chapter 8, Web page surfing prediction is a key aspect of Web data management and mining. Surfing prediction is an important research area on which many application improvements depend. Applications such as latency reduction, Web search, and personalization systems utilize surfing prediction to improve their performance. This in turn improves applications such as E-commerce, social networking, and knowledge management.

There are several problems with the current state-of-the-art solutions. First, the predictive accuracy using a proposed solution such as a Markov model is low; for example, the maximum training accuracy is 41%. Second, prediction using association rule mining (ARM) and longest repeating subsequence (LRS) pattern extraction is done by choosing the path with highest probability in the training set; hence, any new surfing path is misclassified because the probability of such a path occurring in the training set is zero. Third, the sparse nature of the user sessions used in training can result in unreliable predictors. Finally, many of the previous methods have ignored domain knowledge as a means of improving prediction. Domain knowledge plays a key role in improving predictive accuracy because it can be used to eliminate irrelevant classifiers during prediction or reduce their effectiveness by assigning them lower weights. In Part III of this book, we will describe our algorithms for Web page prediction. In this chapter, we will present our hybrid model. For details of related work, we refer the reader to [1, 2].

The organization of this chapter is as follows: Our overall approach is presented in Section 9.2. Feature extraction, which is key to our approach, is elaborated in Section 9.3. Incorporating domain knowledge and classifier reduction, which would enhance the data mining techniques, will be discussed in Section 9.4. The chapter is summarized in Section 9.5.

9.2 Our Approach

WWW prediction is a multiclass problem, and prediction can resolve into many classes. Most multiclass techniques, such as one-vs-one and one-vs-all, are based on binary classification. Prediction is required to check any new instance against all classes. In WWW prediction, the number of classes is very large (11,700 classes in our experiments). Hence, prediction accuracy is very low because it fails to choose the right class. For a given instance, domain knowledge can be used to eliminate irrelevant classes [3].

We use several classification techniques, namely, support vector machines (SVM), artificial neural networks (ANN), association rule mining (ARM), and Markov model in WWW prediction. We propose a hybrid prediction model by combining two or more of them using Dempster's rule [4]. The Markov model is a powerful technique for predicting seen data; however, it cannot predict unseen data. On the other hand, SVM is a powerful technique, which can predict not only for the seen data but also for the unseen data. However, when dealing with too many classes or when there is a possibility that one instance may belong to many classes, SVM predictive power may decrease because such examples confuse the training process. To overcome these drawbacks with SVM, we extract domain knowledge from the training set and incorporate this knowledge in the testing set, to improve prediction accuracy of SVM by reducing the number of classifiers during prediction.

ANN is also a powerful technique, which can predict not only for the seen data but also for the unseen data. Nonetheless, ANN has similar shortcomings as SVM when dealing with too many classes or when there is a possibility that one instance may belong to many classes. Furthermore, the design of the ANN becomes complex with a large number of input and output nodes. To overcome these drawbacks with ANN, we employ domain knowledge from the training set and incorporate this knowledge in the testing set by reducing the number of classifiers to consult during prediction. This improves the prediction accuracy and reduces the prediction time.

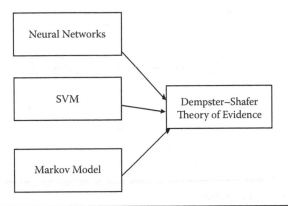

Figure 9.1   Overview of our approach.

Improvements in Web search engines can also be achieved using predictive models. Surfers can be viewed as having traversed the entire WWW link structure. The distribution of visits over all WWW pages is computed and used for reweighting and reranking results. Surfer path information is considered more important than the text keywords entered by the surfers; hence, the more accurate the predictive models, the better the search results [5]. Our approach is illustrated in Figure 9.1.

9.3   Feature Extraction

In Web prediction, the available source of training data is the users' sessions, which are sequences of pages that users visit within a period of time. In order to improve the predictive ability using different classification techniques, we need to extract additional features besides the pages' IDs. In this section, we first introduce some of the problematic aspects of the dataset we are handling, namely, the user session logs. Next, we discuss the feature extraction process and introduce the concept of the sliding window.

In mining the Web, the only source of training examples is the logs that contain the sequences of pages or clicks users have visited or made, time, date, and the period of time the user stays in each page. Many models, such as the Markov model, ARM, and our approach, apply a sliding window on the user sessions to make training instances the same length [6]. If we apply a sliding window, we will end up with many repeated instances that will precipitate the probability calculation. Furthermore, the page IDs in the user sessions are nominal attributes.

Nominal attributes have no internal structure and take one of a finite number of possible values [7]. Many data mining techniques, such as SVM, require continuous attributes because they use a metric measure in their computations (dot product in

	1	2	...	N
1	0	*freq (1, 2)*	...	*freq (1, N)*
2	*freq (2, 1)*	0	...	*freq (2, N)*
...	*freq (..., 1)*	*freq (..., 2)*	...	*freq (..., N)*
N	0	*freq (N, 2)*	...	0

Figure 9.2 Frequency matrix.

the case of SVM). In our implementation, we use bit vectors to represent the page IDs. We keep only the index of the page ID in the vector and its numeric value, if that value is not zero. Missing attributes are assumed to have zero values.

To extract more knowledge from the user sessions, we use what we call frequency matrix shown in Figure 9.2. The first row and column represent the enumeration of Web page IDs. Each cell in the matrix represents the number of times (frequency) users have visited two pages in a sequence. $freq(x, y)$ is the number of times users have visited page y after page x. For example, cell $(1, 2)$ contains the number of times users have visited page 2 after page 1. Note that $freq(1, 2)$ is not necessarily equal to $freq(2, 1)$, and $freq(x, x)$ is always equal to zero.

In this research, we apply a sliding window of size N to break long user sessions into N-size sessions. In our implementation, we use a sliding window of sizes 3 to 7. To further elaborate on the sliding window concept, we present the following example.

Example

Suppose we have a user session $A = \langle 1, 2, 3, 4, 5, 6, 7 \rangle$, where 1, 2,..., 7 is the sequence of pages a user has visited. Suppose, also, that we use a sliding window of size 5. We apply feature extraction to $A = \langle 1, 2, 3, 4, 5, 6, 7 \rangle$ and end up with the following user sessions of 5-page length: $B = \langle 1, 2, 3, 4, 5 \rangle$, $C = \langle 2, 3, 4, 5, 6 \rangle$, and $D = \langle 3, 4, 5, 6, 7 \rangle$. Note that the outcome or label of the sessions A, B, C, and D are 7, 5, 6, and 7, respectively. This way, we end up with the following four user sessions: A, B, C, and D. In general, the total number of extracted sessions using a sliding window of size w and original session of size A is $|A| - w + 1$.

9.4 Domain Knowledge and Classifier Reduction

With regard to WWW surfing, the number of classifiers used to predict one new instance using one-vs-all is still very high. One way to reduce the number of classifiers, consulted during prediction is to use the domain knowledge that we already possess. The domain knowledge here is the frequency matrix shown in Figure 9.2. We use the frequency matrix to reduce the number of classifiers needed to predict for a given instance. Specifically, for a testing example $X = \langle x_1, x_2, \ldots, x_N \rangle$ and a classifier C_i, we exclude C_i in the prediction process if $freq(x_N, i) = 0$ in the frequency matrix, where x_N is the last page ID the user has visited in the testing session. There are two possibilities when the $freq(x, y)$ is 0 in the frequency matrix. First, there is no hyperlink of page y in page x. Second, no user has visited page y directly after page x. We do not distinguish between these two events and simply exclude any classifier f_i when $freq(x_N, i) = 0$.

9.5 Summary

Web page prediction during Web surfing is about predicting the Web pages that a user will visit next based on his or her surfing patterns. This is a key aspect of Web usage mining and has many applications in customer relationship management and E-commerce. In this chapter, we described our tool for Web page surfing prediction. We use feature extraction and classification as our data mining technique. We also use domain knowledge to make the technique more efficient. More details of our tools will be described in Chapters 10 and 11.

There are many areas for further improvement. We would like to analyze the content of the Web pages and take this into consideration when giving advice to users. This means the Web pages that will be useful to a user will not only depend on his or her surfing patterns but will also depend on the content of the Web pages browsed. Another area for improvement is enhancement of the data mining techniques to provide better accuracy and to reduce false positives and negatives. With a growing market for E-commerce and customer relationship management, we believe that there will be an extensive demand for such Web usage mining tools.

References

1. Piton, J. and Pirolli, P., Mining longest repeating subsequences to predict World Wide Web surfing, in *Proceedings of the 2nd USENIX Symposium on Internet Technologies and Systems (USITS'99)*, Boulder, Colorado, October 1999, pp. 139–150.
2. Grcar, M., Fortuna, B., Mladenic, D., *k*NN versus SVM in the collaborative filtering framework, *WebKDD '05*, August 21, Chicago, IL.
3. Burke, R., Hybrid recommender systems: Survey and experiments, *User Modeling and User-Adapted Interaction*, Vol. 12, No. 4, 331–370, 2002.
4. Shafer, G., *A Mathematical Theory of Evidence*, Princeton University Press, Princeton, NJ, 1976.

5. Chung, V., Li, C.H., and Kwok, J., Dissimilarity learning for nominal data, *Pattern Recognition*, Vol. 37, No. 7, 1471–1477, 2004.
6. Brin, S. and Page, L., The anatomy of a large-scale hypertextual Web search engine, in *Proceedings of the 7th International WWW Conference*, Brisbane, Australia, 1998, pp. 107–117.
7. Mobasher, B., Dai, H., Luo, T., and Nakagawa, M., Effective personalization based on association rule discovery from Web usage data, in *Proceedings of the ACM Workshop on Web Information and Data Management (WIDM01)*, 2001, pp. 9–15.

Chapter 10

Multiple Evidence Combination for WWW Prediction

10.1 Overview

In Chapter 9, we described our approach to Web page surfing prediction. We essentially extract features and use domain-based classification. Our approach combines multiple classifiers so that the resulting classifier has the advantages of each of the individual classifiers. In this chapter, we discuss details of our hybrid model for World Wide Web (WWW) prediction using the support vector machine (SVM), artificial neural network (ANN), and the Markov model as evidence based on the Dempster's rule for evidence combination.

Figure 10.1 shows that prediction of a testing point is based on the fusion of two or more separate models. Recall that prediction using SVM (and ANN) has an extra advantage over the Markov model, namely, that they can predict for the unseen data, whereas the Markov model works better with the seen data. Hence, this hybrid model takes advantage of the best of both models in making a final prediction.

Dempster's rule is one part of the Dempster–Shafer evidence combination frame for combining independent bodies of evidence. According to this rule, the sources of evidence should be in the form of basic probability. Because SVM and ANN produce an uncalibrated value that is not a probability [1], we first need to convert or map this output into a posterior probability $P(class \mid input)$.

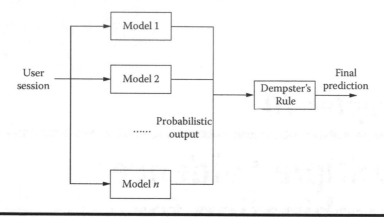

Figure 10.1 **A hybrid model using the Dempster's rule for evidence.**

In the following sections, we will present, first, a method to convert SVM output into a posterior probability by fitting a sigmoid function after SVM output [2]. Second, we apply sigmoid fitting to the output of ANN. Finally, we will present the background of Dempster–Shafer theory.

The organization of this chapter is as follows: We discuss SVM and sigmoid fitting in Section 10.2. ANN model with sigmoid fitting is discussed in Section 10.3. The Markov model is discussed in Section 10.4. Dempster–Shafer theory is discussed in Section 10.5. Applying Dempster–Shafer theory to combine SVM, ANN, and Markov model outputs is discussed in Section 10.6. The chapter is summarized in Section 10.7.

10.2 Fitting a Sigmoid after SVM

The uncalibrated value produced by SVMs is not a probability [1]. The output must be mapped to a posterior probability before SVM output can be used in Dempster's rule. A number of ways in which this can be accomplished have been presented in [1, 3]. Vapnik proposes decomposing the feature space F into orthogonal and nonorthogonal directions [1]. The separating hyperplane can then be considered. First, the direction that is orthogonal to the hyperplane is examined and, second, the $N - 1$ other directions that are not orthogonal to the separating hyperplane are reviewed. As a parameter for the orthogonal direction, a scaled version of $f(x)$, t, is employed. A vector u is used to represent all other directions. The posterior probability is fitted using the sum of cosine terms, and depends on both t and $\boldsymbol{u}$: $P(y = 1 \mid t, u)$ as follows:

$$P(y = 1 \mid t, u) = a_0(u) + \sum_{n=1}^{N} a_n(u)\cos(nf) \qquad (10.1)$$

This promising method has some limitations because it requires a solution of a linear system for every evaluation of the SVM. The sum of the cosine terms is not restricted to lie between 0 and 1 and is not constrained to be monotonic in f. In order to consider the probability $P(y=1|f)$, there is a very strong requirement that f be monotonic [2]. Hastie and Tibshirani in [4] fit Gaussians to the class-conditional densities $p(f|y=1)$ and $p(f|y=-1)$. Here, a single tied variance is estimated for both Gaussians. The posterior probability $P(y=1|f)$ is a sigmoid, whose slope is determined by a tied variance. One can compute the mean and the variance for each Gaussian from the dataset and apply Bayes' rule to obtain the posterior probability as follows:

$$P(y=1|f) = \frac{p(f|y=1)P(y=1)}{\sum_{i=-1,1} p(f|y=i)P(y=i)} \tag{10.2}$$

where $P(y=i)$ are prior probabilities computed from the training set, and f is defined as in Equation 2.14. The posterior is an analytic function of f with the form:

$$P(y=1|f) = \frac{1}{1+\exp(af^2+bf+c)} \tag{10.3}$$

The problem with this method is that Equation 10.3 is not monotonic, and the assumption of Gaussian class-conditional densities is often violated [2].

In this study, we implement a parametric method to fit the posterior $P(y=1|f)$ directly instead of estimating the class-conditional densities $p(f|y)$. It follows that class-conditional densities between the margins are apparently exponential [2]. Bayes' rule (Equation 10.2) on two exponentials suggests using a parametric form of sigmoid as follows:

$$P(y=1|f) = \frac{1}{1+\exp(Af+B)} \tag{10.4}$$

where f is defined as in Equation 2.14 (Chapter 2). This sigmoid model is equivalent to assuming that the output of the SVM is proportional to the log odds of a positive example. The parameters A and B of Equation 10.4 are fitted using maximum likelihood estimation from a training set (f_i, t_i), where the t_i's are the target probabilities defined as follows:

$$t_i = \frac{y_i+1}{2} \tag{10.5}$$

The parameters A and B are found by minimizing the negative log likelihood of the training data, which is a cross-entropy error function:

$$\text{minimize} -\sum_i t_i \log(p_i) + (1-t_i)\log(1-p_i) \tag{10.6}$$

where p_i is as follows:

$$p_i = \frac{1}{1+\exp(Af_i + B)} \tag{10.7}$$

The minimization in Equation 10.6 is a two-parameter minimization. Hence, it can be performed using any number of optimization algorithms. For robustness, we implement the model-trust minimization algorithm based on the Levenberg–Marquardt algorithm [5], whose pseudocode is shown in Appendix A.

10.3 Fitting a Sigmoid after ANN Output

In many typical scenarios, prediction is not resolved using one type of classifier. Instead, we consult many classifiers and combine their output together for a final decision. This requires that for a given input, each classifier produce a probability of class membership. Methods for combining such probabilities include Bayesian theory and Dempster–Shafer theory.

We have implemented the back-propagation learning algorithm based on minimizing the squared error function of the output. Hence, the output of our network cannot be considered a measure of probability. Because we are using Dempster's rule for the combination of evidence to resolve prediction of different classifiers, we should consequently map the output of our neural network into probability.

One important interpretation of the output of the ANN, in the context of the classification problem, is an estimate of the probability distribution. There are several ways to interpret the ANN output in terms of probability. One traditional way is to estimate the probability density function (p.d.f.) from the training data. The assumption here is that the training data follows some distribution (typically, the normal distribution). The normal distribution is widely used as a model parameter in which analytical techniques can be applied to estimate such parameters (mean and standard deviation). The problem is that the assumption of normality is often not justified [6].

An alternative approach to p.d.f. estimation is the kernel-based approximation [6–8]. The reasoning behind kernel-based approximation is that when a particular instance, such as a user session, is present, some probability density is indicated. The probability density is higher in areas where many instances are close to one another. Our confidence in such probability densities is high when we get close to such areas, and low when we move away. In kernel-based estimation, simple functions are located for each available case and aggregated together to estimate the overall p.d.f. A common kernel function used for each case is the Gaussian kernel. A good approximation of the p.d.f. is subject to the existence of sufficient training points. Parzen windows classifiers are an example of such an approach. The Parzen windows method is a nonparametric procedure that synthesizes an estimate of a p.d.f. by superimposing a number of windows to create replicas of a function (often, the Gaussian) [9].

Another approach is to consider learning to minimize a probabilistic function, instead of squared error, such as the cross-entropy shown in Equation 10.8. Once learning is done, the output of the network is an estimate of the p.d.f. [10]. In Equation 10.8, D is the training set, t_d is the target class of example d, and o_d is the output of the network, where f and o_d are defined by Equation 10.9 and Equation 10.10.

$$\text{minimize} - \sum_{d \in D} t_d \log(o_d) + (1 - t_d) \log(1 - o_d) \tag{10.8}$$

$$f(I) = \begin{cases} 1 & \text{if } \sigma \geq 0.5 \\ -1 & \text{otherwise} \end{cases} \tag{10.9}$$

$$o_d = \frac{1}{1 + \exp(Af_d + B)} \tag{10.10}$$

Because the back-propagation algorithm in our implementation minimizes the squared error function, Equation 2.4 (Chapter 2), we choose to implement a parametric method to fit the posterior directly instead of estimating the class-conditional densities $p(f \mid y)$ [2], where y is the target class and f is the output function for the neural network. The output of the neural network is computed as in Equation 10.9, where I is the input to the network and σ is the output of the sigmoid transfer function defined as in Equation 2.3. It follows that class-conditional densities between the margins are apparently exponential [2]. Bayes' rule on two exponentials suggests using a parametric form of sigmoid as in Equation 10.4.

This sigmoid model is equivalent to assuming that the output of the ANN is proportional to the log odds of a positive example. The parameters A and B of Equation 10.4 are fitted using maximum likelihood estimation and can be found by minimizing the negative log likelihood of the training data, which is a cross-entropy error function (Equation 10.8). o_d in Equation 10.8 is defined as in Equation 10.10.

The minimization in Equation 10.8 is a two-parameter minimization. Hence, it can be performed using many optimization algorithms. For robustness, we implement the model-trust minimization algorithm based on the Levenberg–Marquardt algorithm [5].

10.4 Dempster–Shafer for Evidence Combination

Dempster–Shafer theory (also known as *theory of belief functions*) is a mathematical theory of evidence [11] that is considered to be a generalization of the Bayesian theory of subjective probability. As a belief function rather than a Bayesian probability distribution is the best representation of a chance, the Dempster–Shafer theory differs from the Bayesian theory. A further difference is that probability values are assigned to sets of possibilities rather than single events. Unlike Bayesian methods, which often map unknown priors to random variables, the Dempster–Shafer framework does not specify priors and conditionals.

The Dempster–Shafer theory is based on two ideas. First, the notion of obtaining degrees of belief for one question based on subjective probabilities for a related question. Second, Dempster's rule for combining such degrees of belief when they are based on independent items of evidence. Because we use three independent sources of evidence, namely, SVM, ANN, and the Markov model, we are interested in the latter part of the Dempster–Shafer theory, namely, Dempster's rule. We use it to combine three bodies of evidence (SVM, ANN, and Markov model) in WWW prediction. The reader is referred to [12–15] for more details regarding this theory and its applications.

10.5 Dempster's Rule for Evidence Combination

Dempster's rule is a well-known method for aggregating many different bodies of evidence in the same reference set. Suppose we want to combine evidence for a hypothesis C. In WWW prediction, C is the assignment of a page during prediction for a user session. For example, what is the next page a user might visit after visiting pages p_1, p_3, p_4, and p_{10}? C is a member of 2^Θ, that is, the power set of Θ, where Θ is our *frame of discernment*. A frame of discernment Θ is an exhaustive set of mutually exclusive elements (hypothesis, propositions). All of the elements in this power set, including the elements of Θ, are propositions. Given two independent sources of evidence, m_1 and m_2, Dempster's rule combines them in the following frame:

$$m_{1,2}(C) = \frac{\displaystyle\sum_{A,B\subseteq\Theta, A\cap B=C} m_1(A)m_2(B)}{\displaystyle\sum_{A,B\subseteq\Theta, A\cap B\neq\phi} m_1(A)m_2(B)} \tag{10.11}$$

Here, A and B are supersets of C, but they are not necessarily proper supersets; that is, they may be equal to C or to the frame of discernment Θ. The independent sources of evidence m_1 and m_2 are functions (also known as a *mass of belief*) that assign a coefficient between 0 and 1 to different parts of 2^Θ. $m_1(A)$ is the portion of belief assigned to A by m_1. $m_{1,2}(C)$ is the combined Dempster–Shafer probability for a hypothesis C. To illustrate the Dempster–Shafer theory, we present the following example.

Example

Consider a Web site that contains three separate Web pages B, C, and D. Each page has a hyperlink to the two other pages. We are interested in predicting the next Web page (i.e., B, C, or D) a user visits after he or she visits several pages. We may form the following propositions, which correspond to proper subsets of Θ:

P_B—The user will visit page B.
P_C—The user will visit page C.
P_D—The user will visit page D.
P_B, P_C—The user will visit either page B or page C.
P_D, P_B—The user will visit either page D or page B.
P_D, P_C—The user will visit either page D or page C.

With these propositions, 2^Θ would consist of the following:

$$2^\Theta = \{\{P_D\}, \{P_B\}, \{P_C\}, \{P_D, P_C\}, \{P_B, P_C\}\{P_D, P_B\}, \{P_B, P_C, P_D\}, \phi\}$$

In many applications, basic probabilities for every proper subset of Θ may not be available. In these cases, a nonzero $m(\Theta)$ accounts for all those subsets for which we have no specific belief. Because we are expecting the user to visit only one Web page (it is impossible to visit two pages at the same time), we have positive evidence for individual pages only, that is,

$$m(A) > 0 : A \in \{\{P_D\}, \{P_B\}, \{P_C\}\}$$

The uncertainty of the evidence $m(\Theta)$ in this scenario is as follows:

$$m(\Theta) = 1 - \sum_{A \subset \Theta} m(A)$$

In Equation 10.11, the numerator accumulates the evidence that supports a particular hypothesis, and the denominator conditions it on the total evidence for those hypotheses supported by both sources. Applying this combination formula to the preceding example, assuming we have two bodies of evidence, namely, SVM and the Markov model, would yield

$$m_{svm,markov}(P_B) = \frac{W}{\sum_{A,B \subseteq \Theta, A \cap B \neq \phi} m_{svm}(A)m_{markov}(B)}$$

$$W = m_{svm}(\{P_B\})m_{markov}(\{P_B\}) + m_{svm}(\{P_B\})m_{markov}(\{P_B, P_C\}) + m_{svm}(\{P_B\})m_{markov}(\{P_B, P_D\})$$

10.6 Using Dempster–Shafer Theory in WWW Prediction

We have three sources of evidence: the output of SVM, ANN, and the Markov model. These models operate independently. Furthermore, we assume that, for any session x for which it does not appear in the training set, the Markov prediction is zero. If we use Dempster's rule to combine SVM and the Markov model as our bodies of evidence, we get the following equation:

$$m_{svm,markov}(C) = \frac{\displaystyle\sum_{A,B \subseteq \Theta, A \cap B = C} m_{svm}(A)m_{markov}(B)}{\displaystyle\sum_{A,B \subseteq \Theta, A \cap B \neq \phi} m_{svm}(A)m_{markov}(B)} \tag{10.12}$$

In the case of WWW prediction, we can simplify this formulation because we have only beliefs for singleton classes (i.e., the final prediction is only one Web page, and it should not have more than one page) and the body of evidence itself ($m(\Theta)$). This means that for any proper subset A of Θ for which we have no specific belief, $m(A) = 0$.

For example, based on the example discussed earlier, we would have the following terms in the numerator of Equation 10.12:

$$m_{svm}(\{P_B\})m_{markov}(\{P_B\}),$$

$$m_{svm}(\{P_B\})m_{markov}(\{P_B, P_C\}),$$

$$m_{svm}(\{P_B\})m_{markov}(\{P_B, P_D\}),$$

$$m_{svm}(\{P_B\})m_{markov}(\Theta),$$

$$m_{markov}(\{P_B\})m_{svm}(\{P_B, P_C\}),$$

$$m_{markov}(\{P_B\})m_{svm}(\{P_B, P_D\}),$$

$$m_{markov}(\{P_B\})m_{svm}(\Theta)$$

Because we have nonzero basic probability assignments for only the singleton subsets of Θ and the Θ itself, this means that

$$m_{svm}(\{P_B\})m_{markov}(\{P_B\}) > 0,$$

$$m_{svm}(\{P_B\})m_{markov}(\{P_B, P_C\}) = 0, \text{ since } m_{markov}(\{P_B, P_C\}) = 0$$

$$m_{svm}(\{P_B\})m_{markov}(\{P_B, P_D\}) = 0, \text{ since } m_{markov}(\{P_B, P_D\}) = 0$$

$$m_{svm}(\{P_B\})m_{markov}(\Theta) > 0,$$

$$m_{markov}(\{P_B\})m_{svm}(\{P_B, P_C\}) = 0, \text{ since } m_{svm}(\{P_B, P_C\}) = 0$$

$$m_{markov}(\{P_B\})m_{svm}(\{P_B, P_D\}) = 0, \text{ since } m_{svm}(\{P_B, P_D\}) = 0$$

$$m_{markov}(\{P_B\})m_{svm}(\Theta) > 0$$

After eliminating zero terms, we get the simplified Dempster's combination rule as follows:

$$m_{svm,markov}(\{P_B\}) = \frac{m_{svm}(\{P_B\})m_{markov}(\{P_B\}) + m_{svm}(\{P_B\})m_{markov}(\Theta) + m_{markov}(\{P_B\})m_{svm}(\Theta)}{\sum_{A,B\subseteq\Theta, A\cap B\neq\phi} m_{markov}(A)m_{svm}(B)}$$

(10.13)

We use Equation 10.13 to rank the hypothesis and resolve prediction. Note that in choosing or presenting the top n hypotheses, instead of one hypothesis, we can generalize our approach to work as a recommendation system. Because we are interested in ranking the hypotheses, we can further simplify Equation 10.13, making the denominator independent of any particular hypothesis as follows:

$$m_{svm,markov}(\{P_B\}) \propto$$

$$m_{svm}(\{P_B\})m_{markov}(\{P_B\}) +$$

$$m_{svm}(\{P_B\})m_{markov}(\Theta) +$$

$$m_{svm}(\Theta)m_{markov}(\{P_B\})$$

(10.14)

The $\propto$ is the "is proportional to" relationship. $m_{svm}(\Theta)$ and $m_{markov}(\Theta)$ represent the uncertainty in the bodies of evidence for SVM and Markov models, respectively. Note the implication of involving the uncertainty of SVM and the Markov model in Equation 10.14. The higher the uncertainty value of one model is, the more credit or weight is given to the other model. For example, if an unseen path B is presented, the Markov model fails to predict the next page; hence, $m_{markov}(\Theta) = 1$, $m_{markov}(\{P_B\}) = 0$, $m_{svm}(\Theta)m_{markov}(\{P_B\}) = 0$, and only SVM prediction, $m_{svm}(\{P_B\})$, will resolve the prediction.

We compute $m_{svm}(\Theta)$ and $m_{markov}(\Theta)$ in Equation 10.14 as follows. For SVM, we use the margin values for SVM to compute the uncertainty. Uncertainty is computed on the basis of the maximum distance of training examples from the margin as in Equations 10.15, 10.16, and 10.17.

$$m_{svm}(\Theta) = \frac{1}{\ln(e + svm_{margin})}$$

(10.15)

$$m_{ANN}(\Theta) = \frac{1}{\ln(e + ANN_{\text{margin}})} \qquad (10.16)$$

$$m_{markov}(\Theta) = \frac{1}{\ln(e + Markov_{\text{probability}})} \qquad (10.17)$$

In Equation 10.15, svm_{margin} is the maximum distance of training examples from the margin, and e is Euler's number. For ANN, we use the output value of the ANN to compute the uncertainty. We call the output of ANN for specific session x the margin because the ANN weights correspond to the separating surface between classes, and the output of ANN is the distance from this surface. Uncertainty is computed based on the maximum margin of all the training examples as in Equation 10.16. The ANN_{margin} is the maximum distance of training examples from the margin, and e is Euler's number. For Markov model uncertainty, we use the maximum probability of training examples as in Equation 10.17. $Markov_{\text{probability}}$ is the maximum probability of a training example. Note that in both models, the uncertainty is inversely proportional to the corresponding maximum value.

Table 10.1 shows the basic steps in our algorithm to predict WWW surfing using multiple evidence combination. Because these steps are similar, we only present the steps of combining SVM and Markov models.

Table 10.1 WWW prediction steps based on combining SVM and Markov models using Dempster's rule

Algorithm: WWW prediction using hybrid model

Input

$S \leftarrow$ *user sessions data*

Output

y_i: *next page prediction for testing session i.*

Begin

1. *$S' \leftarrow$ Apply-Feature-Extraction(S) // See Section 9.3.*
2. *svm-models $\leftarrow$ Train-SVM(S') // train SVM using one-vs-all, see Section 2.4.*
3. *svm-prob-models $\leftarrow$ Map-SVM-Models(svm-models) // map SVM output to a probability, See Section 10.2.*
4. *svm-uncertainty $\leftarrow$ ComputeUncertainty(SVM) // See Section 10.6., Equation 10.15.*
5. *Construct MakovModel(S') // See Section 10.5.*
6. *markov-uncertainty $\leftarrow$ Compute-Uncertainty (Markov) //See Section 10.6, Equation 10.17.*

Table 10.1 WWW prediction steps based on combining SVM and Markov models using Dempster's rule (*Continued*)

7. *For each testing session x in S', do*

   7.1 Compute and output SVM probabilities for different pages.

   7.2 Compute and output Markov probabilities for different pages.

   7.3 Compute using Equation **10.14** *and output the final prediction y_x.*

End

10.7 Summary and Directions

In this chapter we have described how results from multiple classifiers can be combined for Web page prediction. Our approach is first to extract features of Web page surfing patterns and then train classifiers such as SVM, ANN, and Markov models. We apply sigmoid fitting to SVM and ANN outputs so that they can be in the appropriate format. We then combine the outputs from SVM + Sigmoid, ANN + Sigmoid, and the Markov model by applying the Dempster–Shafer theory of evidence. The combined result is a significant improvement over the application of the individual classifiers (e.g., ANN, Markov, SVM). Our results will be presented in Chapter 11.

Future work will include examining other classification techniques for Web page prediction. These may include decision trees as well as nearest-neighbor algorithms. In addition, we also need to improve on our knowledge-based classification so that we can obtain better accuracy as well as reduce false positives and false negatives.

References

1. Vapnik, V.N., *The Nature of Statistical Learning Theory*, Springer-Verlag, New York, 1995.
2. Platt, J., Probabilities for support vector machines, in *Advances in Large Margin Classifiers*, Smola, A., Bartlett, P., Schölkopf, B., Schuurmans, D., Eds., MIT Press, 1999, original title: Probabilistic Outputs for Support Vector Machines and Comparisons to Regularized Likelihood Methods, pp. 61–74.
3. Wahba, G., Multivariate function and operator estimation, based on smoothing splines and reproducing kernels, in M. Casdagli and S. Eubank, Eds, *Nonlinear Modeling and Forecasting, SFI Studies in Sciences of Complexity*, Vol. XII, 1992, pp. 95–112.
4. Hastie, T. and Tibshirani, R., Classification by pairwise coupling, in *Proceedings of the 1997 Conference on Advances in Neural Information Processing Systems 10*, Denver, CO, pp. 507–513.
5. Press, W.H., Teukolsky, S.A., Vetterling, W.T., and Flannery, B.P., *Numerical Recipes in C: The Art of Scientific Computing*, 2nd ed., Cambridge University Press, Cambridge, 1992.

6. Bishop, C.M., *Neural Networks for Pattern Recognition*, Oxford University Press, Oxford, 1995.
7. Patterson, D.W., *Artificial Neural Networks: Theory and Applications*, Prentice Hall, Englewood Cliffs, NJ, 1996.
8. Parzen, E., On the estimation of a probability density function and mode, *Annual of Mathematical Statistics*, Vol. 33, 1065–1076, 1962.
9. Specht, D.F., Probabilistic neural networks, *Neural Networks*, Vol. 3, 1990, pp. 109–118.
10. Mitchell, T., *Machine Learning*, McGraw Hill, New York, 1997.
11. Lalmas, M., Dempster–Shafer's theory of evidence applied to structured documents: Modelling uncertainty, in *Proceedings of the 20th Annual International ACM SIGIR*, Philadelphia, PA, 1997, pp. 110–118.
12. Aslandogan, Y.A. and Clement T.Y., Evaluating strategies and systems for content based indexing of person images on the Web, in *Proceedings of the eighth ACM international conference on Multimedia*, Marina del Rey, CA, United States 2000, pp. 313–321.
13. Aslandogan, Y.A., Mahajani, G.A., and Taylor, S., Evidence combination in medical data mining, in *Proceedings of the International Conference on Information Technology: Coding and Computing (ITCC'04)*, Vol. 2, 2004, p. 465.
14. Bendjebbour, A., Delignon, Y., Fouque, L., Samson, V., and Pieczynski, W., Multisensor image segmentation using Dempster–Shafer fusion in Markov fields context, *IEEE Transactions on Geoscience and Remote Sensing*, Vol. 39, No. 8, August 2001, pp. 1789–1798.
15. Shafer, G., *A Mathematical Theory of Evidence*, Princeton University Press, Princeton, NJ, 1976.

Chapter 11

WWW Prediction Results

11.1 Overview

As we have stated in Chapter 9, Web page surfing prediction will support many applications, including E-commerce and customer relationship management. In Chapters 9 and 10, we described our tool for Web page surfing prediction. In particular, we combine the outputs of support vector machine (SVM), artificial neural network (ANN), and the Markov model with the Dempster–Shafer theory of evidence for classification. The models are built by extracting features based on the Web pages surfed.

In this chapter, we present experimental results for WWW surfing prediction using five prediction models, namely, Markov model (LRS model), SVM, the association rule model (ARM), ANN, and a hybrid method (HMDR) based on Dempster's rule for evidence combination. Here, we first define the prediction measurements that we use in our results. Second, we present the dataset that we use in this research. Third, we present the experimental setup. Finally, we present our results.

The organization of this chapter is as follows. Our terminology is discussed in Section 11.2, and the data utilized is discussed in Section 11.3. The experimental setup is discussed in Section 11.4. Our results are presented in Section 11.5, and we discuss the results in Section 11.6. The chapter is summarized in Section 11.7.

11.2 Terminology

In all models, we used the N-gram representation of paths [1, 2]. The N-grams are tuples of the form $\langle X_1, X_2, \ldots, X_N \rangle$ that represent the sequence of page clicks by a set of surfers of a Web page. One may choose any length N for N-grams to record. The following definitions will be used in the following sections to measure the performance of the prediction. Pitkow et al. [1] have used these parameters to measure the performance of the Markov model. As we are considering the generalization accuracy and the training accuracy, we include two additional measurements that take into consideration the generalization accuracy, namely, Pr(Hit|MisMatch) and overall accuracy.

- Pr(Match), the probability that a penultimate path, $\langle x_{n-1}, x_{n-2}, \ldots, x_{2n-k} \rangle$, observed in the validation set was matched by the same penultimate path in the training set.
- Pr(Hit|Match), the conditional probability that page x_n is correctly predicted for the testing instance $\langle x_{n-1}, x_{n-2}, \ldots, x_{n-k} \rangle$ and $\langle x_{n-1}, x_{n-2}, \ldots, x_{n-k} \rangle$ matches a penultimate path in the training set.
- Pr(Hit) = Pr(Match) $\times$ Pr(Hit|Match), the probability that the page visited in the test set is the one estimated from the training as the most likely to occur.
- Pr(Miss|Match), the conditional probability that the page is incorrectly classified, given that its penultimate path $\langle x_{n-1}, x_{n-2}, \ldots, x_{n-k} \rangle$ matches a penultimate path in the training set.
- Pr(Miss) = Pr(Match) Pr(Miss|Match), the probability that a page x_n with a matched penultimate path is incorrectly classified.
- Pr(Hit|MisMatch), the conditional probability that a page x_n is correctly predicted for the testing instance $\langle x_{n-1}, x_{n-2}, \ldots, x_{n-k} \rangle$ and $\langle x_{n-1}, x_{n-2}, \ldots, x_{n-k} \rangle$ does not match any penultimate path in the training set. This measurement corresponds to the generalization accuracy, and it is considered more accurate than the training accuracy (represented by Pr(Hit|Match)).
- Overall accuracy A is defined as the overall accuracy that combines both matching/seen and mismatching/unseen testing examples in computing the accuracy (Equation 11.1).

$$A = \Pr(hit \mid mismatch) \times \Pr(mismatch) + \Pr(hit \mid match) \times pr(match) \quad (11.1)$$

The following relations hold for the preceding measurements:

$$\Pr(hit \mid match) = 1 - \Pr(miss \mid match) \quad (11.2)$$

$$\Pr(hit)/\Pr(miss) = \frac{\Pr(hit \mid match)}{\Pr(miss \mid match)} \quad (11.3)$$

Pr(Hit|Match) corresponds to the training accuracy because it shows the proportion of training examples that are correctly classified. Pr(Hit|MisMatch) corresponds to the generalization accuracy because it shows the proportion of unseen examples that are correctly classified. The overall accuracy A combines both.

11.3 Data Processing

In this section, we will first give the process used to collect raw data and then the steps for processing this data. These preprocessing steps include collecting information from user's sessions, data cleaning, user identification, and session identification. As the details of each of these preprocessing tasks can be found in [3], in this section we will briefly discuss them for the purpose of understanding the structure of the processed dataset.

For equal comparison purposes, and to avoid duplicating already existing work, we have used the data collected by Pitkow et al. from Xerox.com on May 10, 1998 and May 13, 1998 [1]. During this period, about 200,000 Web hits were received each day in the form of about 15,000 Web documents or files. The raw data is collected by embedding cookies to the users' desktop. In cases in which cookies did not exist, a set of fallback heuristics was used to collect users' Web browsing information. Several attributes are collected using the preceding method, which includes the IP address of the user, time stamp with date and starting time, visiting URL address, referred URL address, and the browser information or agent.

Once we have the access logs data for the period under consideration, the next step is to uniquely identify the users and their sessions. Without identifying unique users with their sessions, it is impossible to trace the pages they visited while surfing. Specially, the modern Web pages with hidden cookies and embedded session IDs, session identification are the most crucial elements for data preprocessing. This task is quite complicated, because any two or more users may have same IP addresses. Pirolli et al. solve this problem by looking into the browser information [4]. If the IP addresses are the same for two log entries in the access logs and if their browser information shows two different browsing software and/or operating systems, then it can be concluded that the IP addresses represent two distinct users. By the same token, if a log entry has the same IP address as other log entries, but its visiting page is not in any way hyperlinked to the pages visited by the previous entries, it can also be concluded that the new entry is for separate user information. Also, any user can surf the Web for a short period of time and then return for browsing after a significant amount of wait time. To manage this situation, a default time of 30 minutes is used to identify a session for that particular user. For example, if the time between page requests for a user exceeds more than 30 minutes, a new session is considered for this particular user [3].

11.4 Experiment Setup

We use the LIBSVM [5] for SVM implementation and use the $v - SVM$ with the RBF kernel. In our experiments, we set v very low ($v = 0.001$). As we address the problem of multiclass classification, we implement a "one-vs-all" scheme due to its reduction of the number of classifiers needed to be computed over the "one-vs-one" classification. In addition, we incorporate the domain knowledge previously mentioned in Section 9.3 in the prediction.

We implement the back-propagation algorithm for multilayer network learning. Our ANN is composed of two fully connected hidden layers. Each layer is composed of three neurons (see Chapter 2, Figure 2.3). In our experiments, we use a dynamic learning-rate setup based on the distribution of the examples from different classes. Specifically, we use a larger learning rate when updating the weights if the distribution of the class of that example is low, and vice versa. That is because the distribution of pages in the dataset varies from page to page; that is, some Web pages are visited more often than others, and some pages are never visited. Thus, the weights of the network converge toward the examples from the larger distribution class; that is, the accuracy of classifying examples from the larger distribution class is greater than that of classifying examples from the smaller distribution class (the error of the network when only examples from the larger distribution class are considered is very low, whereas it is very high when only examples from the smaller distribution class are considered). For the network to converge toward a reasonable error for both classes, the learning process of these classes should vary. For example, if we have a dataset of two classes with the following distribution: "25% of the examples are from class 1 and 75% are from class 2," then we use a learning rate of 0.25 when processing examples from class 2 and 0.75 when processing examples from class 1. Also, we incorporate the domain knowledge previously mentioned in Section 11.3 into the prediction.

In the ARM, we generate the rules using the Apriori algorithm proposed in [6]. We set *minsupp* to a very low value (*minsupp* = 0.0001) to capture rarely visited pages. We implement the idea of the recommendation engine, proposed by Mobasher et al. [2].

We divide the dataset into three partitions. Two partitions will be used for training, and the third will be used for testing accuracy. In addition, we have removed redundant paths from the testing set so that all repeated testing points are counted once in computing accuracy. Table 11.1 presents the distribution of the training and testing data points for each hop.

Table 11.1 The distribution of the training and testing sets for each hop

Number of hops	Size of training set	Size of testing set
1	23028	12060
2	24222	12481
3	22790	11574
4	21795	10931
5	20031	9946
6	18352	8895
7	16506	7834

11.5 Results

In this section, we present the experimental results obtained using different prediction models, namely, ARM, SVM, Markov models, ANN, and the multiple evidence combination model.

In our experiments, we consider up to seven hops for prediction for all models. Recall that we break long sessions using a sliding window, and a sliding window of size 3 corresponds to one hop because the surfer hops once before reaching an outcome, that is, the last page. Results vary, based on the number of hops, because different patterns are revealed for different number of hops. Also, we show the effect of including domain knowledge on the accuracy of prediction using SVM.

Furthermore, we present the concept of ranking in our results. Rank n means that the prediction is considered correct if the predicted next page happens to be among the top n pages. For example, suppose that we use rank 5 and the prediction output of user session x is {P1, P2, P3, P4, P5} with confidence 0.4, 0.3, 0.2, 0.19, and 0.15, respectively. Suppose that the correct next page is P5 (based on the label in the testing set); then, based on rank 5, this prediction is considered correct because P5 is among the top five pages. On the other hand, it will be considered incorrect if we use rank 2 because P5 is not among the top two predicted pages.

Regarding the training time, it is important to mention that we assume an offline training process. The training time for the Markov model is very small (a few milliseconds) for all window sizes because building the model requires only one pass over the training set. The training time for the ARM is also small (a few seconds) but greater than that of the Markov model because generating the itemsets requires more passes over the training set. The training times for SVM and ANN are very large.

WWW prediction is a complex multiclass problem with a large number of classes. Because we are using the one-vs-all scheme and we have 5430 different Web pages, we create 5430 classifiers. The average training times for SVM and ANN are 26.3 and 35.1 hours, respectively.

Even though, in all prediction models, we need to consult a large number of classifiers to resolve the final prediction outcome, the average prediction time for one instance is very small, as can be seen from Table 11.2.

Table 11.2 Average prediction time for all methods

Method	Time in milliseconds
ANN	31.2
ARM	0.10
Markov	0.12
Dempster's rule	51.1
SVM	49.8

Table 11.3   Using all probability measurements with one hop and rank 1

Method	pr (match)	pr (hit|match)	pr (hit)	pr (miss|match)	pr (miss)	pr (hit)/ pr (miss)	overall pr (hit)/ pr (miss)	pr (hit| mismatch)	overall accuracy
ARM	0.592	0.077	0.046	0.922	0.546	0.084	0.048	0	0.046
SVM	0.59	0.141	0.083	0.858	0.509	0.164	0.133	0.083	0.117
ANN	0.59	0.149	0.088	0.850	0.504	0.175	0.146	0.095	0.127
Markov	0.59	0.19	0.118	0.800	0.474	0.249	0.134	0	0.118
SVM and ANN	0.59	0.151	0.089	0.848	0.502	0.178	0.153	0.106	0.133
ANN and Markov	0.59	0.188	0.111	0.811	0.480	0.232	0.185	0.108	0.156
SVM and Markov	0.59	0.194	0.115	0.805	0.477	0.241	0.184	0.098	0.155
SVM, Markov, and ANN	0.59	0.189	0.112	0.810	0.480	0.233	0.183	0.106	0.155

Table 11.3 shows the prediction results of all techniques using all measurements with one hop. The first column of this table presents different prediction models, namely, ARM, SVM, ANN, Markov, SVM–ANN, ANN–Markov, SVM–Markov, and SVM–ANN–Markov. Subsequent columns correspond to the different measurements we are using as mentioned earlier.

There are several points to note. First, the value of Pr(Match|Mismatch) is zero for both ARM and Markov models because neither model can predict for the unseen or mismatched data. Second, combining more than one prediction method using Dempster's rule achieves the best scores when all measurements are taken into account. For example, the training accuracy (Pr(Hit|Match)) for ARM, Markov, SVM, ANN, SVM–ANN, SVM–Markov, and SVM–ANN–Markov is 7%, 19%, 14%, 15%, 14%, 19%, and 18%, respectively. The overall accuracy for ARM, Markov, SVM, ANN, SVM–ANN, SVM–Markov, ANN–Markov, and SVM–ANN–Markov is 4%, 11%, 11%, 12%, 13%, 15%, 15%, and 15%, respectively. This proves that our hybrid method improves the predictive accuracy. Third, even though the Pr(Hit|Match) in SVM (and ANN) is lower than that in the Markov model, the overall accuracy of SVM is better than that in the Markov model. That is because the Pr(Hit|Mismatch) is zero in the case of the Markov model, whereas it is 8% in the case of SVM (and 9% in the case of ANN). Finally, note that the ARM has the poorest prediction results. The ARM uses the concept of itemsets instead of itemlist (ordered itemset); hence, the *support* of one path is computed on the basis of frequencies of that path and the frequencies of all its combinations. Also, it is very sensitive to *minsupp* values. This might cause important patterns to be lost or mixed.

Figure 11.1 depicts the Pr(Hit|Match) for all prediction techniques using different numbers of hops and rank 1. The *x*-axis represents the number of hops, and the *y*-axis represents Pr(Hit|Match). In this figure, combining models using Dempster's

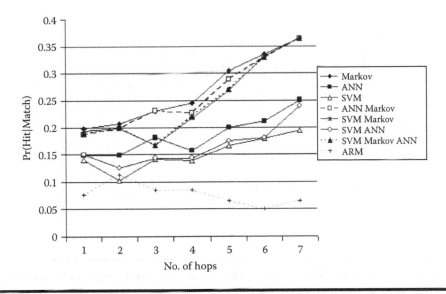

Figure 11.1 Comparable results of all techniques based on pr(Hit | Match) for hops from 1 to 7 and using rank 1.

rule achieves good training accuracy using different numbers of hops. For example, the Pr(Hit|Match), that is, training accuracies, using three hops for Markov, ANN, SVM, ARM, SVM–Markov, SVM–ANN, ANN–Markov, and SVM–ANN–Markov are 23%, 18%, 14%, 8%, 16%, 14%, 23%, and 16%, respectively. Note that the Markov model accuracy is relatively high. That is because we are considering the training accuracy over the seen or matched testing data, and the Markov model can predict well in the case of the seen data. Also, the combination of the Markov model with other models, such as SVM–Markov, has positively affected the final training accuracy; that is, the SVM–Markov training accuracy is better than with SVM alone. Furthermore, the combination of SVM and ANN has reduced the training accuracy. That is because there might be a conflict between the outputs of these models. Figures 11.2 and 11.3 present similar results. For example, Figure 11.3 uses three hops and rank 1 (see also Tables 11.3 and 11.4).

Figure 11.2 depicts the change of Pr(hit | match) with the rank. Recall that when we say rank n, that means we consider the prediction to be correct if the predicted page is among the top n pages. Hence, prediction accuracy is expected to improve with larger rank. For example, the Pr(hit | match), using two hops, has improved from 10%, 19% (using rank 1) to 24%, 34% (using rank 4) for SVM and SVM–Markov, respectively.

The Pr(Match), in general, is high, as we can see from Table 11.5. Recall that we break the dataset into two parts for each number of hops: two-thirds are used for training and one-third for testing. The Pr(Match) is the probability that an example in the testing set is also present in the training set. Because we get a different dataset

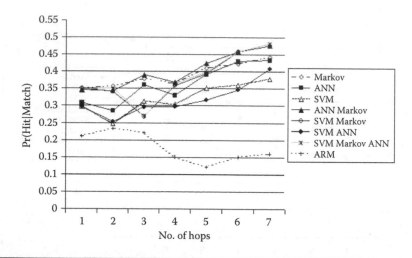

Figure 11.2 **Comparable results of all techniques based on pr(Hit | Match) for hops from 1 to 7 and using rank 4.**

for each different number of hops, the Pr(Match) is different. The Pr(Match) is 37% regardless of techniques in the case of three hops. When we increase the number of hops (sliding window is larger), the number of training points decreases, because Pr(Match) is adversely affected. Note that the values of Pr(match) are the same for all prediction models, namely, SVM, Markov, ARM, and multiple combination.

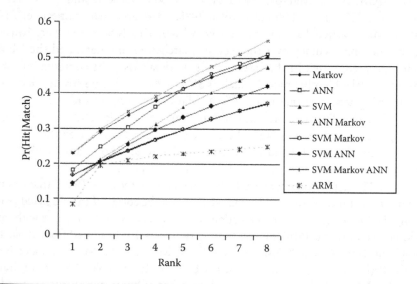

Figure 11.3 **Comparable results of all techniques based on pr(Hit | Match) for 3 hops and using ranks from 1 to 8.**

Table 11.4   Using all probability measurements with one hop and rank 4

Method	pr (match)	pr (hit|match)	pr (hit)	pr (miss|match)	pr (miss)	pr (hit)/ pr (miss)	overall pr (hit)/ pr (miss)	pr (hit| mismatch)	overall accuracy
ARM	0.592	0.211	0.125	0.788	0.467	0.268	0.143	0	0.125
SVM	0.592	0.298	0.177	0.701	0.415	0.425	0.315	0.154	0.24
ANN	0.592	0.308	0.182	0.691	0.409	0.445	0.332	0.164	0.249
Markov	0.592	0.35	0.207	0.64	0.385	0.539	0.262	0	0.207
ANN and Markov	0.592	0.346	0.205	0.653	0.387	0.53	0.368	0.157	0.269
SVM and Markov	0.592	0.351	0.208	0.648	0.384	0.542	0.375	0.158	0.273
SVM and ANN	0.592	0.297	0.176	0.702	0.416	0.423	0.314	0.154	0.239
SVM, Markov, ANN	0.592	0.348	0.206	0.651	0.386	0.534	0.368	0.154	0.269

Figure 11.4 represents the generalization accuracy for all techniques using rank 1. The x-axis represents the number of hops, and the y-axis depicts the Pr(Hit | MisMatch). Recall that generalization is the ability to predict correctly based on unseen data. The ARM and Markov models have zero generalization accuracy because they are proba bilistic models. Note that combining two or more models produces relatively good results. For example, the generalization accuracies for ANN, SVM, ANN–SVM are 17%, 14%, and 14%, respectively. Also, combining SVM (or ANN) with the Markov model affected the generalization accuracy negatively. In general, the prediction accuracy in WWW surfing is low; hence, this increase of the generalization accuracy is considered very important. Figure 11.5 illustrates the generalization accuracy (i.e., pr(Hit | Mismatch)) using all prediction methods and rank 2.

Table 11.5   The pr(Hit), that is, probability of seen data, in the dataset using different number of hops

Number of hops	Pr(Match)
1	0.59
2	0.40
3	0.37
4	0.29
5	0.25
6	0.21
7	0.22

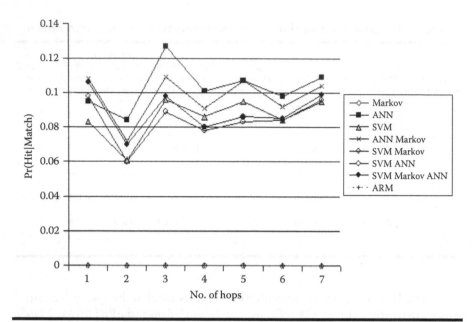

Figure 11.4   Generalization accuracy (i.e., pr(Hit | Mismatch)) using all prediction methods and rank 1.

Figure 11.6 illustrates comparable results of all techniques based on the overall accuracy for three hops and using ranks from 1 to 8. Figure 11.7 presents the overall accuracy (represented in the *y*-axis) of all techniques using a different number of hops (represented in the *x*-axis) and rank 1. As we can see, combining more than

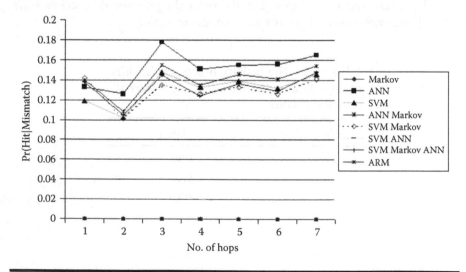

Figure 11.5   Generalization accuracy (i.e., pr(Hit | Mismatch)) using all prediction methods and rank 2.

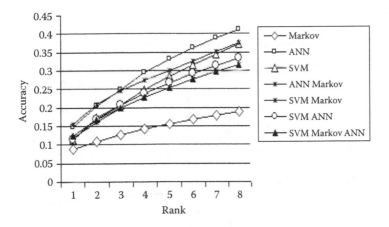

Figure 11.6 Comparable results of all techniques based on overall accuracy for three hops and using ranks from 1 to 8.

one model using Dempster's rule achieved the best overall accuracy. For example, the overall accuracies, using six hops, for ANN–Markov, SVM–Markov, SVM–ANN, and SVM–ANN–Markov, are 16%, 15%, 15%, and 15%, respectively. On the other hand, the overall accuracies for SVM, ANN, Markov, and ARM are 11%, 14%, 8%, and 1%, respectively. Note that SVM (and ANN) has outperformed the Markov model on the basis of overall accuracy. This is because SVM (and ANN) generalizes better than the Markov model. Dempster's rule proves to combine the best of different models because it has kept its superiority over all solo techniques, using all measurements and different number of hops.

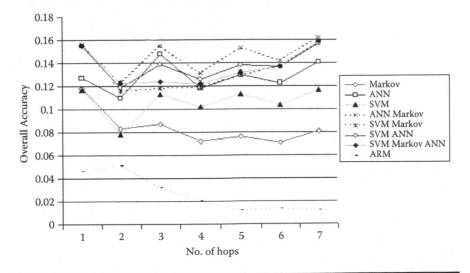

Figure 11.7 Comparable results based on the overall accuracy for rank 1.

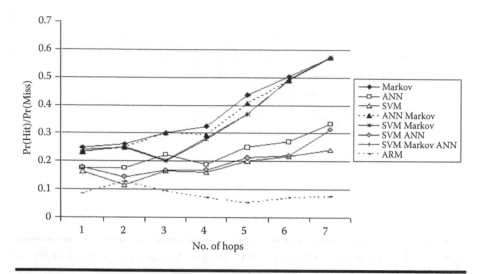

Figure 11.8 **pr(Hit)/pr(Miss) for all methods and using different number of hops and rank 1.**

Figure 11.8 shows the results of all methods measured with the Pr(Hit)/Pr(Miss) using rank 1. It is very similar to the Figure 11.1 because of the relationships between these two measurements (see Equations 11.2 and 11.3). We use this measurement because it does not depend on Pr(Match), which might vary from one dataset to another (see Equations 11.2 and 11.3). As can be seen, Dempster's rule method achieves good results here. For example, using seven hops, Pr(Hit)/Pr(Miss) for the Markov, ANN, SVM, ARM, ANN–Markov, SVM–Markov, SVM–ANN, and SVM–Markov–ANN is 0.57, 0.33, 0.24, 0.07, 0.57, 0.57, 0.31, and 0.57, respectively.

Similarly, Figure 11.9 presents the results of all methods measured with Pr(Hit)/Pr(Miss) using rank 5. Note that Pr(Hit)/Pr(Miss) is almost double that in Figure 11.8. This is expected because we use higher ranks. For example, Pr(hit)/Pr(miss) using rank 1 for SVM–Markov–ANN is 0.23, 0.25, 0.20, 0.28, 0.37, 0.49, and 0.57, for hops from 1 to 7, respectively, whereas Pr(hit)/Pr(miss) using rank 7 for SVM–Markov–ANN is 0.62, 0.63, 0.42, 0.68, 0.76, 1.01, and 1.08, for hops from 1 to 7, respectively.

Figure 11.10 shows the results of all methods measured with the overall ratio of hit/miss using rank 1, that is, $overall\,(hit/miss) = \frac{number\ of\ correct\ predictions}{number\ of\ incorrect\ predicitons}$. The x-axis depicts the number of hops, whereas the y-axis represents the overall hit/miss ratio. Because overall Pr(hit)/Pr(miss) considers both generalization and training accuracy, it is a more realistic measure than Pr(hit)/Pr(miss). As we can see in Tables 11.3 and 11.4, the models are grouped into two categories: single models (SVM, ARM, ANN, and Markov) and combination of models using Dempster's rule (SVM–Markov, SVM–ANN, ANN–Markov, and SVM–ANN–Markov). Note that the models in the second group perform better than those in the first group.

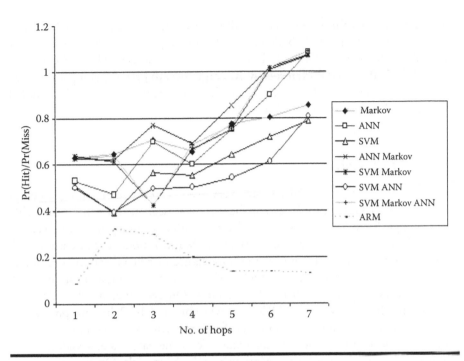

Figure 11.9   pr(Hit)/pr(Miss) for all methods and using different number of hops and rank 5.

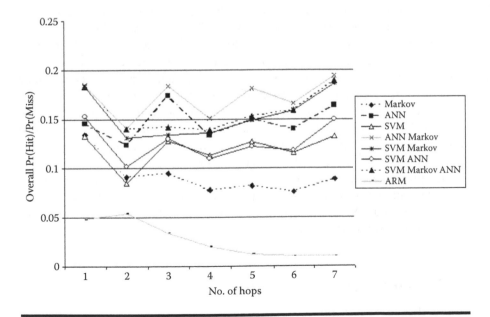

Figure 11.10   Overall pr(hit)/pr(miss) for all methods and using different number of hops and rank 1.

For example, using three hops, the overall Pr(hit)/Pr(miss) ratios for ARM, SVM, Markov, and ANN are 0.03, 0.09, 0.17, and 0.12, respectively. The corresponding values for SVM–ANN, SVM–Markov, ANN–Markov, and SVM–Markov–ANN are 0.13, 0.13, 0.18, and 0.14, respectively. Larger overall Pr(hit)/Pr(miss) means we have higher hit value and lower miss value. Therefore, this confirms the superiority of Dempster's rule over other techniques.

11.6   Discussion

The Markov model proves to perform very well in terms of training accuracy (Pr(hit|match)). However, it fails to predict for the unseen data (Pr(hit|mismatch)). Even though SVM and ANN achieved less training accuracy from the Markov model, their overall accuracy is better than the Markov model because both models can generalize well. This proves the importance of generalization accuracy in such applications. The accuracy of SVM, ANN, and their combination, using all measurements, improves with number of hops. On the other hand, it does not dramatically improve with the ARM and Markov models. When we process the dataset using a large number of hops, less frequent sessions will be produced. This will create a lack of frequencies in the dataset for some patterns or sessions; hence, the inability of prediction for the Markov and ARM models. On the other hand, less frequent sessions mean less confusion in the training set for SVM and ANN, reliable training process, and better prediction accuracy. As expected, all models performed better when using a larger rank. Although this improvement varies from one model to another, it seems to be linear (see Figures 11.3 and 11.6).

Combining all three models, namely, SVM, ANN, and Markov, did not produce the best results all the time. This is related to the inherent shortcoming of Dempster's rule. The problem arises when there is a conflict between two or more models. In this case, the combination of all models affects the results negatively. This scenario occurs when two or more models conflict with their prediction and their prediction confidence (certainty) is low or close. On the other hand, using two models seems a better choice because, even if there is a conflict between models, the model with higher confidence (less uncertainty) will win.

The prediction time, in general, is very small; however, it can be further reduced using domain knowledge or fast computers. The training time is still a concern in case of SVM and ANN. However, this can be mitigated using more memory, fast CPUs, caching techniques, etc.

11.7   Summary and Directions

In this chapter we have provided our results for Web page surfing prediction. As mentioned in the earlier chapters, we extract features of Web surfing patterns and train various classifiers. We combine the results of the classifiers to produce the final result. We believe that combining multiple classifiers is better than using one classifier. We need to conduct more experiments using other classifiers as well as different combinations. We also need to use more recent datasets.

We believe that the tool we have developed could be used for customer relationship management as well as for Web usage mining. Web usage mining is a key aspect of Web data mining. As more and more data is placed on the Web, we need efficient data mining tools tailored to work on different kinds of Web data.

References

1. Pitkow, J. and Pirolli, P., Mining longest repeating subsequences to predict World Wide Web surfing, in *Proceedings of 2nd USENIX Symposium on Internet Technologies and Systems (USITS'99)*, Boulder, CO, October 1999, pp. 139–150.
2. Mobasher, B., Dai, H., Luo, T., and Nakagawa, M., Effective personalization based on association rule discovery from Web usage data, in *Proceedings of the ACM Workshop on Web Information and Data Management (WIDM01)*, 2001, pp. 9–15.
3. Cooley, R., Mobasher, B., and Srivastava, J., Data preparation for mining World Wide Web browsing patterns, *Journal of Knowledge and Information Systems*, Vol. 1, No. 1, 1999.
4. Pirolli, P., Pitkow, J., and Rao, R., Silk from a sow's ear: Extracting usable structures from the Web, in *Proceedings of 1996 Conference on Human Factors in Computing Systems (CHI-96)*, Vancouver, British Columbia, Canada, 1996, pp. 118–125.
5. Chang, C. and Lin, C., LIBSVM: A Library for Support Vector Machines, 2001, http://www.csie.ntu.edu.tw/cjlin/libsvm.
6. Agrawal, R. and Srikant, R., Fast algorithms for mining association rules in large database, in *Proceedings of the 20th International Conference on Very Large Data Bases*, San Francisco, CA, 1994, pp. 487–499.

Conclusion to Part III

In Part III, we have described our tool for Web page surfing prediction. In WWW prediction area, we use Dempster's rule for evidence combination to combine more than one prediction model to improve prediction accuracy. The improvements in WWW prediction contribute to many applications such as Web search engines, latency reduction, and recommendation systems. We used three sources of evidence or prediction in our hybrid method, namely, SVM, Markov, and ANN. To improve the prediction of our hybrid model, we incorporated domain knowledge in prediction to improve the prediction accuracy.

Dempster's rule proves its effectiveness by combining the best of SVM, Markov, and ANN models. This is demonstrated by the fact that its predictive accuracy has outperformed all other techniques. We compared the results obtained using all techniques, namely, SVM, ARM, Markov, ANN, and hybrid models (i.e., combination of these models) against a standard benchmark dataset. Our results show that the hybrid method (Dempster's rule) outperforms all other techniques mainly because of the incorporation of domain knowledge, the ability to generalize for unseen instances, and the incorporation of the Markov model.

DATA MINING TOOL FOR IMAGE CLASSIFICATION

Introduction to Part IV

In Part II, we described our data mining tool for intrusion detection, and in Part III, we described our data mining tool for Web page surfing prediction. In this part, we will describe our tool for image classification. Image classification has many applications in medicine, defense, and entertainment. To classify images, a useful tool is to annotate images automatically. Therefore, our approach consists of a framework for image classification.

Part IV consists of five chapters. Chapter 12 describes data mining for multimedia applications, which includes text, image, audio, and video mining. In Chapter 13, we present image classification models that have influenced our work. In Chapter 14, we discuss subspace clustering algorithms, which are a key approach to our work. Weighted feature selection for medical imaging is discussed in Chapter 15. Experimental results are given in Chapter 16.

Introduction to Faculty

Chapter 12

Multimedia Data Management and Mining

12.1 Overview

Much of the data on the Web is increasingly becoming unstructured. We need tools and techniques to mine these unstructured databases. Such databases consist of multimedia data such as text, images, audio, and video data. Therefore, we need techniques for managing the large multimedia databases and mining these databases to extract patterns and trends.

A lot of research and development has been undertaken on managing multimedia databases [1, 2]. More recently, tools are being developed to mine multimedia databases. However, many of these tools essentially extract concepts from the multimedia data and subsequently mine the concepts to extract patterns. Much of the focus of the data mining tools for mining unstructured data includes mining the text in reports, classifying images, analyzing video to determine suspicious events and to mine the image and geospatial databases to detect unusual patterns. In this part of the book, we will describe one such tool we have developed on image mining. We will classify images as well as automatically annotate images. The details of our tool will be described in Chapters 13 to 16. In this chapter, we will describe the broader area of managing and mining multimedia databases.

The organization of this chapter is as follows: In Section 12.2, we discuss managing and mining multimedia data. Note that, to mine the multimedia data, we first need techniques to mine text, image, audio, and video data. Therefore, in

Section 12.3, we will describe approaches to mining text, image, audio, and video data. The chapter is summarized in Section 12.4.

12.2 Managing and Mining Multimedia Data

There is a need to manage combinations of data types, and the systems that manage them are multimedia database systems (see [1–3]). In addition, the multimedia data has to be mined so that patterns can be extracted. A multimedia database management system (MM-DBMS) provides support for storing, manipulating, and retrieving multimedia data from a multimedia database. In a sense, a multimedia database system is a type of heterogeneous database system, as it manages heterogeneous data types. Heterogeneity is due to the media of the data such as text, image, video, and audio.

An MM-DBMS must provide support for typical database management system functions. These include query processing, update processing, transaction management, storage management, metadata management, security, and integrity. In addition, in many cases, the various types of data such as voice and video have to be synchronized for display, and therefore, real-time processing is also a major issue in an MM-DBMS.

Various architectures are being examined to design and develop an MM-DBMS. In one approach, the DBMS is used to manage just the metadata, and a multimedia file manager is used to manage the multimedia data. There is a module for integrating the DBMS and the multimedia file manager. In this case, the MM-DBMS consists of the following three modules: the DBMS managing the metadata, the multimedia file manager, and the module for integrating the two. The second architecture is the tight coupling approach. In this architecture, the DBMS manages both the multimedia database and the metadata. That is, the DBMS is an MM-DBMS. The tight coupling architecture has an advantage because all of the DBMS functions could be applied on the multimedia database. This includes query processing, transaction management, metadata management, storage management, and security and integrity management.

There are also other aspects to architectures as discussed in [1–3]. For example, a multimedia database system could use a commercial database system, such as an object-oriented database system, to manage multimedia objects. However, relationships between objects and the representation of temporal relationships may involve extensions to the database management system. That is, a DBMS together with an extension layer provide complete support to manage multimedia data. In the alternative case, both the extensions and the database management functions are integrated so that there is one database management system to manage multimedia objects and the relationships between the objects.

Much of the work of mining multimedia data involves mining individual data types such as text, image, audio, and video. The basic idea is to extract concepts

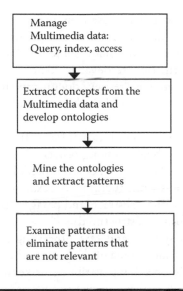

Figure 12.1   Mining multimedia data.

from the multimedia data, and then mine them using techniques developed for mining structured data. Ontologies are utilized to support the mining process. This is illustrated in Figure 12.1. For more details on managing and mining the multimedia data, we refer the reader to [3].

12.3   Management and Mining Text, Image, Audio, and Video Data

In this section, we discuss approaches for managing and mining individual data types such as text, images, audio, and video. Note that much of the discussion in Chapters 13 through 16 focuses on image data management and mining, In particular, we will discuss approaches to mining images so that they can be classified and annotated automatically. In the remainder of this section, we will discuss approaches to managing and mining text, image, audio, and video data.

12.3.1   Text Retrieval

A text retrieval system is essentially a database management system for handling text data. Text data could be documents such as books, journals, magazines, etc. One needs a good data model for document representation. Considerable work has gone into developing semantic data models and object models for document management.

Querying documents could be based on many factors. One could specify keywords and request the documents with the keywords to be retrieved. One could also retrieve documents that share some relationships with one another. Recent research on information retrieval is focusing on querying documents based on semantics. For example, "retrieve documents that describe scenic views" or "retrieve documents that are useful to children under ten years" are examples of such queries.

Much of the information is now in textual form. This could be data on the Web or library data or electronic books, among others. One of the problems with text data is that, unlike relational data, it is not structured. In many cases it is unstructured, and in some cases, it is semistructured. An example of semistructured data is an article that has a title, author, abstract, and paragraphs. The paragraphs are not structured, whereas the format is structured.

Information retrieval systems and text processing systems have been developed over the past few decades. Some of these systems are quite sophisticated and can retrieve documents by specifying attributes or keywords. There are also text processing systems that can retrieve associations between documents. Figure 12.2 illustrates an approach to mining text data.

12.3.2   Image Retrieval

An image retrieval system is essentially a database management system for handling image data. The image data could be x-rays, pictures, satellite images, and photographs. One needs a good data model for image representation. Some work has gone into developing semantic data models and object models for image management.

Querying images could be based on many factors. One could extract text from images and then query the text. One could tag images and then query the tags.

Text Mining

Mine the text and make associations between words

Mine the text and detect unusual or suspicious words

Cluster documents

Classify document

Figure 12.2   Mining text data.

```
┌─────────────────────────────────────────┐
│                                           │
│   Image Mining                            │
│                                           │
│   Mine images and extract buildings, lakes,│
│   and related objects                     │
│                                           │
│   Mine images and detect unusual patterns:│
│   e.g., detect a new building             │
│                                           │
│   Mine images and find associations between│
│   various images                          │
│                                           │
└─────────────────────────────────────────┘
```

Figure 12.3 Mining image data.

One could also retrieve images from patterns. For example, an image could contain several squares. With a picture of a square, one could query the image and retrieve all the squares in it. We can also query images depending on the content. For example, "retrieve images that illustrate sunset" or "retrieve images that illustrate Victorian buildings" are different types of queries.

Image processing has been around for quite a while. We have image processing applications in various domains, including medical imaging for cancer detection, processing satellite images for space and intelligence applications, and also handling hyperspectral images. Images include maps, geological structures, biological structures, and many other entities. Image processing has dealt with areas such as detecting abnormal patterns that deviate from the norm, retrieving images by content, and pattern matching. Figure 12.3 illustrates an approach to mining image data. Note that we have developed a tool based on this approach, which will be described in Chapters 13 to 16.

12.3.3 Video Retrieval

A video retrieval system is essentially a database management system for handling video data. Video data could be in various formats such as wmv, mpeg, avi. There are various issues that need to be considered. A good data model is needed for video representation. Some work has gone into developing semantic data models and object models for video data management (see [1]).

Querying documents could be based on many factors. One could extract text from the video and query the text. One could also extract images from the video and query the images. One could store short video scripts and carry out pattern matching; for example, "find the video that contains the following script." Examples of queries include "find films where the hero is John Wayne" or "find video scripts that show two presidents shaking hands." Recently, there

> **Video Mining**
>
> Mine video and surveillance data and determine suspicious behavior of people
>
> Mine video and extract interesting associations between objects in the video
>
> Automatically annotate video documents

Figure 12.4 Mining video data.

have been some efforts at mining video data. Figure 12.4 illustrates an approach to video mining.

12.3.4 Audio Retrieval

An audio retrieval system is essentially a database management system for handling audio data. Similar to video data audio data has various formats as well. One needs a good data model for audio representation. Some work has gone into developing semantic data models and objects models for audio data management (see [1]).

Querying documents could be based on many factors. One could extract text from the audio and query it. One could store short audio scripts and carry out pattern matching; for example, "find the audio that contains the following script." Examples include "find audio tapes containing the speeches of President John" or "find audio tapes of poems recited by female narrators." Recently, there have been some efforts at audio mining [4]. Figure 12.5 illustrates an approach to mining audio data.

> **Audio Mining**
>
> Mine audio data and determine the speaker
>
> Mine audio data and detect any unusual words in the speech
>
> Understand the audio document and summarize the document

Figure 12.5 Mining audio data.

12.4 Summary and Directions

This chapter has provided an overview of various approaches to managing and mining multimedia data. First, we discussed issues regarding handling multimedia data, and then we focused on individual data types such as text, images, audio, and video. The idea is to extract concepts from unstructured data and then mine them. Ontologies may be used to support the mining task.

There are many challenges in managing and mining multimedia data. Much of the work has focused on developing data models for multimedia data. We need techniques to manage large multimedia databases, including techniques for access methods and indexing. We also need techniques to extract concepts from the unstructured data. These techniques may themselves include data mining techniques. The concepts developed from the data will then have to be mined to extract the nuggets.

Chapters 13 to 16 will describe our multimedia data mining tool. In particular, we will describe our image mining tool. We use various data mining techniques to annotate and classify images. The results could be used to better understand the images. Our research also includes mining text and video data. Descriptions of these tools are given in [5].

References

1. Woelk, D. et al., An object-oriented approach to multimedia databases, *Proceedings of the ACM SIGMOD Conference*, Washington, D.C., June 1986.
2. Prabhakaran, B., *Multimedia Databases*, Kluwer Publishers, Norwell, MA, 1997.
3. Thuraisingham, B., *Managing and Mining Multimedia Databases for the Electronic Enterprise*, CRC Press, Boca Raton, FL, 2001.
4. Special Issue in Audio Mining, *IEEE Computer*, Vol. 36, No. 2, 2003.

Chapter 13

Image Classification Models

13.1 Overview

In Chapter 12, we discussed multimedia data management and mining. In particular, we discussed text, image, audio, and video mining. One approach is to extract concepts from the data, and then mine them. The data also has to be mined to extract the concepts. In this chapter, we elaborate on image mining. In particular, we discuss the tool we have developed for image classification and annotation. To understand our approach in this chapter, we will describe various image classification models that have guided our image classification algorithms. Our tool will be detailed in Chapters 13, 14, and 15.

The organization of this chapter is as follows. In Section 13.2, we discuss the various example models that have influenced our research. In particular, we describe various statistical models and some other published models for image classification. In Section 13.3, we discuss image classification algorithms. In particular, we discuss various aspects of dimensionality reduction, feature transformation, and optimal feature subset selection, and then provide an overview of subspace clustering. Section 13.4 concludes the chapter. Figure 13.1 illustrates the various models we have considered in developing the tool. Details of data mining for image classification and related applications can be found in [1–5].

Image Classification Models
Statistical Models
Translations Models
Relevance Models

Figure 13.1 Image classification models.

13.2 Example Models

13.2.1 Statistical Models for Image Annotation

Given a set of images in which each image is captioned with a set of terms that describe image content, researchers have already proposed various algorithms to determine the correlation between high-level semantics and low-level visual features. Algorithms can also produce annotation for images without captions. Currently, most methods are trying to combine both text and visual image features to uncover hidden semantics using Latent Semantic Indexing (LSI), which has proved successful in the field of cross-language retrieval [6–8]. LSI is based on the reasonable assumption that documents using similar terms are probably semantically related. It analyzes the co-occurrence statistics of terms to discover semantic relations hidden behind terms. By analyzing the statistical relations between visual features and words in the image domain, these kinds of methods can discover some hidden semantics, and the performance of indexing and retrieval result of large image databases is improved. Several statistical models for automatic image annotation have been published [9].

13.2.2 Co-Occurrence Model for Image Annotation

It estimates the correct probability by counting the co-occurrence of words with image objects. First, grid all training images into rectangular subimages. The annotation keywords for each image are inherited by all its subimages. Generate feature vectors for all subimages, and group them using simple centroid-based clustering. The conditional probability $P(w_i \mid b_j)$ for each keyword w_i and each centroid b_j can be evaluated by counting the frequencies of keywords. The conditional probability is $P(w_i \mid b_j) = m_{ji}/M_j$, where m_{ji} is the number of words w_i in centroid b_j and M_j the total number of all keywords in centroid b_j. All conditional probabilities $P(w_i \mid b_j)$ are learned correlations. To annotate an unknown image, divide the unknown image into subimages and generate feature vectors for each of them. For each of these unknown subimages, they must have a closest centroid. Using the closest centroid, calculate the average of conditional probabilities of the nearest centroids of all subimages. Finally, words having the largest average probability value are used to annotate this unknown image. The co-occurrence model is a simple model, but it is an essential idea underlying almost all current models.

13.2.3 Translation Model

In [6], Barnard et al. tried to map keywords to individual image objects. They treated keywords as one language and blob tokens as another language, so that the image annotation problem could be viewed as the translation between two languages. Using some classical machine translation models, they annotated a set of testing images based on the correlation between keywords and blob tokens, which is calculated from analyzing a large number of annotated training images. Similar to the co-occurrence model, a translation model is also based on co-occurrence statistics. However, there are two major differences between the translation and co-occurrence models. One difference is the method of calculating conditional probabilities $P(w_i | b_j)$; the other difference is the image annotation mechanism. In a translation model, conditional probabilities $P(w_i | b_j)$ are calculated using a method based on the expectation maximization (EM) algorithm rather than counting frequencies of co-occurrences. According to all conditional probabilities $P(w_i | b_j)$, a translation model generates one keyword for each blob token. Thus, for a specific blob token b^*, the system will assign a specific word w^* to the blob token that has the maximal $P(w | b^*)$. As shown in Figure 13.2, the third column contains two blob tokens assigned with the keywords *Tiger* and *Grass*. As for image annotation, an unknown image is segmented first to generate some unknown image segments. Each unknown

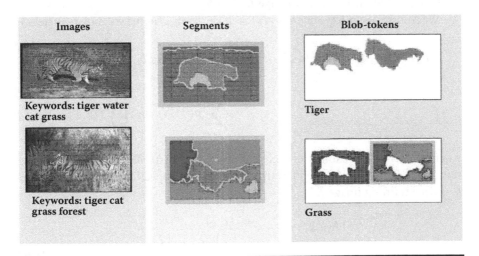

Figure 13.2 Demonstration of correspondence between image objects and keywords.

segment obtains a keyword from its closest blob token in feature space. Keywords for all unknown segments are used as the annotation for the entire unknown image.

The translation model can annotate each segment rather than the whole image. This is very helpful for object recognition and can be used to generate a ranking list of retrieved images based on some query words. However, the translation model also has problems. Because the model is still based on co-occurrence statistics, it is highly likely that the conditional probabilities $P(w_i | b_j)$ of frequent words are higher than those for rare words. As a result, only some keywords could be used to annotate new images. To solve this problem, Kang et al. propose regularized translation models by introducing certain prior preference of translation models into the machine translation model [8]. For our research, we use the basic translation model (TM). More details can also be found in [10].

13.2.4 Cross-Media Relevance Model (CMRM)

It was introduced by J. Jeon et al. [11]. Similar to the co-occurrence and translation models, it also needs to generate blob tokens. After this step, each training image J can be represented as $\{b_{1Z}, \ldots, b_m; w_1, \ldots, w_n\}$. $\{b_1, \ldots, b_m\}$ are the blobs corresponding to regions of the image, and $\{w_1, \ldots, w_n\}$ are the keywords in the image annotation. In CMRM, there is not a one-to-one correspondence between the blob tokens and keywords as in the translation model. Instead, CMRM assumes that a set of keywords $\{w_1, \ldots, w_n\}$ is related to the set of blobs $\{b_1, \ldots, b_m\}$ in an image. Any unannotated image I can be represented by a set of blob tokens $\{b_1, \ldots, b_m\}$. Based on the joint distribution of blobs and keywords learned from a training set of annotated images, the CMRM will select a set of keywords $\{w_1, \ldots, w_n\}$ automatically to describe the content of image I.

We estimate the probability $P(w | I)$ for all keywords w in the vocabulary as follows:

$$P(w | I) \propto P(w, I) \approx P(w, b_1, \ldots, b_m) = \sum_{J \in T} P(J) P(w, b_1, \ldots, b_m | J)$$

$$= \sum_{J \in T} P(J) P(w | J) \prod_{i=1}^{m} P(b_i | J) \quad (13.1)$$

where $P(J)$ is the probability of each training image that follows uniform distribution. $P(w | J)$ and $P(b_i | J)$ denotes the probability of a specific keyword w and blob b_j given a training image J.

$$P(w | I) = (1 - \alpha) \frac{\#(w, J)}{|J|} + \alpha \frac{\#(w, T)}{|T|}$$

$$P(b | J) = (1 - \beta) \frac{\#(b, J)}{|J|} + \beta \frac{\#(b, T)}{|T|} \quad (13.2)$$

where $\#(w, J)$ is the number of times the word w appears in the image J's annotation, and $\#(w, T)$ is the number of times the word w appears in the training dataset. Similarly, $\#(b, J)$ is the number of regions in the image J that belong to the blob b. $\#(b, T)$ reflects the number of training images in which the blob b ever appeared. $|J|$ denotes the aggregate number of all words and blobs in the image J, and $|T|$ stands for the size of the training dataset. α and β are both smoothing constants. The keywords having the highest $P(w \mid I)$ will be selected to annotate the image I.

The CMRM model does not consider the correlations between keywords. However, there are correlations between words. For instance, the word *plane* is more likely to appear with the word *airport* rather than the word *boat*. To solve this problem, Jin et al. proposed an improved CMRM model by applying a coherent language model to an image [12].

13.2.5 *Continuous Relevance Model*

Lavrenko et al. extended the CMRM model and proposed the continuous relevance model (CRM) in [13]. In this model, they introduced a special function G that maps image regions r to real-valued vectors g, and calculated the joint probability of a word w and a region r rather than the joint probability of a word w and a blob b in CMRM (as shown in Figure 13.3). The joint distribution probability is calculated as follows:

$$P(w, r_1, \ldots, r_m) = \sum_J P(J) P(w \mid J) \prod_{i=1}^{m} P(r_i \mid J) \qquad (13.3)$$

$P(J)$ is assumed to be uniform. $P(w \mid J)$ is same as the CMRM model in [12]. $P(r \mid J)$ is based on the kernel density estimate $P(r \mid J) = 1/n \sum_{i=1}^{n} K\left(\| r - r_i \| / \beta\right)$.

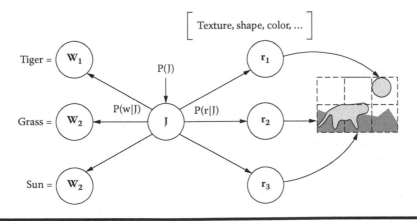

Figure 13.3 Continuous relevance model (CRM).

The CRM model applies the continuous probability density functions to visual features directly. The concept of the blob and clustering algorithms is not applied in this model; therefore, the corresponding loss of information is avoided.

13.2.6 Other Models

Feng et al. [14] modified the CRM model and proposed the multiple Bernoulli relevance model (MBRM). In MBRM, an image is represented by a set of tiles that are generated by dividing images into rectangular blocks. Because image segmentation is avoided in MBRM, computational cost is reduced significantly. The parameter estimation process is simplified because each image has the same number of regions. The keywords are modeled with multiple Bernoulli distribution.

Monay et al. [15] applied standard latent semantic analysis (LSA) and probabilistic latent semantic analysis (PLSA) to image annotation. Some graphical models such as the Latent Dirichlet Allocation (LDA) model and the Gaussian mixture model (GMM) have been applied to image annotation as well [8]. In addition, classification approaches are used to generate semantic labels for images (see, for example, [16, 17]). In classification approaches, keywords are treated as independent classes. Different classifiers will be trained for each keyword. An ensemble of trained classifiers will be applied to generate semantic labels for images.

13.3   Image Classification

Image classification means to classify images into categories in a supervised way. In supervised classification, training images with class labels are given to train classifiers, which in turn are used to generate labels for new unlabeled images. Classifying images by content is an important step to finding useful information from a large image collection. Basically, all classifiers can be put into two categories: parametric and nonparametric. Wang et al. [18] proposed Image-based Classification of Objectionable Websites (IBCOW) to classify if a Web site is objectionable based on the image content in WebPages. Uehara et al. [19] applied the binary Bayesian classifier to classify images into indoor and outdoor categories. In [5], Antonie et al. applied neural networks to classify breast cancer images. As a new classification algorithm, the support vector machine (SVM) has been successfully applied for use in the image classification area [20]. In addition, relevance feedback techniques attracted researchers' attention. The system produced results, and users gave the system feedback that the system could use to update parameters. In short, the feedback can help the system to understand users' perception better and improve classification accuracy. Hu et al. [16] generated a Bayesian frame with one-step feedback for semantic image classification. Rui et al. [21, 22] considered multilevel image content and produced a solid theoretical relevance feedback framework.

In our work, we studied the performances of various KNN algorithms for medical image classification. We modified the evidence-theory-based KNN algorithm. All algorithms are implemented and tested on ImageCLEFmed 2006 dataset. The modified evidence-theory-based KNN algorithm has the best classification accuracy.

13.3.1 Dimensionality Reduction

Data representation in the reduced number of dimensions is a fundamental problem in data mining. Dimensionality reduction can save data storage space and decrease computational cost. There are two strategies to reduce dimensionality. One is to find the best possible subset of features, which is called *feature selection*. The other strategy is to transform data to a lower-dimensional space. Each dimension in this lower-dimensional space will be a linear combination of original dimensions.

13.3.2 Feature Transformation

The most popular techniques for data transformation are *principle component analysis* (PCA) and *singular value decomposition* (SVD). These two methods are very similar. After transformation, the data is projected to a lower-dimensional space where dimensions having bigger variances are kept. Therefore, feature transformation may provide better discriminative ability than feature selection. In [23], the authors proposed a recursive clustering singular value decomposition (RCSVD), which reduces the dimension of feature space locally (i.e., for each cluster). The results show that RCSVD reduces dimension significantly without losing much search efficiency. However, new features after transformation will be a linear or nonlinear combination of original features. They are not interpretable because new features do not have a clear physical meaning as original features. In many applications where physical meaning of features has to be preserved, feature transformation is not applicable.

13.3.3 Feature Selection

Feature selection started to be a research field in the 1970s. The purpose of feature selection is to find the optimal subset of features that are most relevant to the data mining task. Its effectiveness and efficiency in removing irrelevant or redundant features have been proved in many published papers. Let us denote P_f as the power set of f features and E a criterion function that will evaluate the qualities of feature subsets. The size of P_f will be $2f$. The feature selection can be formulated as: find the optimal feature subset X_f that satisfies $E(X_f) = \max_{X \in P_f} E(X)$. An exhaustive search can generate a global optimal solution. However, it is not feasible for high-dimensional data. Thus, feature selection algorithms balance between optimality and computational feasibility. Normally, they can only guarantee a local optimal solution rather than a global optimal solution.

Feature selection includes two major steps: searching and evaluation. Normally, during searching, we need to generate various candidate feature subsets and evaluate each of these with some criterion during evaluation. Candidate subsets are generated by applying different types of heuristics through the feature space, such as greedy sequential searches (forward or backward), floating search, and genetic search. Based on the applied evaluation criterion, most existing feature selection algorithms can be put into two broad categories: filter and wrapper. Filter models apply general properties of data to evaluate feature subsets. There is no learning algorithm involved. For instance, in [24], entropy measurements are used to determine feature subset relevance based on the argument that data containing dense clusters usually have low entropy. RELIEF [25] is the representative of filter models. On the other hand, wrapper models include learning algorithms to assist feature subset evaluation. The preselected feature subset is the input to the learning algorithm. The quality of the selected feature subset is evaluated according to the output of the training algorithm based on some criterion such as classification accuracy. In some wrapper models, the output of the learning algorithm will be sent back to the feature-searching phase as feedback to modify the feature subset. The modified feature subset will be input to the learning algorithm again. The same process will be repeated until we cannot get any more improvement. For example, if we use information gain as the feature evaluation criterion, the algorithm will converge when we cannot obtain more information gain value based on the output of the learning algorithm. The feature subset producing the biggest information gain will be the optimal feature subset. Because of the involvement of the learning algorithm, wrapper models are normally more computationally intensive than filter models.

Feature weighting is a general form of feature selection. In feature weighting, each feature will be assigned a weight between 0 and 1. If the feature is more interesting, then the feature weight will be larger. In feature selection, the weight will be either 0 or 1. Assigning different weights for different features is not new in the data mining area. For example, You et al. extended the use of the Symmetrical Tau criterion [26] to find the optimal weights for visual features. In particular, Tau value will be calculated for each given weight set. The weight set that has the maximum Tau value will be chosen. However, the assumed weight will be given. In almost all approaches except ours, weight is assigned for each feature manually according to domain knowledge.

Most of the feature selection algorithms are used for supervised learning. In unsupervised learning, feature selection is harder because we do not have class information for the data. Therefore, there are no obvious criteria to guide feature selection.

13.3.4 Subspace Clustering Algorithms

Due to the curse of dimensionality, data becomes sparse and distance measures gradually become meaningless as the number of dimensions increases. Because almost all clustering algorithms are based on distance measurement, the curse of dimensionality will confuse clustering algorithms when the dimension is high, and degrade the quality of the results of traditional clustering algorithms. Subspace clustering is able to mitigate the curse of dimensionality. Compared with feature selection, subspace clustering is more complicated. First of all, subspace clustering is a simultaneous clustering and feature-discriminating process, which means subspace clustering will handle clustering and feature discrimination at the same time. Second, feature selection only needs to find one optimal feature subset for the whole dataset, but subspace clustering algorithms find the most relevant feature subset for each cluster.

The idea of subspace clustering has been proposed in the past. The CLIQUE algorithm in [3] is a bottom-up subspace clustering algorithm. The key idea is based on the downward closure property of density, which means that if there are dense units in k dimensions, there are dense units in all $(k - 1)$ dimensional projections. The algorithm first finds dense units in each dimension. According to the downward closure property of density, the dense units in higher-dimensional space can only appear in the combination of dense lower-dimensional space. The algorithm propagates high-dimensional space from low-dimensional space until there are no dense units present. The CLIQUE was the first subspace clustering algorithm. Since then, various subspace clustering algorithms have been published. Some of them follow the bottom-up strategy of CLIQUE and extend it in different directions. For example, ENCLUS [24] measures entropy rather than density or coverage. MAFIA [27] improves cluster quality by introducing an adaptive grid and parallelism. Aggarwal et al. [2] proposed the PROCLUS algorithm, which is the first top–down subspace clustering algorithm. Basically, the top–down subspace clustering approaches find the initial approximation of clusters at the beginning. Full feature space is considered, and each dimension is weighted equally. Each dimension is assigned a weight for each cluster, based on clustering results. The updated weights are applied in the following iteration to regenerate the clusters. Many subspace clustering algorithms follow top–down strategy such as ORCLUS, FINDIT, and δ-Clusters. In our approach, we generate a weighted feature selection algorithm on the basis of top–down subspace clustering. The input is the whole dataset, and the output is the weight sets for all clusters. The most challenging part of feature weighting for unsupervised learning is how to quantify the degree of feature relevance for each cluster in the unsupervised learning cases. It is very critical because the estimated feature weights will affect the output of unsupervised learning in the next iteration. We estimate feature weights for each cluster according to feature value distribution. We applied our weighted feature selection algorithm to generate visual tokens in the proposed automatic image annotation framework. To the best of our knowledge, this is the first attempt to apply an automatic weighted feature selection algorithm to automatic image annotation.

13.4 Summary

Much of the data on the Web and elsewhere is unstructured. This data could be text, images, audio, and video. Recently, there has been much interest in managing images, including geospatial and spatiotemporal data. In Part IV of this book, we describe the data mining tool we have developed to mine image data. In particular, we discuss image classification. In this chapter, we described various image classification models we have utilized.

There are numerous challenges in mining image and geospatial data. First, we need appropriate feature extraction techniques. These techniques have to "understand" images and extract features. Next we need appropriate classification models that will provide better accuracy and reduce false positives and false negatives. We need to develop ways of combining multiple models so that we can develop the most appropriate model for particular images. In Chapters 14, 15, and 16, we will describe our tool.

References

1. Aggarwal, C.C., Wolf, J.L. Yu, P.S., Procopiuc, C., and Park, J.S., Fast algorithms for projected clustering, in *Proceedings of the 1999 ACM SIGMOD International Conference on Management of Data*, ACM Press, 1999, pp. 61–72.
2. Aggarwal, C.C. and Yu, P.S., Finding generalized projected clusters in high dimensional spaces, in *Proceedings of the 2000 ACM SIGMOD International Conference on Management of Data*, May 16–18, 2000, Dallas, TX, ACM Press, 2000, pp. 70–81.
3. Agrawal, R., Gehrke, J., Gunopulos, D., and Raghavan, P., Automatic subspace clustering of high dimensional data for data mining applications, in *Proceedings of the 1998 ACM SIGMOD International Conference on Management of Data*, ACM Press, Seattle, WA, 1998, pp. 94–105.
4. Yang, J. and Honavar, V., Feature subset selection using a genetic algorithm, *IEEE Intelligence Systems*, Vol. 13, 44–49, 1998.
5. Antonie, M., Zaiane, O.R., and Coman, A., Application of data mining techniques for medical image classification, in *Second International Workshop on Multimedia Data Mining (MDM/KDD)*, San Francisco, CA, 2001.
6. Barnard, K., Duygulu, P., de Freitas, N., Forsyth, D., Blei, D., and Jordan, M., Matching words and pictures, *Journal of Machine Learning Research*, 3, 1107–1135, 2003.
7. Blei, D. and Jordan, M., Modeling annotated data, in *Proceedings of the ACM SIGIR Conference on Research and Development in Information Retrieval*, 2003, pp. 127–134.
8. Blei, D., Ng, A., and Jordan, M., Latent Dirichlet allocation, *Journal of Machine Learning Research*, 3, 993–1022, 2003.
9. Blum, A. and Langley, P., Selection of relevant features and examples in machine learning, *Artificial Intelligence*, 97(1–2), 245–271, 1997.
10. Brown, P.F., Della Pietra, S.A., Della Pietra, V.J., and Mercer, R.L., The mathematics of machine translation: Parameter estimation, *Computational Linguistics*, 19(10), 263–311, 1993.
11. Jeon, J., Lavrenko, V., Manmatha, R., Automatic image annotation and retrieval using cross-media relevance models, *26th Annual International ACM SIGIR Conference*, Toronto, Canada, 2003.

12. Jin, R., Chai, J.Y., and Si, L., Effective automatic image annotation via a coherent language model and active learning, *ACM Multimedia*, 892–899, 2004.
13. Lavrenko, V., Manmatha, R., and Jeon, J., A model for learning the semantics of pictures, in *Proceedings of the 16th Conference on Advances in Neural Information Processing Systems NIPS*, December 8–13, 2003, Vancovver and Whistler, British Columbia, Canada, MIT Press, Boston, MA, 2004.
14. Feng, S., Manmatha, R., and Lavrenko, V., Multiple Bernoulli relevance models for image and video annotation, in *IEEE Conference on Computer Vision and Pattern Recognition*, June 27 to July 2, 2004, Washington, D.C., IEEE Computer Society, 2004, pp. 1002–1009.
15. Monay, F. and Gatica-Perez, D., On image auto-annotation with latent space models, in *Proceedings ACM International Conference on Multimedia*, November 2–8, 2003, Berkeley, CA.
16. Hu, G., Bu, J., and Chen, C., Semantic image classification based on Bayesian framework and one-step relevance feedback, *IEEE International Conference on Systems, Man and Cybernetics*, Vol. 1, 268–273, 2003.
17. Jiang, J. and Conrath, D., Semantic similarity based on corpus statistics and lexical taxonomy, in *Proceedings of the International Conference on Research in Computational Linguistics*, Taiwan, 1997.
18. Wang, J.Z., Wiederhold, G., and Firschien, O., System for screening objectionable images using Daubechies' wavelets and color histograms, *Computer Communications*, 1355–1360, 1998.
19. Uehara, Y., Endo, S., Shiitani, S., Masumoto, D., and Nagata, S., A computer-aided visual exploration system for knowledge discovery from images, in *Second International Workshop on Multimedia Data Mining* (MDM/KDD '2001).
20. Khan, L. and Awad, M., Classification problems using support vector machine in data mining, Ed., John Wang, *Encyclopedia of Data Warehousing and Mining*, Idea Group Publishing, Toronto, Canada, 2005.
21. Yong Rui and Thomas S. Huang, A novel relevance feedback technique in image retrieval, *ACM Multimedia*, 2, 67–70, 1999.
22. Rui, Y., Huang, T.S., and Chang, S.-F., Image retrieval: Current techniques, promising directions and open issues, *Journal of Visual Communication and Image Representation*, Vol. 10, 39–62, March 1999.
23. Thomasian, A., Castelli, V., and Li, C.-S., RCSVD: Recursive Clustering with Singular Value Decomposition for Dimension Reduction in Content-Based Retrieval of Large Image/Video Databases, IBM Research Report RJ 20704 (91772), 1997.
24. Cheng, C.-H., Fu, A.W., and Zhang, Y., Entropy-based subspace clustering for mining numerical data, in *Proceedings of the 5th ACM SIGKDD International Conference on Knowledge Discovery and Data Mining*, ACM Press, 1999, pp. 84–93.
25. Kononenko, I., Estimating attributes: Analysis and extensions of relief, *Proceedings of the 7th European Conference on Machine Learning*, 1994, pp. 171–182.
26. You, T., Dillon, S., and Liu, J., An integration of data mining and data warehousing for hierarchical multimedia information retrieval, *IEEE International Symposium on Intelligent Multimedia, Video and Speech Processing* (ISIMP'2001), 2001, pp. 373–376.
27. Goil, S., Nagesh, H., and Choudhary, A., Mafia: Efficient and Scalable Subspace Clustering for Very Large Data Sets, Technical Report CPDC-TR-9906-010, Northwestern University, Evanston IL 60208, June 1999.

Chapter 14

Subspace Clustering and Automatic Image Annotation

14.1 Introduction

In Chapter 13 we described various image classification models. One particular approach we have utilized is to annotate images, which is a key aspect of our tool. In particular, we have utilized the subspace clustering algorithm. Compared to low-level visual features such as color, texture, and shape, high-level conceptual information represented by using text descriptors can describe image semantics better. If we can generate image annotation automatically, a context-based image retrieval system will be a good choice. As we discussed Chapter 13, automatic image annotation is an unsolved problem in general. However, it is possible to generate good results for a specific domain even though it is still a challenging problem.

Most of the current image annotation and retrieval algorithms follow a similar methodology (as shown in Figure 14.1). That is, first take images and create segments (visual tokens or objects) by using image segmentation algorithms or simply an image grid. Second, extract visual features and generate mathematical representation such as a vector for each segment. Third, group segments using clustering algorithms to construct blob tokens. Finally, analyze the correlation between words and blob tokens to discover hidden semantics. Train the system

153

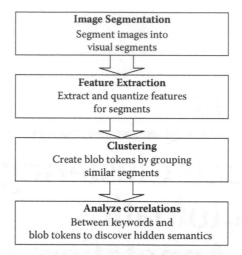

Figure 14.1   Methodology of automatic image annotation.

with large amount of annotated images, and use the learned correlation to predict words for unknown images. This chapter will elaborate on the image annotation tool we have developed.

The organization of this chapter is as follows: In Section 14.2 we describe our framework for image annotation. The Vector Space Model we have utilized will be discussed in Section 14.3. Clustering algorithms for the blob (binary large objects) tokens will be discussed in Section 14.4. Constructing the probability table will be discussed in Section 14.5. Automatic annotation methods will be discussed in Section 14.6. Experimental setup is given in Section 14.7. Valuation methods will be discussed in Section 14.8. Performance results will be given in Section 14.9. The chapter is summarized in Section 14.10.

14.2   Proposed Automatic Image Annotation Framework

We have proposed an automated image annotation framework based on a translation model (as shown in Figure 14.2). Training images are segmented into visual tokens first. The correlations between keywords and visual tokens are learned in the "Linking Objects with Keywords" module. The learning results will be saved in an "Image Object Library." Testing images are segmented into visual tokens as well. Each visual token in the testing image will be recognized in the "Object Recognition" module based on knowledge saved in the Image Object Library. Annotation for testing images comes from keywords linked to visual tokens in the testing image.

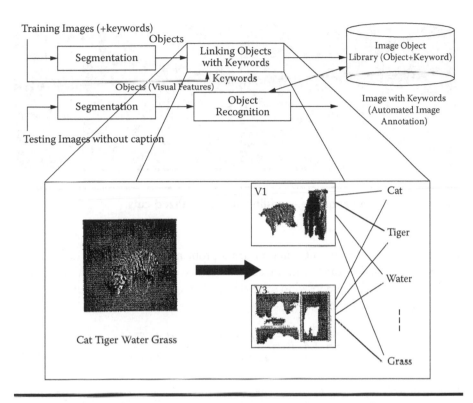

Figure 14.2   Flow diagram of automated image annotation mechanism.

14.2.1   Segmentation

We segment images into a number of visual tokens using normalized cuts [1]. Normalized cuts is an image segmentation algorithm. For example, suppose each pixel in image is represented as a node in a graph, and edge between any two nodes is weighted by a certain similarity estimate between two corresponding pixels; then the image will be modeled as a fully connected undirected graph $G = (V, E)$. The image segmentation problem will become a partition graph problem. Normalized cuts is a graph–theoretic criterion to measure how good a graph partition is. Compared with other image segmentation algorithms such as image griding and region growing, the normalized cuts algorithm is based on global properties of the graph rather than local properties. This is more similar to perceptual process for a human being. Perceptually significant parts will be detected first. Figure 14.3 shows examples of normalized cuts and image griding.

In graph theory, *cut* means a set of edges whose removal will cause a graph to be disconnected. The cost of a cut is the sum of edge weights of all removed edges. The optimal bi-partitioning of a graph is the cut having minimal cut cost.

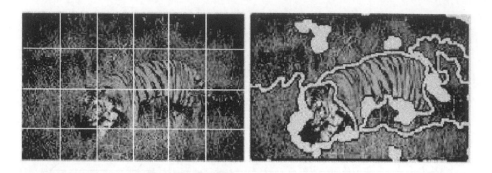

Figure 14.3   Example of image griding and normalized cuts.

However, the minimum cut criterion has a problem by nature. The definition of cuts as determined by the minimum cut criterion favors generating small partitions. Normalized cuts was proposed to solve this problem by normalizing cut cost by the size of segments as follows:

$$Ncut(A, B) = \frac{cut(A, B)}{assoc(A, V)} + \frac{cut(A, B)}{assoc(B, V)} \qquad (14.1)$$

In Equation 14.1, $cut(A, B)$ means the cost of the cut that partitions the graph into A and B. Segment $assoc(A, V)$ represents the sum of costs of all edges that touch A. Segment $assoc(B, V)$ is defined similarly. So, the bias of the minimum cut criterion is fixed by normalizing the size of the segments.

After image segmentation, we need to extract various visual features to describe visual tokens generated by the normalized cuts. Each visual token will be described by colors, textures, shapes, area, and other features. For example, in the COREL dataset, each visual token or image segment is represented by 30 visual features (see, for example, [2], [3], and [4], [5]). However, most of the visual features do not occupy a discrete space. Now, the problem is how to determine the correlation between keywords and visual tokens. The similarity of visual tokens is ill defined compared to keywords. For example, tiger visual tokens that appear in various images are supposed to be the same but may not be matched exactly. Hence, first, similar visual tokens will be grouped together based on clustering. Next, we will determine the correlation between keywords and visual tokens.

Image segmentation and feature extraction are fundamental and very important because they determine how much semantic information we can get from images. However, in this chapter, we focus on the clustering algorithms used to generate the blob token and a method to construct the probability table linking blob tokens with keywords.

14.3 The Vector Space Model

Vector space representation is a successful model applied to natural language processing. In this model, a document d_i in a collection consists of a set of words from vocabulary $(w_1, w_2, \ldots, w_N)$. The document d_i can be represented by an N-dimensional vector. The j-th vector component is the frequency of the j-th word in the vocabulary that appeared in document d_i. Thus, a document collection that contains M documents can be represented by a term-by-document matrix with N rows and M columns, where N is the number of terms in the vocabulary. Many powerful text analysis algorithms are based on the vector space model. In order to apply text analysis approaches to images, we generate a vector space representation for images via a quantized image representation.

14.3.1 Blob Tokens: Keywords of Visual Language

Note that each image will be represented by a set of keywords and visual tokens. Here, a visual token means a segmented region or object, and it will be described by a set of low-level features using the vector space model. Because all of these visual features do not occupy a discrete space, and the concept of the similarity of visual tokens is ill defined as compared to keywords, we need to quantize the visual features associated with the visual token or object. The straightforward solution is to use the clustering algorithm to quantize the image object representation. The idea is to generate discrete blob tokens for visual features by using the K-means algorithm to cluster similar visual tokens together to generate a finite set of blob tokens. Blob tokens can be thought of as keywords of visual language, which is similar to keywords of a natural language. It is obvious that the clustering algorithm will directly affect the quality of blob tokens.

We propose an algorithm based on subspace clustering to avoid the curse of dimensions during the clustering of visual tokens. Image data is usually highly dimensional, and normal clustering algorithms (e.g., K-means) assign equal weights to all dimensions. Due to the curse of dimensionality, the data becomes sparse, and distance measures become gradually meaningless as the number of dimensions increase. This will degrade the quality of the clustering result for traditional clustering algorithms. To solve this problem, we propose a top-down subspace clustering algorithm in this chapter. In each cluster, each visual feature is weighted according to how relevant this feature is to the cluster. We present a method estimating this relevance based on histogram analysis. To the best of our knowledge, subspace clustering algorithms have never been applied in automatic image annotation and retrieval. We implemented our subspace clustering algorithm and K-means algorithm used in [6] to generate blob tokens.

14.3.2 Probability Table

As discussed earlier, to analyze the correlation between keywords and blob tokens we need to apply statistical models that estimate the relation between each pair of keyword and blob token, and then construct a $P_{W \times B}$ matrix based on these estimates. W is the total number of keywords, and B is the total number of blob tokens. $P_{i,j}$ is the element in the matrix P that is in i-th row and j-th column. $P_{i,j}$ represents the conditional probability of i-th keyword for the given j-th blob token. This matrix $P_{W \times B}$ is the probability table we want to obtain. It is a difficult task to generate the probability table because image datasets usually do not provide explicit correspondence. Duygulu et al. applied the EM algorithm, calculating correspondences based on an initial estimate of the probability table, and used the correspondences to update the estimates of the probability table [6].

To construct the probability table, we implement four different approaches to analyze relations between keywords and blob tokens, based on two blob token sets generated by K-means and the proposed subspace clustering algorithm. Performance is compared based on precision, recall, and annotation accuracy using a benchmark dataset.

14.4 Clustering Algorithm for Blob Token Generation

Because low-level image features such as colors, textures, and shape do not occupy a discrete space, most image retrieval models use clustering algorithms (e.g., K-means) to quantize image object representation and construct a set of visual vocabulary. As each blob token is usually high in dimension, and normal clustering algorithms assign equal weights to all dimensions, the data becomes sparse and distance measures become gradually meaningless as the number of dimensions increase due to the curse of dimensionality. This will degrade the quality of the clustering result for traditional clustering algorithms. Finally, it will degrade the quality of the image annotation. To solve this problem, we generate a weighted feature selection algorithm. In other words, some features will be more relevant than other features for a set of visual tokens. For example, for a "ball" visual token, the shape feature will be more important than the color or texture feature. On the other hand, for a "rose" visual token, the color feature will be the dominating feature. Thus, we need to determine dominating features across a set of visual tokens instantaneously and assign more weight over others. Furthermore, during the clustering process, dominating features may vary from cluster to cluster. We need to determine the weight for a cluster on the fly, and the membership of a cluster may be changed based on the weight. Thus, this is a very challenging task.

We discuss the K-means algorithm, which is one popular clustering algorithm for a large dataset. In [6], Duygulu et al. used the K-means algorithm to generate discrete blob tokens. Then we describe our clustering algorithm in detail.

14.4.1 K-Means

K-means is a classic clustering algorithm. Its aim is to partition N data points $\langle x_1, x_2, \ldots, x_N \rangle$ into K clusters. The centers of K clusters $\langle c_1, c_2, \ldots, c_K \rangle$ are preassigned randomly and will be modified in an adaptive way. The algorithm works as follows.

- Decide the number K and assign values to centers or centroids $\langle c_1, c_2, \ldots, c_K \rangle$.
- The given data point x_i will be assigned into j-th cluster if $j = \arg\min_{1 \leq r \leq k} \| x_i - c_r \|^2$.
- Update the winning center c_j by $C_j^{new} = C_j^{old} + \eta \left(x_i - C_j^{old} \right)$.

Implement the second and the third steps iteratively for each input data point until all centers converge. K-means is preferable for clustering large datasets due to its faster running time O(KNrD), where K is the number of clusters, N is total number of input, r is the number of iterations before converging, and D is the dimension of the data point.

There are some problems with the K-means algorithm. First, the preassigned K could be not optimal. Even if K is the optimal, because the initial K centers are selected randomly, we still cannot ensure that the clustering result is optimal. In addition, because K-means is essentiality a hill-climbing algorithm, it is guaranteed to converge on a local but not necessarily a global optimum. In other words, the choices of the initial centers are critical to the quality of the results.

Aiming at these problems, many K-means-based algorithms have been published. In this chapter, we have implemented a general K-means algorithm and compared it with our algorithm.

14.4.2 Fuzzy K-Means Algorithm

K-means has hard membership, which means a data point will belong to only a single cluster (i.e., not shared). Sometimes we prefer soft membership, which means one data point can belong to more than one cluster (i.e., shared). Given the dataset $\langle x_1, x_2, \ldots, x_N \rangle$ and fuzzy partition $\langle A_1, A_2, \ldots, A_K \rangle$, the membership function μ needs to satisfy two conditions as follows:

$$\sum_{i=1}^{K} \mu_{A_i}(x_j) = 1 \tag{14.2}$$

$$0 < \sum_{j=1}^{N} \mu_{A_i}(x_j) < 1 \quad for \quad \forall i \tag{14.3}$$

Equation 14.2 means that each data point must be completely distributed, and Equation 14.3 says that there are no empty partitions and that a partition must contain some elements to some degree. The center of each partition will be estimated as

$$v_i = \frac{\sum_{j=1}^{N} [\mu_{A_i}(x_j)]^m \, x_j}{\sum_{j=1}^{N} [\mu_{A_i}(x_j)]^m} \tag{14.4}$$

where m is a fuzzy factor that governs the effect of the membership grade. The performance of the partition is estimated as follows:

$$J_m(P) = \sum_{j=1}^{N} \sum_{i=1}^{K} [\mu_{A_i}(x_j)]^m \| x_j - v_i \|^2 \tag{14.5}$$

Step 1: Set $k = 0$, select an initial partition $P(0)$.

Step 2: Calculate centers $v_i(k)$ according to Equation 14.4.

Step 3: Update the partition to $P(k + 1)$ according to

$\forall x_j$, if $\| x_j - v_i^{(k)} \|^2 > 0$ and then the membership of x_j to the partition A_i will be updated by

$$\mu_{A_i}^{(k+1)}(x_j) = \left[\sum_l^K \left(\frac{\left\| x_j - v_i^{(k)} \right\|^2}{\left\| x_j - v_l^{(k)} \right\|^2} \right)^{\frac{1}{m-1}} \right]^{-1} \tag{14.6}$$

If $\exists v_i, i \in \{1, 2, \ldots, K\}$ makes $\left\| x_j - v_i^{(k)} \right\|^2 = 0$, we assign an extremely small value arbitrarily.

Step 4: Compare $P(k)$ to $P(k + 1)$. If $\| P(k) - P(k+1) \| < \varepsilon$, then stop. Otherwise set $k = k + 1$ and go to step 2.

14.4.3 Weighted Feature Selection Algorithm

To link semantic concepts (keywords) with blob tokens accurately, we hope that the blob tokens generated by clustering algorithms have rich semantic information. This means we expect that all or at least most segmented image objects in the same blob have the same semantic meanings. For objects having the same semantic meaning, they must have some relevant low-level features. The set of relevant features is different for different semantic concepts. For example, all segmented "tiger" objects have the same color; the color features are relevant to tiger objects. Shape or position features are not relevant for the tiger concept. In another case, if the concept is "ball," the relevant features are shape, but color features are not relevant. The relevant features or dominant features are very useful when we do clustering and classification. The problem is, most current image clustering algorithms do not consider the relevant features and assign the same weight to all low-level features; but image data is normally high-dimensional data, and many of the dimensions are not relevant. These irrelevant dimensions will hide clusters in noisy data and confuse the clustering algorithms. The objects in the same cluster are very similar in the dominant feature dimension, but the distance or similarity measures may indicate dissimilar results due to the noisy data in an irrelevant dimension. The problem could become even worse when the data has different scales in different dimensions. Figure 14.4

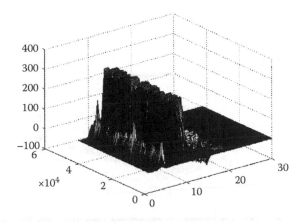

Figure 14.4   Surface plot of original data.

shows the surface plot of 42379 data points in the Corel dataset. We can see that the scales of some features are much larger than those of others. Thus, if we use the original data to calculate distance or similarity, these features will neutralize the effects of all other features. We normalize data $\langle x_{i1}, x_{i2}, \ldots, x_{im} \rangle$ into its normal form using mean (μ_j) and variance (σ_j) for the j-th low-level feature as $<(x_{i1} - \mu_1)/\sigma_1, (x_{i2} - \mu_2)/\sigma_2, \ldots, (x_{im} - \mu_m)/\sigma_m>$. The similarity measures computed from the normal form are invariant to amplitude scaling and shifting.

Calculating the variance is an important part of many statistical applications and analyses. The variance of j-th feature can be calculated usually as $\sigma_j^2 = \frac{\sum_{i=1}^{N}(x_{ij}-\mu_j)}{N}$, which is actually a biased estimate of variance. The most common formula for computing variance by far is $\sigma_j^2 = \frac{\sum_{i=1}^{N}(x_{ij}-\mu_j)}{N-1}$, which gives an unbiased estimate of variance and is the most commonly used measure of variance. We accept the unbiased estimate of variance. The surface plot of the normal form of the dataset is shown in Figure 14.5. We use this plot to train the system.

In this chapter, we propose an adaptive clustering algorithm to build connections between concepts and low-level features by assigning different weights to features in different blobs. We represent the m low-level features in the j-th cluster as $\langle f_{j1}, f_{j2}, \ldots, f_{jm} \rangle$, and the corresponding weights of these features are $\langle w_{j1}, w_{j2}, \ldots, w_{jm} \rangle$. We have a total of N data points, which corresponds to segmented image objects. The dimension of the data point is m, and the i-th data point in the dataset is represented as $\langle x_{i1}, x_{i2}, \ldots, x_{im} \rangle$. The major steps of our algorithm are as follows.

Step 1: As in the case of K-means, we predecide the number of clusters k and randomly select k data points from dataset as initialized cluster centroids. For example, the centroid for the j-th cluster is $\langle c_{j1}, c_{j2}, \ldots, c_{jm} \rangle$. Initialize the weights of the features for clusters to make sure that $\sum_{l=1}^{m} w_{jl} = 1$ for all $1 \leq j \leq k$.

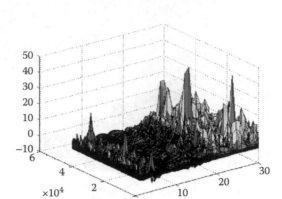

Figure 14.5 Surface plot of normalized data.

Step 2: Distribute all N data points. The i-th data points $\langle x_{i1}, x_{i2}, \ldots, x_{im} \rangle$ in the j-th cluster if $j = \arg\min_{1 \leq j \leq k} \sum_{l=1}^{m} w_{jl} \times \| x_{il} - c_{jl} \|^2$. Update the centroid of the j-th cluster $c_{jl}^{new} = c_{jl}^{old} + \eta(x_{il} - c_{jl}^{old})$ for all $1 \leq l \leq m$.

Step 3: After distributing N data points, we need to update the weights of features for all clusters based on the current clustering result.

Step 4: Repeat steps 2 and 3 until the centroids of all clusters converge.

The idea of our algorithm is to update the weights of features in each cluster adaptively. After the program terminates, based on the $\langle w_{j1}, w_{j2}, \ldots, w_{jm} \rangle$, we can decide which feature is more relevant or dominant than another feature for the j-th cluster. Step 3 is important. As we discussed earlier, the value of the relevant features in the same cluster should be similar. According to this heuristic, for the l-th feature in the j-th cluster f_{jl}, we assume that the denser the distribution of f_{jl}, the more possible the l-th feature is the dominant feature for the j-th cluster. The problem is how to evaluate the degree of density of the f_{jl} and assign weight correspondingly. After clustering, we say that the number of data points in each cluster is $\langle N1, N2, \ldots, Nk \rangle$, $\sum_{i=1}^{k} Ni = N$. For values of the l-th feature in the j-th cluster, if Nj values follow only one distribution, variance can represent the degree of density. The less the variance, the more dense the data. However, in our study, we did not use variance. The reason is that variance cannot always represent the degree of density or the pattern of data distribution, especially when we have more than one distribution. The counterexample is shown in Figure 14.6.

Two histograms have the same variance value 1012. However, all the data in the left histogram has only two values, 1 and 21. The right histogram is similar to the uniform distribution. Obviously, variance cannot show this kind of difference, but it is very important for some applications. In our case, for example, if the distribution of some feature values is similar to the left histogram in Figure 14.6,

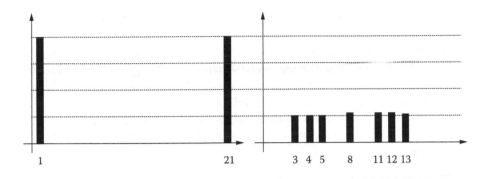

Figure 14.6 Two histograms having same variance.

it would be very possible that the feature is relevant. On the other hand, if data values have no tendency that looks like the right histogram, it is highly possible that the feature is irrelevant. That is the reason why we do not use variance to evaluate the weight of features.

In our algorithm, we use a heuristic method to estimate the weight of each feature. After step 2, all the data points in the j-th cluster can be represented using an $Nj \times m$ matrix. We make a histogram for each feature or each column in this matrix. For example, assume that the histogram of the l-th feature is shown as in Figure 14.7. The value in the X-coordinates is the value of the l-th feature, which is $\Re_l \in (0,1)$ in this example. We define the range of the l-th feature value as $\Re_{lX}$ and divide $\Re_{lX}$ into 100 equally spaced interval $[I_{l1}, I_{l2}, \ldots, I_{l100}]$ where $(i-1) \times 0.01 \times \Re_{lX} < I_{li} \leq i \times 0.01 \times \Re_{lX}$. The value Y_{li} in the Y-coordinates is the

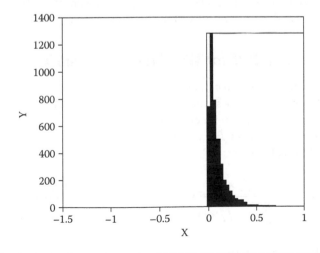

Figure 14.7 Black/solid part is the area of the histogram and rectangular is $Max(Y_{li})$ $\Re_{lX}$.

number of data points whose *l*-th feature values are located within the corresponding interval I_j. The area of the histogram is $Area_{hist(l)} = \sum_{i=1}^{100} Y_{li} \times I_{li}$. We define the ratio for the *l*-th feature as $Ratio_l = 1 - \frac{Area_{hist(l)}}{Max(Y_{li}) \times \Re_{lx}}$. The value of $Ratio_l$ can show how dense the *l*-th feature value distribution is. When $Ratio_l$ is larger, the value distribution for the *l*-th feature is denser. In other words, the *l*-th feature is more likely to be the dominant feature for the corresponding cluster.

Now we calculate the new weight values by normalizing $Ratio_l$. We define $Ratio_l$ in the *j*-th cluster as $Ratio_{jl}$; the new weight of the *l*-th feature for the *j*-th cluster is defined as $w_{jl} = \frac{Ratio_{jl}}{\sum_{l=1}^{m} Ratio_{jl}}$.

14.5 Construction of the Probability Table

Assume that there are W keywords and B blob tokens. The whole annotated training image dataset has N images. Then, the dataset can be represented by a matrix $M_{N \times (W+B)}$.

14.5.1 Method 1: Unweighted Data Matrix

First of all, we generate $M_{N \times (W+B)}$ by counting the frequency of keywords and blob tokens. $M_{N \times (W+B)} = [M_{N \times W} \mid M_{N \times B}] = [M_{W1} \mid M_{B1}] = M$. $M_{W1}[i, j]$ is the item of *i*-th row and *j*-th column in M_{W1}, which means the frequency of *j*-th keyword appeared in the *i*-th image. Similarly, $M_{B1}[i, j]$ is the item of the *i*-th row and *j*-th column in M_{B1}, which means the frequency of the *j*-th blob token appeared in the *i*-th image. We use $M_{W1}^T \times M_{B1}$ and normalize each column to get the probability table T_{Corr1} based on co-occurrence. $T_{Corr1}[i, j]$ is an estimate of $p(w_i \mid b_j)$, which is a conditional probability of the keyword w_i given the blob b_j.

14.5.2 Method 2: tf*idf Weighted Data Matrix

The term *tf* means *term frequency*, and *idf* stands for *inverse document frequency*. In text retrieval, some terms appear much more often than average, such as "of," "the," etc. These words are not useful for classification, and should be assigned less weight. For the term k in document D_i, which is represented as T_k, the normalized term weight should be as follows:

$$w_{ik} = \frac{tf_{ik} \times idf_k}{\sqrt{\sum_{k=1}^{t} (tf_{ik} \times idf_k)^2}} = \frac{tf_{ik} \log(N / n_k)}{\sqrt{\sum_{k=1}^{t} (tf_{ik})^2 [\log(N / n_k)]^2}}$$

where tf_{ik} is frequency of term T_k in document D_i, idf_k is the reverse document frequency, N is the total number of documents, and n_k is the total number of documents that contain T_k. We tried a similar method for the image case. Images correspond to documents, and blob tokens generated by the clustering algorithm correspond to the terms. Each item in the image vector is the weight for the corresponding blob token in the image. For example, $w_{i,\,l}$ is the weight of the blob token b_i in image l. Let N be the total number of images, and n_i the number of images in which the blob token b_i appears. Define the normalized frequency tf_{il} as $tf_{il} = \frac{freq_{il}}{\max_h\,freq_{hl}}$.

The term $freq_{i,\,l}$ is the number of times the blob b_i appears in the image l. The maximum of appearance is calculated over all blobs that appeared in the image l. Such frequency is normally referred to as the tf factor, which indicates how well the blob describes the image. We assume that, if a blob token appears in most of the images, it is not very useful for distinguishing a relevant image from a nonrelevant one. So, we need to define an inverse document frequency idf_i for b_i as $idf_i = \log N/n_i$.

Balancing the two foregoing factors, we have the weight of blobs:

$$w_{il} = tf_{il} \times idf_i = tf_{il} \times \log\frac{N}{n_i}$$

We generate $M_2 = [M_{W2} | M_{B2}]$ using the preceding two weights for the keyword and blob token instead of the frequency in M_1. Based on M_2, we calculate the probability table T_{Corr2} in the same manner as in Method 1.

14.5.3 *Method 3: Singular Value Decomposition (SVD)*

SVD and PCA are common techniques for the analysis of multivariate data. SVD can be used to reduce the dimension of data or clean up noise and reveal the information structure. SVD is widely applied to reduce high-dimensional data (Figure 14.8).

$$
\begin{bmatrix}
99 & 1 & 2 \\
80 & 7 & 6 \\
81 & 88 & 86 \\
87 & 19 & 20 \\
93 & 25 & 24 \\
24 & 76 & 77 \\
5 & 82 & 84 \\
6 & 13 & 14 \\
12 & 94 & 96 \\
18 & 100 & 98
\end{bmatrix}
= USV^T =
$$

$$
\begin{bmatrix}
-0.1437 & -0.5224 & 0.3123 \\
-0.1386 & -0.4037 & -0.1440 \\
-0.4809 & -0.1278 & -0.4207 \\
-0.2033 & -0.3956 & 0.2870 \\
-0.2328 & -0.4101 & -0.1449 \\
-0.3573 & 0.1393 & 0.1627 \\
-0.3585 & 0.2633 & 0.3764 \\
-0.0655 & 0.0152 & 0.2127 \\
-0.4190 & 0.2679 & 0.3741 \\
-0.4443 & 0.2498 & -0.4911
\end{bmatrix}
\times
\begin{bmatrix}
302.9726 & 0 & 0 \\
0 & 170.2350 & 0 \\
0 & 0 & 3.2584
\end{bmatrix}
\times
\begin{bmatrix}
-0.4205 & -0.9073 & 0.0032 \\
-0.6414 & 0.2948 & -0.7083 \\
-0.6417 & 0.2999 & 0.7059
\end{bmatrix}^T
$$

Figure 14.8   Illustration of SVD.

However, the transformed features can be a linear or nonlinear combination of old features and often have no physical meaning anymore, and thus, the clustering result based on transformed data is hard to interpret. So, we use SVD to clean up noise rather than reduce the dimension.

To remove noise, we generate a new matrix S' by keeping r the largest singular value $\sigma_1, \sigma_2, \dots, \sigma_r, r < \min(m, n)$ and setting the others to zero. We make $\sum_{i=1}^{r} \sigma_i / \sum_{j=1}^{\min(m, n)} \sigma_j \approx \beta$, which means we preserve the β (say, at 95%) variance of the distribution and only lose 5% information. Then we can calculate the optimal low-rank representation of $X_{m \times n}$ as $X_{m \times n}' = US'V^T$. Note that this new matrix will not reduce any dimension (still $m \times n$), but it will remove/reduce noise across all dimensions. We then apply SVD to $M_{W1}, M_{B1}, M_{W2}, M_{B2}$ one by one to calculate $M_3 = [M_{W3}|M_{B3}]$ and $M_4 = [M_{W4}|M_{B4}]$ correspondingly, and based on M_3 and M_4, we derive the probability table.

Let $X_{m \times n}$ denote a matrix with m rows and n columns. SVD can always decompose $X_{m \times n}$ into the product of three matrices as $X_{m \times n} = USV^T$ (as shown in Figure 14.2), where U is an $m \times n$ matrix, S is an $n \times n$ diagonal matrix, and V^T is also an $n \times n$ matrix. $S = diag(\sigma_1, \sigma_2, \dots, \sigma_{\min(m, n)})$, $\sigma_1 > \sigma_2 > \dots, \sigma_{\min(m, n)}$, and $\sigma_j > 0$ for all $j > \text{rank}(X_{m \times n})$.

14.5.4 Method 4: EM Algorithm

The expectation maximization (EM) algorithm is an iterative optimization method that is usually used to calculate maximum likelihood estimates of certain parameters when the given samples are incomplete. During the Expectation (E) step, we estimate the likelihood by including a certain set of parameters θ that describe a hidden probability distribution. The maximization (M) step computes the maximum likelihood of parameters by maximizing the expected likelihood found on the E step. Then the found parameters will be used in another E step. The process keeps repeating until no further improvement can be achieved. We followed the translation model to sum over all the possible assignments of keywords to blob tokens as follows:

$$p(w \mid b) = \prod_{n=1}^{N} \prod_{j=1}^{M_n} \sum_{i=1}^{L_n} p(a_{nj} = i) t(w = w_{nj} \mid b = b_{ni})$$

where M_n is the number of keywords in the n-th image, L_n is the number of blob tokens in the n-th image. $p(a_{nj} = i)$ is the probability that a blob token b_i is associated with a keyword w_j, and $t(w = w_{nj} \mid b = b_{ni})$ is the probability of obtaining the word w given the instance of blob b. $p(a_{nj} = i)$ and $t(w = w_{nj} \mid b = b_{ni})$ are parameters. The likelihood $p(w \mid b)$ is maximized by using the EM algorithm. We initialize two parameters $p(a_{nj} = i)$ and $t(w = w_{nj} \mid b = b_{ni})$ according to T_{Corr1} and T_{Corr2} and update the parameters iteratively based on two constraints $\sum_i p(a_{nj} = i) = 1$ and $\sum_w t(w^* \mid b^*) = 1$, where w^* is a specific keyword and b^* is a specific blob token. Finally, we get probability tables T_{Corr5} and T_{Corr6}, which correspond to Method 1 plus EM algorithm, and Method 2 plus EM algorithm. The detailed steps are as follows:

Step 1: Initialize parameters

$p(a_{nj} = i)$: Because there is no a priori knowledge, we take the average as the initial value. For example, if there are 5 blobs in image n, the probability of assigning a specific word w_j to the blob b_i would be 14.2.

$t(w = w_{nj} \mid b = b_{ni})$: Generate initial estimates using Method 1 or Method 2

Step 2: E step

For each image n and word j, calculate the likelihood as $p' = \frac{p(a_{nj}=i)t(w_{nj}|b=b_{ni})}{\sum_{i=1}^{L_n} p(a_{nj}=i)t(w_{nj}|b_{ni})}$

Step 3: M step

Re-estimate two parameters using p'

$p(a_{nj} = i)$: Calculate the average of p' across images having the same number of keywords and blobs.

$t(w = w_{nj} \mid b = b_{ni})$: Find all pairs of words and blobs that appear together at least once, sum over p', and normalize to get new $t(w = w_{nj} \mid b = b_{ni})$.

Step 4: Evaluation

Check the difference between values of the new parameters and the old parameters. If there is no difference, or the difference is less than certain preselected threshold, then converge. Otherwise, go back to Step 2.

According to the probability table, we can build the connection between keywords and blob tokens. We assign a keyword w_i to a blob token b_j if $p(w_i \mid b_j)$ is the maximum in the j-th column of the probability table.

14.5.5 Fuzzy Method

We generate another statistical model to generate the probability table. We apply the fuzzy K-means algorithm to generate $P(b \mid o)$, where $P(b \mid o)$, is the probability of a specific blob b for a given specific segment (object) o. We define probability $P(o \mid J)$ as the probability of a specific segment o for a given image J. If the object o is not in the image J, this probability is 0; otherwise $P(o \mid J)$ equals $1/\#J$, where $\#J$ means the number of objects in image J. We calculate the probability $P(b \mid J)$ based on $P(b \mid o)$ and $P(o \mid J)$ as follows:

$$P(b \mid J) = \sum_{i=1}^{N} P(b \mid o_i)P(o_i \mid J)$$

where N is the total number of objects. The probability $P(w \mid J)$ is calculated using Equation 13.2, where w is a particular keyword. $P(b)$ is an estimate based on $P(b \mid o)$. Finally, we apply Bayes' rule and the probability theory to generate the matrix

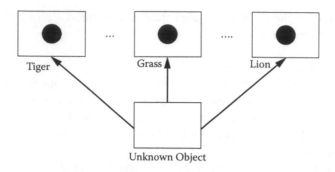

Figure 14.9   Illustration of automatic annotation.

$W * B$ in which W is the number of keywords (size of vocabulary) and B is the number of blobs. Each element is the probability $P(w|b)$.

14.6   AutoAnnotation

To annotate the image automatically, we calculate the distance between the given image object and all centroids of blob tokens, and represent this image object with the keyword of the closest blob token (see Figure 14.9). The annotation is generated using keywords assigned to all objects in the image. For example, in Figure 14.9, the test image object is similar to the centroid of the second blob; the second blob corresponds to the keyword "grass." Therefore, the keyword for the test image object will be grass.

In addition, we applied another approach to generate the image annotation. In some models, the keywords are decided by certain estimated parameters such as conditional probability or values of the membership function. In these cases, it is not binary. One segment could have more than one keyword, which is decided by a certain threshold. If the estimated parameter is larger than the threshold, the keyword will be used to represent the segment, or we can choose x keywords having top x parameters.

14.7   Experimental Setup

14.7.1   Corel Dataset

The dataset used in this chapter is downloaded from [2, 3]. All detailed information is as shown in Table 14.1.

There are 5000 images from 50 stock photo CDs in this dataset. Each CD contains 100 images on the same topic.

Table 14.1 Information of dataset and experiments

Number of images	5,000
Number of training images	4,500
Number of testing images	500
Number of training objects	42,379
Number of testing objects	4,637
Number of testing objects for corresponding accuracy	299
Number of concepts	374
Number of features	30
Number of blobs	500

Figure 14.10 shows some sample images from different topics. We use 4500 images as a training set, and the remaining 500 images as testing set. From the 500 testing images we manually labeled 50 images to test correspondence accuracy. The image segmentation algorithm is normalized cut. Each image is represented as a 36-dimensional vector, which corresponds to 36 low-level features.

Figure 14.10 Sample images of Corel dataset.

Six features in this dataset are duplicated. We ignore the duplications and use only 30 features. The feature extraction and quantization ensures that there are 1–10 blobs and 1–5 keywords for each image. The vocabulary contains 374 different keywords.

14.7.2 Feature Description

Each image is represented as a 30-dimensional vector, which corresponds to 30 low-level features.

The features represent, rather roughly, major visual features/properties:

Size is represented by the portion of the image covered by the region.

Position is represented using the coordinates of the region center of mass normalized by the image dimensions.

Color is represented by using the average and standard deviation of (R, G, B), (L, A, B) over the region.

Texture is represented by using the average and variance of 16 filter responses. Four differences of Gaussian filters with different sigmas, and 12 oriented filters, aligned in 30-degree increments.

Shape is represented by the ratio of the area to the perimeter squared, the moment of inertia (about the center of mass), and the ratio of the region area to that of its convex hull.

For color features of an image, we use six features (i.e., average and standard deviation of RGB and LAB color space); for texture we use 12 features (mean-oriented energy along with 30 degree increments); and for shape, we use six features (i.e., area, x, y, boundary, convexity, and moment of inertia). The vocabulary contains 374 different keywords.

14.8 Evaluation Methods

Because we use the same dataset and need to compare with its results, the evaluation methods are also similar. We clustered a total of 42,379 image objects from 4,500 training images into 500 blobs using the K-means algorithm and the proposed top-down subspace clustering algorithm. We follow the four models discussed in Section 14.5 to calculate probability tables based on the two clustering results, respectively. Finally, we have 12 different probability tables, which correspond to the 12 different methods shown in Table 14.2.

14.8.1 Evaluation of Annotation

To evaluate the annotation, we retrieve images from the testing dataset using 20 frequent keywords from the vocabulary. The image will be retrieved if the

Table 14.2 Twelve probability tables and corresponding methods

PTK1: K-means + unweighted matrix (method1)	**PTK2:** K-means + weighted tf*idf (method2)	**PTK3:** K-means + unweighted matrix + SVD (method3)
PTK4: K-means + weighted tf*idf + SVD (method3)	**PTK5:** K-means + unweighted matrix + EM (method4)	**PTK6:** K-means + weighted tf*idf + EM (method4)
PTS1: Subspace + unweighted matrix (method1)	**PTS2:** Subspace + weighted tf*idf (method2)	**PTS3:** Subspace + unweighted matrix + SVD (method3)
PTS4: Subspace + weighted tf*idf + SVD (method3)	**PTS5:** Subspace + unweighted matrix + EM (method4)	**PTS6:** Subspace + weighted tf*idf + EM (method4)

automatically established annotation contains the query keyword. We evaluate the result using precision, recall, and the common E measure, which are defined as $p = Num_{Correct}/Num_{Retrieved}$, $r = Num_{Correct}/Num_{Exist}$, and $E(p, r) = 1 - 2/1/p + 1/r$, respectively.

$Num_{Correct}$ means the number of retrieved images that contain the query keyword in its annotation. $Num_{Retrievedt}$ is the number of retrieved images, and Num_{Exist} is the total number of images in the test set containing the query keyword in the annotation.

14.8.2 Evaluation of Correspondence

We manually labeled the image objects of 50 images to test the correspondence. If the word predicted by the blob contained manually generated keywords of this object, we can say that the blob predicts the word correctly in the right place. It is possible that the predicted word is contained in the image rather than in the object.

14.9 Results

Table 14.3 shows some examples of automatic image annotation. The order of keywords in automatic annotation is the same as the decreasing order of the size of the corresponding segmented image objects.

We compare pairwise PTK and PTS based on precision and recall from Figures 14.11 to 14.16. Not every word in the vocabulary can appear in automatic annotation; only a subset of words S_W can be predicted by blobs. For different clustering algorithms and probability table construction methods, this

Table 14.3   Examples of automatic annotations compared with the original annotation

Images	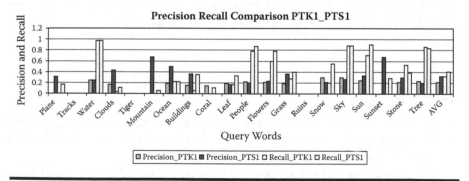				
Original annotation	sunset trees sky Hawaii	house flowers garden windows	sun clouds sky glow	grizzly bear meadow grass	cougar trees forest
Automatic annotation of PTS6	water people shops sky sun sunset	buildings garden flowers snow	water clouds sky sun	field grass tree bear birds	rocks snow tree water
Automatic annotation of PTK6	clouds buildings people sky sun	field garden people flowers sky	petals sun sunset stone	water field people tree	water snow street

subset of keywords S_W could be different, which is why the precision or recall of some query words is zero. Twenty frequent query words are selected from the vocabulary. From these clustered column figures, we can see that the precision and recall of PTS are better than those of PTK for most of the query words. The average precision and recall of PTS in each case are better than those of PTK.

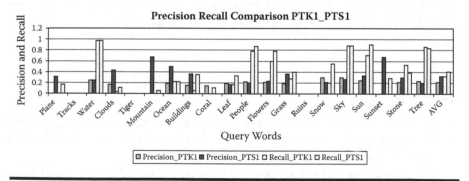

Figure 14.11   Precision recall comparison of PTK1 and PTS1.

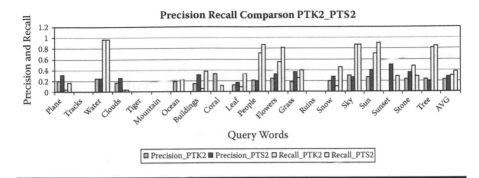

Figure 14.12   Precision recall comparison of PTK2 and PTS2.

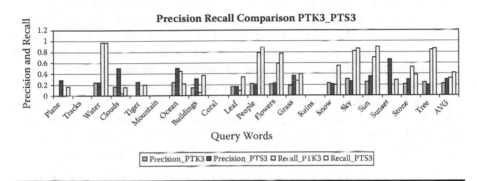

Figure 14.13   Precision recall comparison of PTK3 and PTS3.

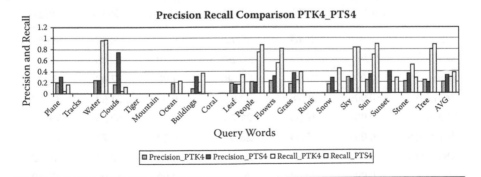

Figure 14.14   Precision recall comparison of PTK4 and PTS4.

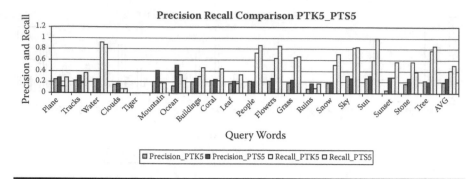

Figure 14.15   Precision recall comparison of PTK5 and PTS5.

The common E measure is calculated based on average precision and recall, and the E measure of PTS is lower than that of PTK (as shown in Figure 14.17).

Figure 14.18 compares correspondence accuracy between PTK and PTS. The results show again that PTS is better than PTK. We tested the correspondence using 50 test images, which included 299 segments labeled manually. Table 14.4 shows the number of segments annotated correctly. The first column PTK$_{correct}$ shows the number of segments that are labeled with the right keywords in the right place for PTK methods. For example, the number in the first row and first column is 14. That means 14 segments among 299 test segments are labeled with the right keyword in the right place using method PTK1. Similarly, the second column PTS$_{correct}$ shows values for PTS methods. The third column PTK$_{img}$ and the

Table 14.4   Performance comparison of fuzzy method, PTK6, and PTS6

	Average precision based on 10 most frequent keywords (%)			Average recall based on 10 most frequent keywords (%)		
	Fuzzy method	PTK6	PTS6	Fuzzy method	PTK6	PTS6
Water	23.34	24.65	25.12	100	90.52	89.66
Sky	37.96	31.52	26.20	78.10	82.86	82.86
Tree	50.00	22.29	20.88	1.08	77.42	86.02
People	0.00	20.78	20.00	0.00	71.62	86.49
Grass	0.00	18.50	21.74	0.00	62.75	68.63
Buildings	0.00	17.44	26.60	0.00	27.78	46.30
Mountain	0.00	17.50	38.89	0.00	18.42	18.42
Flowers	0.00	22.08	26.44	0.00	62.96	85.19
Snow	0.00	17.98	18.03	0.00	51.61	70.97
Clouds	0.00	15.38	10.53	0.00	7.69	7.69
Average	11.13	20.81	23.44	17.92	55.36	64.22

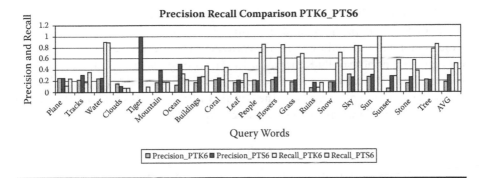

Figure 14.16   Precision recall comparison of PTK6 and PTS6.

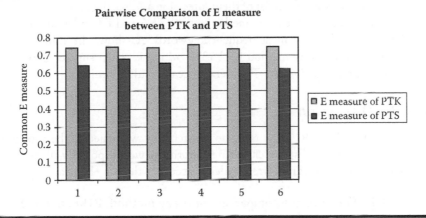

Figure 14.17   The first two columns are E measures of PTK1 and PTS1, the second two columns are E measure of PTK2 and PTS2. X-coordinates in Figure 14.18 have same meaning.

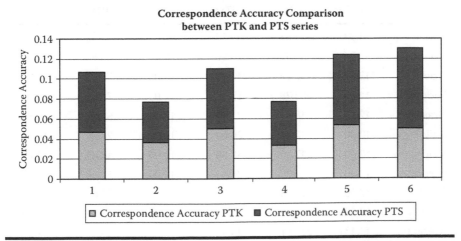

Figure 14.18   Correspondence accuracy comparison between PTK and PTS.

fourth column PTS$_{img}$ show the number of segments labeled with right keywords but not necessarily in the right places, using PTK and PTS methods, respectively. Results in Table 14.2 indicate that the correspondence accuracies of PTS methods are higher than those of PTK methods. The factor of *tf* idf* and SVD are not helpful for improving correspondence accuracy. In some cases, *tf* idf* makes the correspondence accuracy even worse. The EM algorithm improves the correspondence accuracy, especially when based on subspace clustering.

14.9.1   Results of Fuzzy Method

We also implemented the fuzzy method. Experimental results show that this method favors frequent keywords. Only a few frequent query keywords generate good precision and recall; however, for most of them, precision and recall are worse than other methods. We compared the fuzzy method with PTK6 and PTS6 based on average precision and recall of 10 most frequent keywords. As shown in Table 14.5, the average precision of fuzzy method is 11.13%, which is much smaller than PTK6 (214.81%) and PTS6 (23.44%). The average recall result is similar.

14.9.2   Discussion

Our experimental results show that, no matter how we generate the probability table, the top-down subspace clustering algorithm we proposed will get better annotation performance and correspondence accuracy than the K-means algorithm.

Table 14.5   Performance comparison of fuzzy method, PTK6, and PTS6

Images	Average precision based on 10 most frequent keywords (%)			Average recall based on 10 most frequent keywords (%)		
	Fuzzy method	PTK6	PTS6	Fuzzy method	PTK6	PTS6
Water	23.34	24.65	25.12	100	912.52	89.66
Sky	37.96	31.52	26.20	78.10	82.86	82.86
Tree	512.00	22.29	212.88	1.08	77.42	86.02
People	12.00	212.78	212.00	12.00	71.62	86.49
Grass	12.00	18.50	21.74	12.00	62.75	68.63
Buildings	12.00	17.44	26.60	12.00	27.78	46.30
Mountain	12.00	17.50	38.89	12.00	18.42	18.42
Flowers	12.00	22.08	26.44	12.00	62.96	85.19
Snow	12.00	17.98	18.03	12.00	51.61	712.97
Clouds	12.00	15.38	112.53	12.00	7.69	7.69
Average	11.13	212.81	23.44	17.92	55.36	64.22

We cannot say that one clustering algorithm is better than the others; some are more suited to certain problems. Image data has a high dimension, which will confuse the clustering algorithm with noise data. In addition, for automatic image annotation, blob tokens generated by the clustering algorithm are expected to have similar semantic meaning. Otherwise it is impossible to predict a keyword well. It is difficult for normal clustering algorithms to overcome the curse of high dimensionality and produce good clustering results. Therefore, we propose one top-down subspace clustering algorithm. This algorithm can assign weights to each dimension and update these weights during the learning process.

14.10 Summary

Image classification is becoming an important area for many applications, including medical, entertainment, defense, and intelligence. It is a key aspect of image data mining. Before we classify and mine the images, one approach is to annotate the images. Much of image annotation is currently performed manually. More recently, some automatic image annotation algorithms have been proposed. We have described in this chapter a tool we have developed that annotates the images. We have also described the experimental results we have conducted and compared them with other approaches.

The tool we have developed is a first step in the image annotation process. We need to examine different models based on different techniques. For example, what is the best approach to extract the blobs from the images? What are the more appropriate approaches to correlate the blobs with the tokens? We need to possibly combine various models to obtain better accuracy as well as reduce the false positives and negatives. Our image classification tool will be described in more detail in the next two chapters.

References

1. Shi J. and Malik, J., Normalized cuts and image segmentation, *IEEE Conference on Computer Vision and Pattern Recognition(CVPR)*, June 1997, Puerto Rico.
2. http://corel.digitalriver.com/.
3. http://kdd.ics.uci.edu/databases/CorelFeatures/CorelFeatures.data.html
4. http://phobos.imib.rwth-aachen.de
5. http://www.cs.arizona.edu/people/kobus/research/data/eccv_2002
6. Duygulu P., Barnard, K., de Freitas, N., and Forsyth, D., Object recognition as machine translation: Learning a lexicon for a fixed image vocabulary, *Seventh European Conference on Computer Vision (ECCV)*, Vol. 4, 2002, pp. 97–112.
7. Kalman, D., A singularly valuable decomposition: The SVD of a matrix, *College Mathematics Journal*, Vol. 27, No. 1, January 1996.

Chapter 15

Enhanced Weighted Feature Selection

15.1 Introduction

In Chapter 13, we discussed image classification models and in Chapter 14 we discussed our approach to subspace clustering. As discussed earlier, our automatic image annotation framework is based on the translation model. After determining visual vocabulary using clusters, we need to determine the correlation between keywords and blob tokens. Hence, we need to apply machine translation models to translate visual vocabulary to keywords. Finally, this learned model will be applied to translate unannotated images into textual keywords. Therefore, the quality of visual vocabulary is very critical.

We proposed a conservative weighted feature selection algorithm in Chapter 14, in which each feature in a cluster will be assigned a weight according to how relevant the feature is to the cluster. We presented a method estimating this relevance based on histogram analysis in Chapter 14. In this chapter, we propose two more weighted feature selection mechanisms. One is an aggressive (compared to the conservative one which we discussed in Chapter 14) histogram analysis, the other one is based on chi-square calculation. For the aggressive method, the idea is similar to the conservative method. If the feature value distribution is denser for a cluster, the feature is more important to, or representative of, the cluster and this feature will carry more weight for that cluster. Intuitively, the feature will carry more weight when its value is sparsely distributed as compared to uniformly distributed. For this, first, we calculate density for a feature in a particular cluster. Next, we compute weight based on density in an aggressive manner. The conservative approach works gracefully; on the other hand, the aggressive approach takes into account the reciprocal of density, which makes density have more effect on weight. The concern of the chi-square method is the difference between the global feature distribution (GD), based on all training data points, and local feature distribution (LD), based on the data points in one specific cluster. If the GD and LD of a feature are very similar, it means the feature is not representative of the corresponding cluster. We will assign less weight to the feature. Now, the question is how we would like to quantify the difference between a feature LD and GD. The chi-square method is applied to measure this difference. We also studied linear discriminative analysis for feature weighting.

In addition, in this chapter we propose another method to determine correlation between keywords and blob tokens. Our proposed method, namely, Conservative Context (C2), takes into account not only keyword-to-blob-token correlation, but also keyword-to-keyword correlation and blob-token-to-blob-token correlation when calculating correlation between keywords and blob tokens. In C2, we evaluate word-to-word and blob-token-to-blob-token correlations on the basis of word frequency and blob-token frequency, respectively. Finally, we recalculate correlations between keywords and blob tokens after combining word-to-word and blob-token-to-blob-token correlations.

The organization of this chapter is as follows. In Section 15.2, we describe an aggressive feature weighting algorithm. Our experimental results are discussed in Section 15.3. The chapter is summarized in Section 15.4. Some related work is provided in [1–3].

15.2 Aggressive Feature Weighting Algorithm

In the aggressive approach, the weight of features will be changed significantly rather than incrementally. As shown in Chapter 14, density/weight will be inversely proportional to the $Area_{hist(l)}$. Thus, density will be given by: $Density_l^A = Max(Y_{li}) \times R_{lx} / Area_{hist(l)}$. Similar to the conservative one, the curve of the histogram is sharper; thus, the density will be higher. The difference from the conservative one is that density will change more aggressively in this method.

15.2.1 Global Data Reduction (GDR)

Normally, SVD could be used to reduce dimension or clean up noise. When using SVD to reduce dimension, the new features will be a linear combination of original features, and it will be hard to explain the meaning of results and determine important original features. We applied SVD to the original dataset to reduce dimension before applying K-means clustering. For weight assignment, we calculate based on features after dimension reduction. Each feature is a linear combination of all original features. We call this method the global data reduction technique (GDR) (see also [4]).

15.2.2   Weighted Feature Using Chi-Square

A density-based feature weighting strategy works fine in many cases, but it has a shortcoming that limits its usage [5]: It does not consider the bias of datasets. For example, if the distribution of one specific feature based on the whole dataset is similar to the distribution of the same feature based on each of the clusters, this feature is not representative, because its feature value distribution is similar for all clusters. Density of distribution cannot represent feature weight in this case.

To solve this problem, we propose an alternative feature weighting approach based on distribution distortion. The statistical distance measure between two distributions is very useful in research areas such as pattern recognition and information theory. In this paper, we apply a chi-square-like method to calculate the distortion between two distributions. In statistics, Pearson's chi-square statistic is $X^2 = \sum_{allcells}(O_i - E_i)^2/E_i$, which is used to assess discrepancy by quantifying the comparison of the observed and expected counts in a table. O_i is the observed counts in the table, and E_i is the expected counts in the table. The larger the value of X^2 is, the worse the fit is. For example, suppose that the ratio of male to female students in the class is exactly 1:1, but in the physics class there have been 80 female and 40 male students over the past 1 year. So, the expected number of male students E_m and female students E_f should be 60 and 60. And the observed number of male students O_m and female students O_f are 40 and 80, respectively. The chi-square of this example is $(40 - 60)^2/60 + (80 - 60)^2/60 = 13.34$. In our case, the purpose is to assess how different two distributions are and generate a distortion value to quantify this difference. The bigger the distortion value, the more different the given two distributions are. The input is a given cluster c and a given feature f, and the output is the weight of feature f in cluster c. First of all, we generate a global feature histogram $H_G = (H_1, H_2, \ldots, H_B)$ based on the whole dataset and a local feature histogram $h_L = (h_1, h_2, \ldots, h_B)$ based on the cluster c, where B is the number of bins for the histogram. Figure 15.1 shows an example of feature distribution. The X axis represents feature values, which are in the range [−25, 100] in this example. The width of the bin is 0.1. The Y-axis represents the number of data points that fall in corresponding bins. Figure 15.1 shows the global distribution, which is based on the whole dataset (left), and the local distribution, which is based on one cluster (right). Before calculating distortion, we need to normalize the two histograms and ensure that all values lie between 0 and 100, which means $0 \le H_i \le B$, $0 \le h_i \le B$ *for* $i = 1, 2, \ldots, B = 100$. We regard histogram values of global distribution H_i as expected counts and h_i for local distribution as observed counts, so we applied chi-square to calculate the distortion between global and local distribution of feature f for cluster c as follows:

$$distortion(c, f) = \sum_{i=1}^{B} \frac{(H_i - h_i)^2}{H_i} \tag{15.1}$$

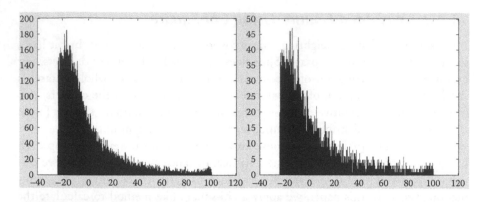

Figure 15.1 **Example of feature value distribution based on the entire dataset (global/left) and one cluster (local/right).**

From the foregoing formula, we can see that the distortion value will be larger when the global and local distributions are more different. The idea is that a larger distortion value means the feature f is more representative for cluster c, and so we should assign more weight to the feature f in cluster c. Thus, larger distortion means more weight. We easily calculate normalized weight value based on distortion values, as follows:

$$w_{cl} = \frac{distortion(c, f_l)}{\sum\limits_{i=1}^{m} distortion(c, f_i)} \quad (15.2)$$

where w_{cl} is the weight of the l-th feature in cluster c and m is the total number of features. Here, we also normalize weight values, which guarantees that the summation of all feature weights for any cluster equals to 1.

15.2.3 Linear Discriminant Analysis

For a semantic concept, we have a set of associated images. From these images, a set of visual tokens will convey this concept. Each of these visual tokens will be represented by a set of low-level features (color, texture, and shape). We know that all visual features are not equally important for a semantic concept; some features will be more relevant than others for a set of visual tokens/images. For example, for a "ball," the shape feature will be more important than the "color," and texture features. On the other hand, for a "rose," the visual token color feature will dominate. Thus, we need to determine dominating features across a set of visual tokens immediately and assign more weight to these features than to others. Then, for a given concept, determining the important features and quantifying the importance of each feature is nontrivial. Given a set of training images $I = \{I_i\}_{i \in \{1, 2, \ldots, J\}}$ and a set of concepts $W = \{w_k\}_{k \in \{1, 2, \ldots, K\}}$, each image I_i is annotated with some concepts from the concept set W. However, for a given image I_i and concept w_k, the problem is that we do not know which segmented region in I_i corresponds to w_k. Also, owing to unsolved object segmentation, each detected region may be associated with more than one concept and vice versa (see also [6], [7], and [8]).

We present a method based on approximation of linear discriminant analysis (ALDA) to find a dominant visual feature for each semantic concept and determine its weight [9]. For this, first, we define four sets: S, T, T_G, and G. For any given feature x and concept w_k, T is the set of x values of all segments included in all images labeled by w_k; G is the set of x values of all segments contained in images that are not labeled by w_k; and S is the set of x values, calculated on all the segments that exactly represent the concept w_k. S is the subset of T, and we define T_G as the supplementary set of S in T. So, $T = S \cup T_G$, and the intersection between T_G and S is empty. In addition, for any feature set F, μ_F is the average of all values of $x_i \in F$, v_F is the variance, and c_F is the cardinal. We also define B_{DE} as the Between Variance between any sets D and E and define W_{DE} as the Within Variance between sets D and E.

For each feature x, discrimination power $F(x; w_k) = 1/1 + V(x; w_k)$ (where $V(x; w_k) = W_{SG}/B_{SG}$) can represent how important x is to w_k. For example, if $F(x_1; w_k) > F(x_2; w_k)$, then we can say feature x_1 is more relevant to w_k than x_2. Based on discrimination power values, we can easily determine dominant features for each concept and calculate corresponding weights. Unfortunately, there is no automatic way to determine the sets S and T_G. Thus, we cannot calculate B_{SG} and W_{SG}. However, it is easy to estimate the other two sets, T and G. We will show that $V(x; w_k)' = W_{TG}/B_{TG}$ is a good approximation of $V(x; w_k)$. Thus, the feature x is based on the approximation $F(x; w_k)' = 1/1 + V(x; w_k)'$. Furthermore, if we sort all features based on $V(x; w_k)$ or $V(x; w_k)'$, the result will be similar. Now, without loss of generality, we will show that $V(x; w_k)' = W_{TG}/B_{TG}$ is a linear function of $V(x; w_k)$. For this, first we will derive W_{TG} and B_{TG} and then plug these into $V(x; w_k)'$. Next, we represent $V(x; w_k)'$ in terms of $V(x; w_k)$. Finally, based on some simple assumptions, we show that $V(x; w_k)'$ is a good approximation of $V(x; w_k)$.

Let $p_S = c_S/c_T$ and $q_S = 1 - p_S = c_T - c_S/c_T = c_{T_G}/c_T$. We assume that $\mu_{T_G} = \mu_G$ and $v_{T_G} = v_G$. So, we have

$$\mu_T = q_S \cdot \mu_{T_G} + p_S \cdot \mu_S = q_S \cdot \mu_G + p_S \cdot \mu_S \tag{15.3}$$

After derivation, we get v_T represented by v_S and v_G.

$$v_T = q_S \cdot v_G + p_S \cdot v_S + p_S \cdot q_S \cdot (\mu_G - \mu_S)^2 \tag{15.4}$$

$$B_{TG} = \frac{c_T}{c_T + c_G}\left(\mu_T - \frac{c_T \cdot \mu_T + c_G \cdot \mu_G}{c_T + c_G}\right)^2 + \frac{c_G}{c_T + c_G}\left(\mu_G - \frac{c_T \cdot \mu_T + c_G \cdot \mu_G}{c_T + c_G}\right)^2$$

$$= \frac{c_T}{c_T + c_G}\left(\frac{c_G \cdot \mu_T - c_G \cdot \mu_G}{c_T + c_G}\right)^2 + \frac{c_G}{c_T + c_G}\left(\frac{c_T \cdot \mu_G - c_T \cdot \mu_T}{c_T + c_G}\right)^2 = \frac{c_T \cdot c_G(\mu_T - \mu_G)^2}{(c_T + c_G)^2}$$

$$= \frac{c_T \cdot c_G \cdot (q_S \cdot \mu_G + p_S \cdot \mu_S - \mu_G)^2}{(c_T + c_G)^2} = \frac{c_T \cdot c_G \cdot p_S^2 (\mu_S - \mu_G)^2}{(c_T + c_G)^2} = \frac{c_G \cdot c_S^2 \cdot (\mu_S - \mu_G)^2}{c_T \cdot (c_T + c_G)^2}$$

(15.5)

Similarly, we have

$$B_{SG} = \frac{c_S \cdot c_G \cdot (\mu_S - \mu_G)^2}{(c_S + c_G)^2}$$ (15.6)

From Equations 15.5 and 15.6, we have

$$B_{TG} = \frac{c_S \cdot (c_S + c_G)^2}{c_T \cdot (c_T + c_G)^2} \cdot B_{SG}$$ (15.7)

We also derive the Within Variance W_{TG} and W_{SG}:

$$W_{TG} = \frac{c_T \cdot v_T + c_G \cdot v_G}{c_T + c_G} = \frac{c_T \cdot (q_S \cdot v_G + p_S \cdot v_S + p_S \cdot q_S \cdot (\mu_G - \mu_S)^2) + c_G \cdot v_G}{c_T + c_G}$$

(15.8)

$$= \frac{(c_T - c_S + c_G) \cdot v_G + c_S \cdot v_S + p_S \cdot q_S \cdot c_T \cdot (\mu_G - \mu_S)^2}{c_T + c_G}$$

By definition of $W_{SG} = \frac{c_S \cdot v_S}{c_S + c_G} + \frac{c_G \cdot v_G}{c_S + c_G}$, we derive $v_G = \frac{c_S + c_G}{c_G} \cdot W_{SG} - \frac{c_S \cdot v_S}{c_G}$. Substituting v_G into Equation 15.8, we have

$$W_{TG} = \frac{(c_T - c_S + c_G) \cdot \left(\frac{c_S + c_G}{c_G} \cdot W_{SG} - \frac{c_S \cdot v_S}{c_G}\right) + c_S \cdot v_S + p_S \cdot q_S \cdot c_T \cdot (\mu_G - \mu_S)^2}{c_T + c_G}$$

Since $p_S = c_S / c_T$ and $q_S = 1 - p_S = c_T - c_S / c_T$, we have

$$W_{TG} = \frac{(c_T - c_S + c_G) \cdot (c_S + c_G)}{c_G \cdot (c_T + c_G)} \cdot W_{SG} - \frac{c_S \cdot (c_T - c_S)}{c_G \cdot (c_T + c_G)} \cdot v_S + \frac{c_S \cdot (c_T - c_S)}{c_T \cdot (c_T + c_G)} \cdot (\mu_G - \mu_S)^2$$

(15.9)

From Equations 15.7 and 15.9, we calculate $V(x; w_k)'$:

$$V(x; w_k)' = \frac{c_T \cdot (c_T - c_S + c_G) \cdot (c_T + c_G)}{c_G \cdot c_S \cdot (c_S + c_G)} \cdot \frac{W_{SG}}{B_{SG}} + \frac{(c_T - c_S) \cdot (c_T + c_G)}{c_S \cdot c_G}$$

$$\times \left(1 - \frac{c_T}{c_G} \cdot \frac{v_S}{(\mu_G - \mu_S)^2}\right) = A(w_k) \cdot V(x; w_k) + B(w_k)(1 - C(x; w_k))$$

$$(15.10)$$

In Equation 15.10, A and B are positive constants for any w_k. When c_T/c_G is small and v_S is insignificant compared with $(\mu_G - \mu_S)^2$, $C(x; w_k)$ will be much smaller than 1 and can be neglected. Then, $V(x; w_k)'$ is a linear function of $V(x; w_k)$, and the order of $V(x; w_k)$ and $V(x; w_k)'$ values should be the same. Thus, we can use for feature x, $F(x; w_k)' = \frac{1}{1+V(x; w_k)'}$. Then, for any given concept w_k, we can decide the most important features by sorting $F(x; w_k)'$ values and assigning normalized weights for features by $f_i = \frac{F(X_i; w_k)'}{\sum_{n=1}^{M} F(X_n; w_k)'}$ where f_i is the weight for the *i-th* feature.

15.2.4 Link between Keyword and Blob Token

To determine a link between keywords and blob tokens, first we construct a probability table. Let us assume that there are W keywords, B blob tokens, and N images. Then, the dataset can be represented by a matrix $M_{N \times (W+B)}$, where row N corresponds to the number of images, the first W column corresponds to W keywords, and the next B column corresponds to B blob tokens. Next, we calculate the probability table by implementing various weight calculation strategies. Finally, the relationship between keywords and blob tokens can be determined by the probability table. For example, we assign a keyword w_i to a blob token b_j if $p(w_i|b_j)$ is the maximum in the *j-th* column of the probability table.

Generate M1 and M2, which are the same as in Chapter 14. Based on these two matrixes, we generate the following different models to calculate the probability table.

15.2.4.1 Correlation Method (CRM)

We use $M_W^T \times M_B$, which gives a matrix with the dimension of $W \times B$ (upper part of Figure 15.2) and normalize each column to get a probability table T_{corr} based on co-occurrence. $T_{corr}[i, j]$ is an estimate of $p(w_i|b_j)$, which is a conditional probability of keyword w_i given blob b_j.

15.2.4.2 Cosine Method (CSM)

Instead of using $M_W^T \times M_B$, we can apply the cosine to calculate the matrix with the dimension of $W \times B$ in which the element of the *i-th* row and *j-th* column is the

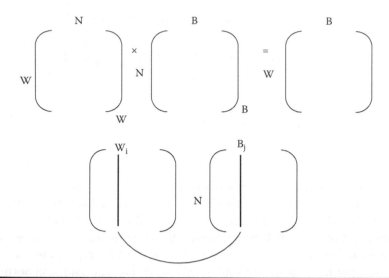

Figure 15.2   Correlation methods.

cosine between the *i-th* column in M_W^T and the *j-th* column in M_B. Then, just as in CRM, we normalize each column to get a probability table T_{corr}. In fact, the correlation method takes into account the following fact: If a keyword appears across a set of images and a blob also appears in the same set of images, then there is a chance that this blob and keyword are correlated (see bottom part of Figure 15.2).

15.2.4.3   Conservative Context (C2)

CRM and CSM consider the correlation between keywords and blobs when calculating the probability table. However, besides the correlation between keywords and blobs, there exist word-to-word correlation and blob-to-blob correlation. Some keywords often appear together, and some keywords never do. For example, the word *tiger* may appear with the word *grass* often, but it never appears with the word *building*. For a given blob, if the probability of *tiger* is high, it will make a positive contribution to the probability of grass and negative contribution to the probability of *building*. It is similar for blob-to-blob correlation. Thinking along these lines, we generate a method named conservative context (C2) to calculate the probability table.

In the C2 method, we generate a matrix M_{WW} by $M_W^T \times M_W$. The diagonal value is the maximum for each column because each word always appears with itself. Based on M_{WW}, we calculate the word-to-word correlation matrix WW. The element $WW_{ij} = (M_{WW})_{ij} / (M_{WW})_{jj}$ means the probability of word i for a given word j. Similarly, we have matrix M_{BB} by $M_B^T \times M_B$ and blob-to-blob correlation

$$\underset{W}{\left(\underset{}{\overset{B}{T}}\right)} = \underset{W}{\left(\underset{}{\overset{W}{WW}}\right)} \times \underset{W}{\left(\underset{}{\overset{B}{T_{corr}}}\right)} \times \underset{B}{\left(\underset{}{\overset{B}{BB}}\right)}$$

Figure 15.3   The Conservative Context (C2) method.

matrix BB. The element $BB_{ij} = (M_{BB})_{ij} / (M_{BB})_{jj}$ means the probability of the blob i for a given blob j.

In the C2 method, we consider word-to-word, word-to-blob, and blob-to-blob correlations. So, the probability table is generated based on matrix WW, BB, and T_{Corr} (as shown in Figure 15.3). For a specific given blob n, the probability of a specific word m is $T_{mn} = \sum_{j=1}^{B} (\sum_{i=1}^{W} (WW_{mi} \times (T_{Corr})_{ij}) \times BB_{jn})$.

In addition, the EM algorithm is another choice to calculate the probability table. SVD can be applied to remove noise or reduce dimension.

15.3   Experiment Results

In this chapter, we use the Corel dataset, which is the same as the one discussed in Chapter 14. After we clustered a total of 42,379 image objects from 4,500 training images into 500 blobs using the proposed aggressive feature weighting algorithm and chi-square-based weighting algorithm, we applied six different methods (M1+CRM, M2+CRM, etc.) to calculate probability tables based on weighted feature selection and without weighted feature selection, respectively. The evaluation method is the same as we discussed earlier.

Table 15.1   Precision for 10 most frequent keywords for top 50 images

	Conservative	Aggressive	K-means	GDR	C2
M1+CRM	0.316	0.214	0.318	0.316	0.344
M2+CRM	0.314	0.21	0.324	0.312	0.35
M1+SVD+CRM	0.32	0.226	0.322	0.316	0.344
M2+SVD+CRM	0.32	0.218	0.322	0.316	0.352
M1+EM	0.314	0.238	0.288	0.27	0.342
M2+EM	0.314	0.242	0.284	0.26	0.346
Average	0.316333333	0.224666667	0.309666667	0.298333333	0.34633333

Table 15.2 Recall for 10 most frequent keywords for top 50 images

	Conservative	Aggressive	K-means	GDR	C2
M1+CRM	0.310111122	0.208856017	0.297930584	0.30019711	0.31999286
M2+CRM	0.311458113	0.192378765	0.306299191	0.29669996	0.329429046
M1+SVD+CRM	0.311140808	0.220687531	0.307343675	0.30303734	0.31999286
M2+SVD+CRM	0.315775606	0.196329119	0.302759189	0.29690512	0.333132746
M1+EM	0.309124439	0.218801776	0.283548792	0.26970244	0.322332576
M2+EM	0.306496009	0.222784705	0.296536134	0.26362258	0.328189962
Average	0.31068435	0.209972986	0.299069594	0.28836076	0.325511675

Results (precision and recall) are reported for the 10 most frequent keywords (each of these keywords appears more than 2 times per 100 words on average in a Corel dataset) in Tables 15.1 and 15.2. Note that annotation works well when keywords and corresponding blobs are frequent. This is because more patterns will be revealed. For fair comparison, we have not set this threshold high enough (say only 2%). In Table 15.1, we observe that on average the C2 (34.63%) outperformed conservative weighted feature selection (31.63%), aggressive (22.47%), K-means (30.97%), and GDR (29.83%) by factors of 9.48%, 54.12%, 11.82%, and 16.09% correspondingly. Hence, the C2 outperformed conservative, aggressive, GDR, and K-means. A similar pattern is also revealed in the case of recall (see Table 15.2). In summary, with regard to precision, we observe that the aggressive approach fares worst. This is because the features of more than 90% of the objects are either equally important or do not differ significantly. Therefore, the conservative selection captures these minor differences successfully. On the other hand, in the Corel dataset used, only a few objects possess features that differ substantially from one another. Although the features of some objects will be represented well by the aggressive method, it will not work well for other objects. Hence, the overall performance is even worse than K-means. Recall that in GDR, SVD will reduce the dimensions, the new features will be linear combinations of original features, and it will be hard to determine important features separately. Hence, results will not be improved.

In Figures 15.4 and 15.5, we demonstrate how precision and recall will be affected by the increasing number of images. The X-axis represents the total number of images retrieved, and the Y-axis represents precision in Figure 15.4 and recall in Figure 15.5. Here, we have reported results only for the M2+EM method. Note that for other methods we have observed similar results.

In Figure 15.4, we observe that with an increasing total number of retrieved images, precision will be decreased. This is because when we retrieve more images in order to increase recall (i.e., include more relevant images), precision is adversely effected. C2 continuously outperforms conservative, aggressive, and K-means.

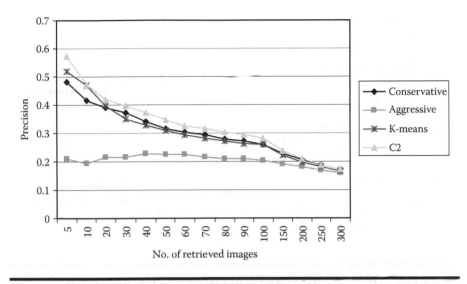

Figure 15.4   Average precision of queries with top 10 most frequent keywords.

For example, when the total number of retrieved images equals to 40, we notice 37.15%, 34.75%, 32.25%, and 25% precision with regard to C2, conservative, K-means, and aggressive.

In Figure 15.5, recall increases with an increasing number of retrieved images. Furthermore, C2 outperforms conservative, aggressive, and K-means in both cases,

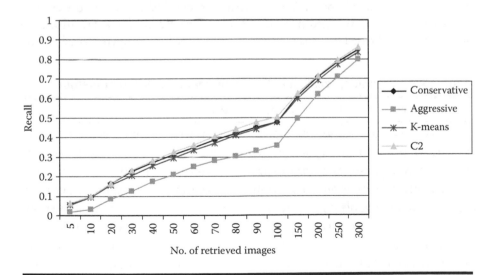

Figure 15.5   Average recall of queries with top 10 most frequent keywords.

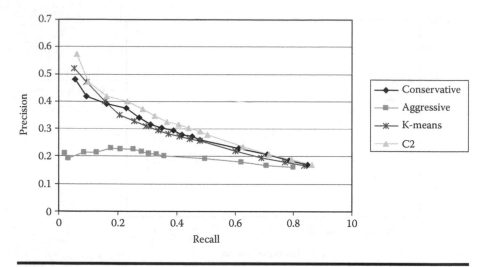

Figure 15.6 Precision versus recall of top 10 most frequent keywords.

with aggressive being the worst. This is because conservative captures weighted features gracefully, and most objects possess features that are equally important or slightly insignificant. Therefore, aggressive fails due to its aggressiveness in selection of weights. Recall that only a few objects in the Corel dataset have features that differ significantly from one another. Curves of precision vs. recall are shown in Figure 15.6.

In Table 15.3, P1, R1, and E1 mean precision, recall, and E measurement for traditional K-means without weighting method, respectively. Next, we present two approaches that are weighted methods. P2, R2, and E2 are for weighted feature selection method based on density. P3, R3, and E3 are for chi-square-based feature

Table 15.3 Precision, recall, and E-measurement for different methods

	M1+CRM	M2+CRM	M1+SVD+CRM	M2+SVD+CRM	M1+EM	M2+EM
P1	0.112833045	0.111907798	0.118421924	0.124403116	0.175397288	0.170531144
R1	0.21191368	0.202170978	0.212069849	0.19916343	0.320936589	0.318640549
E1	0.852741451	0.855930992	0.84802212	0.846853443	0.773171206	0.777836133
P2	0.15004107	0.120306797	0.138239901	0.138848815	0.14878761	0.142294627
R2	0.231283549	0.223190455	0.240866339	0.226010433	0.300307726	0.299297001
E2	0.81799218	0.843659135	0.824337691	0.827981442	0.801012992	0.8071143
P3	0.165437462	0.171850467	0.161117175	0.161860196	0.171150572	0.174210784
R3	0.258180044	0.349971276	0.258804863	0.352684909	0.342235952	0.346053028
E3	0.798343314	0.769489378	0.801401667	0.77811217	0.771813727	0.768247693

Images					
Original Annotation	mountain, sky, water, snow	sky, water, people, sand	city, mountain, sky, sun	sky, water, boats, buildings	field, horses, mare, foals
Annotation based on Chi-square	city, mountain, sky, water, snow, cars	city, sky, water, tree, people, buildings, snow	city, sky, sun, water, people, snow, sunset	sky, water, tree, people, buildings, flowers, street	field, horses, foals, city

Figure 15.7 Examples of automated annotation generated by distortion-based feature weighting using M2+EM to link keywords and blob tokens.

weighting method. Each column corresponds to one method that links keywords and blob tokens (discussed in Section 14.5). For all methods, the chi-square-based weighted approach has the largest precision and recall and smaller E measurement. For example, for the M2+EM method, the E for chi-square, density, and traditional K-means are 0.768247693, 0.8071143, and 0.777836133 respectively.

Figure 15.7 shows some examples of automatic image annotation. The first row displays original images that are from different image categories. The second row shows manually assigned annotations for each image. The last row is automated annotation generated by chi-square-based feature weighting. Here, the association between keywords and blob tokens is analyzed by the M2+EM method. From the annotation results, we can see that some chi-square-based annotations cover all relevant keywords that appeared in manual annotations, but also include a few irrelevant keywords. For example, for the first image in Figure 15.7, the chi-square-based annotation includes all keywords in original annotation and some irrelevant keywords such as *city* and *cars*. In the other case, the chi-square-based annotation misses some relevant keywords and generates some irrelevant keywords too. The last image in Figure 15.7 is an example of this case. The chi-square-based annotation misses the keyword *mare* in the original annotation and includes an irrelevant keyword *city*.

Table 15.4 Precision and recall of LDA and conservative feature weighted method for top 20 most frequent keywords

	Precision % (LDA)	Recall % (LDA)	Precision % (Conservative)	Recall % (Conservative)
water	24.32	93.10	24.18	88.79
sky	27.60	50.48	27.78	80.95
tree	20.46	86.02	18.78	76.34
people	18.78	62.16	18.99	81.08
grass	16.05	76.47	16.57	54.90
buildings	19.23	27.78	29.58	38.89
mountain	11.11	2.63	17.24	13.16
flowers	16.88	48.15	23.53	74.07
snow	7.94	16.13	17.43	61.29
clouds	10.00	11.54	11.11	7.69
rocks	6.45	9.09	8.16	18.18
stone	16.67	38.10	13.83	61.90
street	23.81	19.23	19.05	15.38
plane	0	0	20.00	24.00
bear	9.52	9.09	11.54	13.63
field	21.21	41.18	16.67	47.06
sand	4.17	5.26	0	0
birds	12.20	29.41	15.15	29.41
beach	0	0	0	0
boats	0	0	0	0
Average	13.32	31.29	15.50	39.34

15.3.1 Results of LDA

We implemented LDA (discussed in Section 15.2.3) to evaluate features' weights. We tested the performance of LDA using the Corel dataset. As shown in Table 15.4, the average precision for the top 20 most frequent keywords is 13.32% and the corresponding average recall is 31.29%, which is worse compared to the conservative feature weighted algorithm (average precision is 15.50% and average recall is 39.34%). However, this method is much faster for features' weight evaluation because iteration is avoided. Decreased performance is the trade-off for speed.

15.4 Summary and Directions

In this chapter, we have addressed the image annotation problem using enhanced feature weighting algorithms. We have proposed aggressive and chi-square-based feature weighting mechanisms. The results show that the aggressive mechanism does not improve clustering and makes clustering algorithms hard to converge sometimes. The chi-square-based weighting algorithm improves the measure of similarity and, consequently, improved annotation performance. We conducted a comparative study of these methods using a benchmark dataset.

In addition, we proposed the Conservative Context (C2) method to estimate correlations between blob tokens and keywords. By considering correlations between words and between blob-tokens, C2 produces more accurate correlations between keywords and blob tokens. The idea is if a keyword w and a blob token b are correlated with each other, it will favor both the correlations between b and keywords closed to w and the correlations between w and blob tokens closed to b. Experiment results show that C2 outperforms other methods.

In future, we would like to extend this work in the following directions. First, we would like to study the impact of weighted feature selection on the continuous relevance model (CRM). Second, we would like to extend this work to the video domain. We believe that such enhancements will improve the feature selection techniques.

References

1. Dudani, S A., The distance-weighted k-nearest neighbor rule, *IEEE Transactions on Systems, Man, and Cybernetics*, Vol. 6, 325–327, 1976.
2. Das, S., Filter, wrappers and a boosting-based hybrid for feature selection, *Proc. of the 18th International Conference on Machine Learning*, 2001, pp. 74–81.
3. Dash, M., Choi, K., Scheuermann, P., and Liu, H., Feature selection for clustering—a filter solution, in *Proceedings of IEEE International Conference on Data Mining 2002*, 2002, pp. 115–122.
4. Xing, E., Jordan, M., and Karp, R., Feature selection for high-dimensional genomic microarray data, *Proceedings of the 18th International Conference on Machine Learning*, 2001, pp. 601–608.
5. Wang, L., Liu, L., and Khan. L., Automatic Image Annotation and Retrieval Using Subspace Clustering Algorithm, in *Proceedings of the ACM MMDB*, November, 2004, pp. 100–108.
6. Fisher, L. and Van Ness, J.W., Admissible discriminant analysis, *Journal of the American Statistical Association*, 68, 603–607, 1973.
7. Fix, E. and Hodges, J L., Discriminatory Analysis, Nonparametric Discrimination: Consistency Properties, Technical Report 4. USAF School of Aviation Medicine, Randolph Field, TX 1951.
8. Dash, M., Liu, H., and Yao, J., Dimensionality reduction of unsupervised data, in *Ninth IEEE International Conference on Tools with AI*, ICTAI '97, November 1997, pp. 532–539.

Chapter 16

Image Classification and Performance Analysis

16.1 Introduction

Classification is a broad-ranging research field that includes many decision-theoretic approaches to identify data. Datum is typically described numerically via a vector $(x_1, x_2, \ldots, x_n)$, and n is the number of data attributes. Therefore, each piece of data can be treated as one point in an n dimensional space, and each data point belongs to one of the distinct and exclusive classes. Classification algorithms normally employ two steps, training and testing. Characteristic properties of data (or partition of n dimensional space) figured out by analyzing labeled training data will be applied to classify unlabeled testing data. Obviously, there is a hidden assumption for classification. That is, training data and testing data share the same distribution in n dimensional space. Image classification analyzes image feature vectors and organizes data into categories.

In the previous chapter, we discussed automatic image annotation where a given image is labeled with text describing its contents. In restricted domains, image annotation can be a classification task if annotation is just a class label from a constrained set of classes. Classifiers trained with training set image features will be used for the prediction of unseen images. Many classification algorithms are available such as K-nearest neighbor (KNN), neural network, decision tree, Bayesian network, and support vector machine (SVM). It is hard to say which classification algorithm is better. We can only say one classification algorithm is better than others for a specific problem. KNN is a very popular classification algorithm having good performance and short period of training time. Various KNN algorithms have been published. SVM is a new classification algorithm compared to other classification algorithms, and many research papers have shown that SVM can produce better classification results than other algorithms. In this chapter, we study different KNN algorithms and SVM in the medical image classification domain. Performance is analyzed based on classification accuracy. We present a data resampling method to solve the data imbalance problem. We also present a modified evidence theory-based KNN algorithm. Results show that resampling is helpful to improve the classification accuracy of KNN classifiers, and our modified evidence theory-based KNN algorithm outperforms other KNN algorithms discussed in this chapter. The 10,000 fully classified medical radiographs used for this study are from ImageCLEF (Cross Language Evaluation Forum) 2006. (See also [1–6]).

The organization of this chapter is as follows: Description of various classifiers that we have used are discussed in Section 16.2. Evidence theory with KNN is discussed in Section 16.3. The experimental setup is given in Section 16.4. Our results are presented in Section 16.5. Overall discussion of our approach and results are given in Section 16.6, and the chapter is summarized in Section 16.7.

16.2 Classifiers

16.2.1 K-Nearest Neighbor Algorithm

The K-nearest neighbor algorithm (KNN) is a very simple and efficient classification algorithm. The algorithm does not require any preprocessing of labeled data samples before use. The KNN classifier simply assigns an unknown input vector f to the class of a majority of its K-nearest neighbors. It is possible to have the same amount of votes from multiple classes, which causes a tie. To break the tie, we can sum up the distances of neighbors in each class that tied and assign vector f to the class with minimal distance, or we can choose the class with the nearest neighbor. Clearly, the tie is still possible. In that case, we will take an arbitrary assignment.

16.2.2 Distance Weighted KNN (DWKNN)

A main drawback of KNN algorithm is that each of the k-nearest neighbors is equally important. Intuitively, the closer the neighbor is, the more possible that the unknown vector f is in the class of this neighbor. Hence, assigning neighbors with different voting weights based on their distances to the vector f is intuitively appealing. Dudani [7] proposed a distance weighted k-nearest neighbor rule. Given the k-nearest neighbor $v_1, v_2, \ldots, v_k$ of the vector f, the $d_1, d_2, \ldots, d_k$ are corresponding distances which are sorted in increasing order. The label of the neighbor v_i will be assigned more voting weight than the label of the neighbor v_j if $d_i < d_j$. Dudani defined the weight w_i of the *i-th* nearest neighbor *vi* as below:

$$w_i = \begin{cases} \dfrac{d_k - d_i}{d_k - d_1} & d_k \neq d_1 \\ 1 & d_k = d_1 \end{cases} \tag{16.1}$$

Each neighbor will vote with this weight. Finally, the unknown vector f is assigned to the class that gets the greatest voting value from the k-nearest neighbors. From the definition of voting weight above, we know if we only consider the closest neighbor, the distance weighted KNN is just same as KNN.

16.2.3 Fuzzy KNN

Keller et al. proposed a fuzzy KNN algorithm [8]. The difference between KNN and fuzzy KNN is that "The fuzzy KNN algorithm assigns class membership to a sample vector rather than assigning the vector to a particular class." Note that $u_i(f)$, the membership of the class i to the unknown vector f, is defined as below:

$$u_i(f) = \frac{\displaystyle\sum_{j=1}^{K} u_{ij} \left(1/\|f - v_j\|^{2/(m-1)}\right)}{\displaystyle\sum_{j=1}^{K} \left(1/\|f - v_j\|^{2/(m-1)}\right)} \tag{16.2}$$

where u_{ij} is the membership of the class i to the j-th neighbor v_j of vector f. As seen by the equation, the memberships of f depend on the inverse of the distance from the nearest neighbors and their class memberships; m is the parameter to determine how important the distance is when evaluating each neighbor's contribution to the membership value.

The membership u_{ij} can be calculated in many different ways. In this study, we investigated two methods. One is a hard membership assignment method, which means that if the sample vector j is labeled as the member of the class i, then u_{ij} equals 1. Otherwise, u_{ij} equals to 0. We name it fuzzy KNN 0. The other method is a soft membership method. We name it fuzzy KNN 1. Soft membership means that the sample membership u_{ij} is weighted in a certain way. We calculate u_{ij} based on distances between the vector j and centroids of various classes as below.

$$u_{ij} = \frac{1/\|v_j - X_i\|^{2/(m-1)}}{\displaystyle\sum_{k=1}^{c} \left(1/\|v_j - X_k\|^{2/(m-1)}\right)} \tag{16.3}$$

The sample membership u_{ij} will be larger when the distance between the sample vector v_j and the centroid of the class i (X_i) is smaller. It is seen that u_{ij} satisfies $u_{ij} \geq 0$ and $\sum_{i=1}^{C} u_{ij} = 1$.

16.2.4 Nearest Prototype Classifier (NPC)

The nearest prototype classifier is very similar to the KNN algorithm. The difference is that the labeled samples in NPC are a set of class prototypes rather than data vectors in KNN. Class prototypes are a set of prototype vectors that represent classes. In our implementation, the prototype vectors are centroid vectors of classes. Let $W = \{X_1, X_2, \ldots, X_c\}$ be the set of c prototype vectors. X_i is the centroid vector of the class i. The membership function associated with the vector f and the class i will be defined as below:

$$u_i(f) = \frac{1/\|f - X_i\|^{2/(m-1)}}{\sum_{j=1}^{c} \left(1/\|f - X_j\|^{2/(m-1)}\right)} \qquad (16.4)$$

The equation above shows that memberships of the vector f are decided only by distances from f to various class prototypes. The closest class prototype will be assigned the highest membership. In another words, the unknown vector f is always assigned to the closest class.

16.3 Evidence Theory and KNN

16.3.1 Dempster–Shafer Evidence Theory

The evidence theory was proposed by Shafer in 1976 (see the discussions in Part I). It represents the degree of belief that may be attributed to a given hypotheses on the basis of given evidence and combines evidences from different sources using Dempster's rule. Evidence theory is applied to combine outputs of multiple classifiers to generate a more accurate classification procedure.

We define Ω as frame of discernment, which is a finite set of mutually exclusive and exhaustive hypotheses in a problem domain. The size of power set of Ω is 2^Ω which includes the empty set $\emptyset$ and the entire set Ω. In evidence theory, the contribution of evidence to our belief in different hypotheses is described by basic probability assignment (BPA) function m, the belief function Bel, and the plausibility function Pl. BPA function m assigns a number between 0 and 1 to each nonempty subset of Ω and 0 to the empty set $\emptyset$. And the sum of BPAs for all subsets A of Ω is equal to 1.

$$\sum_{A \subset \Omega} m(A) = 1 \qquad (16.5)$$

$$m(\emptyset) = 0 \qquad (16.6)$$

The mass $m(A)$ measures the amount of belief that is contributed exactly to A. The subsets A of Ω are called the focal elements of the belief function if $m(A) > 0$. It is obvious that the belief committed to a hypothesis A must be committed to all hypotheses it implies. For example, an animal is a subset of creatures, if the evidence shows that X is an animal, and then this evidence also shows that X is a creature. Therefore, to obtain the total belief in hypotheses A, we must add BPAs for all subsets B of A. The definition of the belief function is as below.

$$Bel(A) = \sum_{B \subseteq A} m(B) \qquad (16.7)$$

It is very easy to prove that summation of the belief of hypotheses A and its contradiction $\overline{A}$ is not necessarily equal to 1. So, $Bel(A)$ cannot show how much our beliefs in $\overline{A}$. The plausibility of A $Pl(A) = 1 - Bel(\overline{A}) = \sum_{B \cap A \neq empty} m(B)$ defines how much A is plausible.

Based on the Dempster rule of combination, two given mass functions, m_1 and m_2 over the same Ω can be combined to generate a new mass function as follows:

$$m(C) = m_1 \oplus m_2(C) = \frac{\sum_{A \cap B = C} m_1(A) \times m_2(B)}{1 - \sum_{A \cap B = empty} m_1(A) \times m_2(B)} \qquad (16.8)$$

$$m(\emptyset) = 0 \qquad (16.9)$$

16.3.2 Evidence-Theory-Based KNN (EKNN)

Various evidence theoretic KNN algorithms have been proposed [9]. In such an approach for example, each neighbor of a pattern is considered as evidence supporting some hypotheses about the class membership of that pattern. The BPAs are calculated for each of the k-nearest neighbors of the pattern. The belief of each hypothesis is obtained by aggregating BPAs using the Dempster's rule of combination. Denoeux et al. show that their evidence theoretic KNN yield lower error rates than other methods using the same information in many situations. However, the complexity of the Dempster–Shafer rule is high.

Wang et al. generate an extended KNN based on evidence theory [10]. Instead of combining k BPAs in [9], they constructed a mass function based on neighborhoods. Because our algorithm is on the basis of their work, we will discuss their work in detail.

As we discussed before, each image is represented by d visual features with a vector of d attributes $\langle x_1, x_2, \ldots, x_d \rangle$. The value range or domain of the i-th feature is $dom(x_i)$. So, the domain of the case is defined by $V = dom(x_1) \times \cdots \times dom(x_d)$ which is a hyper cube in a d dimensional space. Each image will belong to one, and only one, class in the finite set $C = \{c_1, c_2, \ldots, c_M\}$. The labeled training dataset will be specified as:

$$D = \{< s_i, c_j >: s_i \in V, c_j \in C, \text{ where } i = 1, 2, \ldots, N \quad j = 1, 2, \ldots, M\}$$

Definition 1: Neighborhood is a region in V that covers a set of neighbors of an unknown pattern s

We consider V as the frame of discernment Ω. In [10], Wang et al. adopt the hypercube interpretation of neighborhood. Each neighborhood is a hypercube in V that contains s. In this dissertation, we choose the hyper sphere interpretation of neighborhood. We define h neighborhoods of s: $H_1, H_2, \ldots, H_h$. Each neighborhood is a hyper sphere in V covering a set of neighbors of s. When we consider k the nearest neighbors, the biggest hyper sphere H_h is the one which covers, and only covers, the k-nearest neighbors. Then, we divide the radius of hyper sphere H_h into h equal intervals and generate multiple hyper spheres with different radius. Each hyper sphere will be one neighborhood.

Figure 16.1 shows projection of all neighborhoods in 2-D space when the number of neighborhoods is 10. The origin in Figure 16.1 represents the pattern s. If any hyper

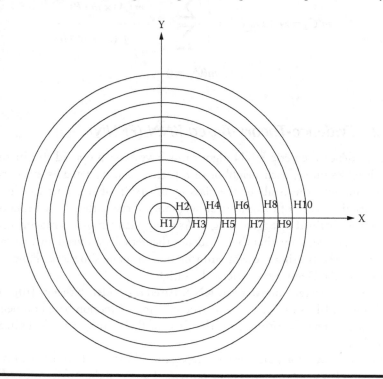

Figure 16.1 Projections of neighborhoods in 2-dimensional space.

sphere is not totally contained in V, only the part of hyper sphere that is in V will be kept and defined as the corresponding neighborhood. Each neighborhood is a source of evidence supporting hypotheses concerning the class membership of the pattern s.

Definition 2: Joint probability $P(H_i, c)$ is the probability of a random data point in the neighborhood $H_i(H_i \in 2^\Omega)$ and belongs to class $c (c \in C)$.

Because information about distribution of data is not available, Wang et al. assume data is uniformly distributed in V and define the joint probability $P(H_i, c)$ as below

$$P(H_i, c) = |H_i^c| / |D| \tag{16.10}$$

$|H_i^c|$ is the size of the subset of H_i that belongs to class c. $|D|$ is the size of the training dataset.

Definition 3: The mass function m_s induced for s from neighborhoods H will be defined as below:

$$m_s(A, c) = \begin{cases} \dfrac{P(A, c)}{\displaystyle\sum_{i=1}^{h} \sum_{c \in C} P(H_i, c)} & if \quad A = H_i \\ 0 & otherwise \end{cases} \tag{16.11}$$

where $A \in 2^\Omega$, and $c \in C$.

New patterns are classified by applying conditional pignistic probability function.

$$\overline{BetP}(A, c) = \sum_{i=1}^{h} m_s(H_i, c) \times \frac{|A \cap H_i|}{|H_i|} \tag{16.12}$$

Wang et al. have shown that $\overline{BetP}$ is a probability function on Ω (see, for example, [10]). Because H_i is the neighborhood of s, so $s \in H_i$. If we consider the pattern s as a singleton set, we have

$$\overline{BetP}(s, c) = \sum_{i=1}^{h} m_s(H_i, c) / |H_i| \tag{16.13}$$

$$\overline{BetP}(s) = \sum_{c \in C} \overline{BetP}(s, c) \tag{16.14}$$

Now, based on Bayes' rule, we can calculate conditional probability $\overline{BetP}(c|s)$ as follows:

$$\overline{BetP}(c|s) = \overline{BetP}(s, c) / \overline{BetP}(s) \tag{16.15}$$

For the pattern s, we calculate $\overline{BetP}(c|s)$ for all $c \in C$, s will be classified as the class having the maximal $\overline{BetP}(c|s)$.

16.3.3 Density-Based EKNN (DEKNN)

In this section, we present another evidence-theory-based KNN. As we discussed, the meaning of the joint probability $P(H_i, c)$ in Equation 16.10 is the probability of a random data point in the neighborhood H_i and belongs to class c. By expanding Equation 16.10, we can see the joint probability $P(H_i, c)$ is the multiplication of two parts (see Equation 16.16). $|H_i|$ is the size of the neighborhood H_i. The first part $|H_i^c|/|H_i|$ is the capability of the neighborhood H_i for discriminating the class c. The second part $|H_i|/|D|$ is the degree of support from the neighborhood H_i. Therefore, we can explain the joint probability $P(H_i, c)$ in another way. $P(H_i, c)$ can be thought of as the support that the class c obtains from the neighborhood H_i.

$$P(H_i, c) = |H_i^c|/|D| = \frac{|H_i^c|}{|H_i|} \times \frac{|H_i|}{|D|} \tag{16.16}$$

$|H_i^c|/|H_i|$ is the percentage of the class c in the neighborhood H_i. If the neighborhood H_i contains more data points of class c than data points of other classes, class c always gets more support from the neighborhood H_i than other classes. Therefore, large classes are always favored, which is also a major problem of the KNN algorithm. To solve this problem, we modify EKNN by changing the probability function $P(H_i, c)$. To describe our algorithm, we need to define two concepts, global density and local density of classes.

Definition 4: Global density G^c is the proportion of class c in the training dataset. Hence, we define global density G^c as follows:

$$G^c = |c|/|D| \tag{16.17}$$

$|c|$ is the size of class c.

Definition 5: Local density L_i^c is the proportion of class c in the neighborhood H_i. We define L_i^c as follows:

$$L_i^c = |H_i^c|/|H_i| \tag{16.18}$$

In EKNN, the capability of the neighborhood H_i for discriminating class c is totally determined by L_i^c, the local density of class c in the neighborhood H_i. Large classes usually have larger local density than small classes; that is why EKNN favors large classes. We solve this problem by considering density. The idea is based on straightforward thinking. In a particular neighborhood, if the local density of a class is larger than its global density, this class will get more support from this neighborhood. If the local density of the class is less than its global density, the class will get less support from this neighborhood. We formalize the idea and modify Equation 16.16 as follows:

$$P(H_i, c) = \left(w1 \times L_i^c + w2 \times \frac{L_i^c - G^c}{L_i^c} \right) \times \frac{|H_i|}{|D|} \tag{16.19}$$

We see $w1$ and $w2$ are weights, and $w1 + w2 = 1$. In our experiment, we assign equal weight 0.5 to $w1$ and $w2$. The construction of mass function in our algorithm is same as EKNN in Equation 16.11.

16.4 Experiment Results

16.4.1 ImageCLEFmed 2006 Dataset

Some examples are shown in Figure 16.2 and detailed information about the dataset is shown in Table 16.1.

Images in ImageCLEFmed 2006 dataset are monochrome images with very specific layouts. The areas under investigation are basically at the center of the images. Considering these facts, we chose a very simple method to extract image features. We resize each image into 16*16 and read intensity values of all 256 pixels. Each image will be represented by a 256-D vector. PCA was applied to reduce dimensionality.

16.4.2 Imbalanced Data Problem

Imbalance of data is a big problem for most classification algorithms. In KNN based algorithms, the classification result totally depends on the majority of voting. The number of samples in each class is a really big issue in influencing the final voting results. When the numbers of labeled samples are very different for classes, this becomes a really serious problem. For example, if we have only one labeled sample for class i and we consider k-nearest neighbors where $k \gg 1$, no matter how we calculate distances or evaluate weights, the class i can get only one vote at most. Basically, it is almost impossible to assign an unknown vector to the class i. In our ImageCLEFmed 2006 dataset, data is imbalanced, too. Among a total of 116 classes, the biggest class has more than 1700 labeled samples, but the smallest class only has around 10 labeled samples. The unknown vector will have a much better chance to be assigned to a large class rather than a small class.

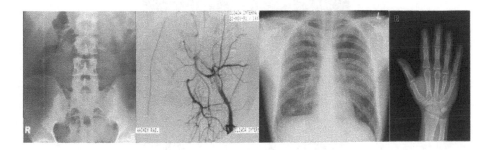

Figure 16.2　Image examples of ImageCLEFmed 2006.

Table 16.1   Information of ImageCLEFmed 2006

Number of training images	9000
Number of testing images	1000
Number of classes	116
Size of the biggest class in training set	1733
Size of the smallest class in training set	10

To solve this problem, we resampled the training dataset. Unlike resampling methods with replacement, we extract subimages from each image rather than picking up one image multiple times. We present two methods for subimage generation in this paper. One is the random subwindow (RSW) resampling method that is shown in Figures 16.3 and 16.4. In the RSW method, both size and position of subimages are randomly determined. We generate more subimages for images in small classes (as shown in Figure 16.4) and less subimages for images in big classes (as shown in Figure 16.3). The number of subimages is decided by the sizes of classes and training dataset. We extract visual features and generate a feature vector for each subimage rather than the whole image. Feature extraction follows the same method discussed in Section 16.4.1. By doing this, we increase the size of the training data of small classes and balance the dataset.

The other method is the partially random subwindow (PRSW) resampling method (as shown in Figures 16.5 and 16.6), which is similar to RSW. The only difference between the two methods is that the sizes and positions of subimages in the PRSW method are not totally random. The width and height will be no less than 80% of the original image; locations of subimages have to guarantee that the subwindow is completely included in the original image. We run KNN and DWKNN with the original dataset and resampled dataset correspondingly. The RSW method makes the classification result even worse. Because the sizes of subimages in the first method are totally random, the subimages will lose a lot of information and can

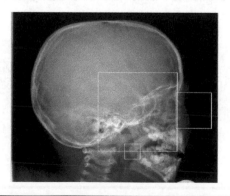

Figure 16.3   RSW resampling for images in small class.

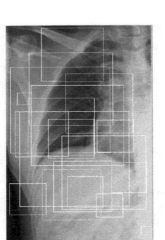

Figure 16.4 RSW resampling for images in big class results.

not always represent the characteristics of the corresponding class. Thus, generating subimages with the RSW method will produce much noise and confuse the classification algorithm. In the PRSW method, we set a lower bound of subimage size. Any subimage covers at least 64% of the central area of the original images, therefore subimages generated by this method will keep most of the information and characteristics of original images. In the following discussion, resampling means PRSW.

Much published research work has shown that resampling improves classification accuracy. However, resampling will increase the computational load

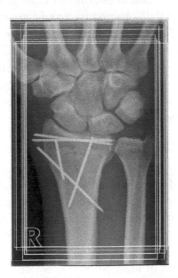

Figure 16.5 PRSW resampling for images in small class.

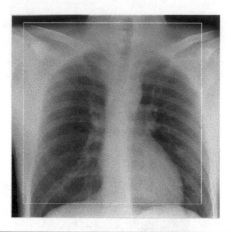

Figure 16.6 PRSW resampling for images in big class.

because it increases the total number of data. In addition, resampling always favors small classes. In some cases, the added data points will become noise and distract classifiers. The DEKNN algorithm will solve the data imbalance problem in a better way.

In DEKNN (see Equation 16.9), similar to EKNN, the classes having larger local density will get more support. This is reasonable in most of the cases. The difference is the support in DEKNN is not totally determined by the local density of the classes. When the local density is larger than global density ($L_i^c > G^c$), the second part in Equation 16.9 will be positive and class c will get more support from the neighborhood H_i. If the local density is less than global density ($L_i^c < G^c$), the second part in Equation 16.9 will be negative, and class c will get less support from the neighborhood H_i. DEKNN does not always favor small classes like resampling methods do. If the local density of a small class in a specific neighborhood is smaller than its global density, the small class will get even less support. At the same time, DEKNN does not increase the computational load because it does not require resampling. Experimental results show that DEKNN has better classification accuracy than EKNN for both large classes and small classes.

16.4.3 Results

We implemented all classifiers discussed in Section 16.2, EKNN and DEKNN. For all of these algorithms, different parameters such as K (the number of closest neighbors) and dimensionality are applied for training and accuracies of all algorithms, with different parameters compared. In another study, we found that the accuracy of fuzzy KNN is insensitive to the fuzzy factor m, and EKNN's accuracy is insensitive to the number of neighborhoods. So we choose $m = 2$ and consider only 10 neighborhoods in this chapter.

First of all, we study how K impacts classification accuracy for different algo-rithms. We chose the dimension to be 256, and evaluate accuracy for various K. Results are shown in Figure 16.7. The X coordinate represents the number of closest neighbors K, which varies from 500 to 1. The Y coordinate represents classification accuracy. We found that, for almost all algorithms, accuracy goes up slightly with decreasing K. For example, the accuracy of KNN is 51.8% when K equals 200, and it goes up to 71.7% when K equals 5. There are two exceptions here. One is NPC. We know the classification accuracy of NPC is decided by class centroids, which is independent of the number of neighbors. So, accuracy of the NPC does not change when the number of neighbors varies. The other exception is EKNN and DEKNN. No matter how many neighbors we consider, the accuracy of EKNN and DEKNN are stable, which is better than with other algorithms. DEKNN improves EKNN slightly and has the best accuracy. KNN, DWKNN, fuzzy KNN 0, EKNN, and DEKNN will have equivalent accuracies when K is less than 10. Fuzzy KNN 1 has the worst accuracy. Similar experiments have been done with different dimensions; the results are similar.

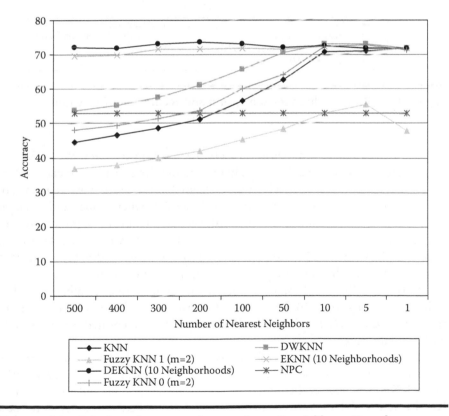

Figure 16.7 Relations between the number of neighbors K and accuracy. Dimension = 256.

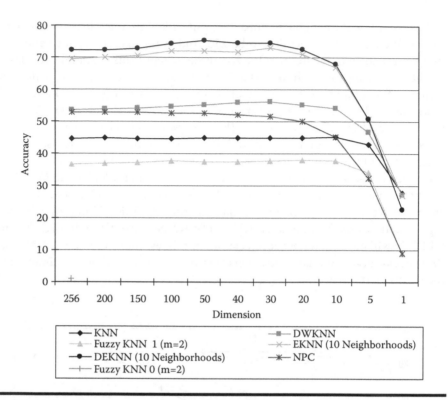

Figure 16.8   Relations between dimension and accuracy for fuzzy KNN 0.

Second, we study how dimension affects classification accuracy. We fix K to be 500, and test accuracy for a different dimension. Results are shown in Figure 16.8. Axis X stands for dimension, which varies from 256 to 1. Axis Y is accuracy. For all algorithms, accuracy is insensitive to dimension when dimension is larger than 10. When dimension is less than 10, accuracy will drop significantly. For example, the mean of EKNN's accuracy is 71.3%, and variance is 1.45% when dimension is larger than 20. However, it drops to 50.7% when dimension equals 5 and to 27% when dimension equals 1. The optimal dimension for most of algorithms is 20 or 30, and classification accuracy will drop due to information lost if dimension is less than 20. For various dimensions, DEKNN has the best accuracy, and fuzzy KNN 1 is the worst. The same study was repeated for different K, with similar results.

Table 16.2 shows accuracies of various algorithms in the best case, worst case, and average case. In the best case and worst case, accuracies of KNN, DWKNN, Fuzzy KNN 0, and EKNN almost have the same value (74.3% and 16.4%). Fuzzy KNN 1 and NPC have lower accuracies. DEKNN has better accuracy in the best case (76.3%) and a little bit worse accuracy (15.5%) in the worst case. However, on

Table 16.2   Classification accuracies of best case, worst case, and average for different algorithms

	Max	Min	Average
KNN	74.30	16.40	54.55
DWKNN	75.50	16.40	60.09
Fuzzy KNN 0	74.90	16.40	56.50
Fuzzy KNN 1	56.10	9.10	41.22
EKNN	74.70	16.40	65.46
DEKNN	76.3	15.5	65.94
NPC	52.90	9.00	45.80

average, DEKNN has the best performance (65.94%). The average is calculated based on accuracies with all different parameters.

In addition, we applied the support vector machine (SVM) to classify images in ImageCLEFmed 2006. SVM type is C-SVC, and multiple kernel types are applied such as linear, polynomial, radial basis, and sigmoid. Classification accuracies are 26.5%, 9.1%, 27.3%, and 12.7%, correspondingly. The result of SVM is much worse than KNN for this dataset. For fuzzy KNN, we changed the fuzzy parameter m from 2 to 5. Results of fuzzy KNN with hard sample membership function are shown in Figures 16.9 and 16.10, each curve illustrating results for a specific m. We can see that accuracy will be improved when we decrease the number of neighbors. When the dimension is 256, the best performance was obtained when we only considered the five closest neighbors. Reducing dimension improves accuracy slightly but not very significant for fuzzy KNN. Fuzzy parameter m does not affect classification accuracy very much. When we compared fuzzy KNN with other algorithms above, we chose $m = 2$.

For EKNN and DEKNN, we tried different numbers of neighborhoods and noticed the number of neighborhoods does not affect accuracy. Similarly, in the previous discussion, the number of neighborhoods for EKNN and DEKNN is 10.

In order to verify the efficiency of our resampling method, we ran KNN and DWKNN for both original dataset and resampled dataset. The result is shown in Figure 16.11. According to results, we can see that resampled data can generate better accuracy for both KNN and DWKNN. For example, when we consider 200 nearest neighbors, the accuracy of KNN with original dataset is 50.4%. The accuracy of KNN with resampled data is 59.8%. Similarly, for the DWKNN, the accuracy is 59.4% for the original dataset and 65.4 for resampled data when K equals 200. The improvement is significant. However, the amount of improvement will decrease when the number of neighbors reduces. If we consider just the closest neighbor, the improvement will be only 1%.

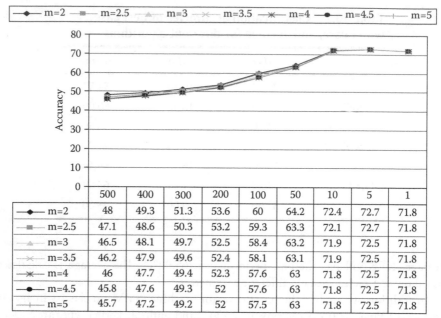

	500	400	300	200	100	50	10	5	1
m=2	48	49.3	51.3	53.6	60	64.2	72.4	72.7	71.8
m=2.5	47.1	48.6	50.3	53.2	59.3	63.3	72.1	72.7	71.8
m=3	46.5	48.1	49.7	52.5	58.4	63.2	71.9	72.5	71.8
m=3.5	46.2	47.9	49.6	52.4	58.1	63.1	71.9	72.5	71.8
m=4	46	47.7	49.4	52.3	57.6	63	71.8	72.5	71.8
m=4.5	45.8	47.6	49.3	52	57.6	63	71.8	72.5	71.8
m=5	45.7	47.2	49.2	52	57.5	63	71.8	72.5	71.8

Number of Neighbors

Figure 16.9 Relations between number of neighbors K and accuracy for fuzzy KNN 0. Dimension = 256.

As we discussed, DEKNN solves data imbalance problem in a better way. In Table 16.3, we compare average classification accuracy of EKNN and DEKNN for large classes, small classes, and all classes. If the size of one class is larger than 1% of the whole training dataset, we think it is a large class. Otherwise, it is a small class. In the ImageICEFmed 2006 dataset, there are only 19 large classes among a total of 116 classes. The data imbalance problem is very serious. As shown in Table 16.3, DEKNN has better average classification accuracy than EKNN for all classes. Compared with EKNN, DEKNN improves the performance of small classes without sacrificing the performance of large classes.

Table 16.3 Average classification accuracies for large classes, small classes, and the whole dataset

	Large classes	Small classes	All classes
EKNN	71.62	32.90	39.47
DEKNN			
	74.84	36.64	43.12

Note: Dimension = 256, K = 500, and H = 10.

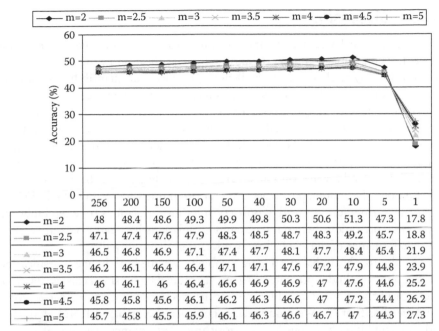

	256	200	150	100	50	40	30	20	10	5	1
m=2	48	48.4	48.6	49.3	49.9	49.8	50.3	50.6	51.3	47.3	17.8
m=2.5	47.1	47.4	47.6	47.9	48.3	48.5	48.7	48.3	49.2	45.7	18.8
m=3	46.5	46.8	46.9	47.1	47.4	47.7	48.1	47.7	48.4	45.4	21.9
m=3.5	46.2	46.1	46.4	46.4	47.1	47.1	47.6	47.2	47.9	44.8	23.9
m=4	46	46.1	46	46.4	46.6	46.9	46.9	47	47.6	44.6	25.2
m=4.5	45.8	45.8	45.6	46.1	46.2	46.3	46.6	47	47.2	44.4	26.2
m=5	45.7	45.8	45.5	45.9	46.1	46.3	46.6	46.7	47	44.3	27.3

Dimension

Figure 16.10 Relations between dimension and accuracy for fuzzy KNN 0. Number of neighbors K = 500.

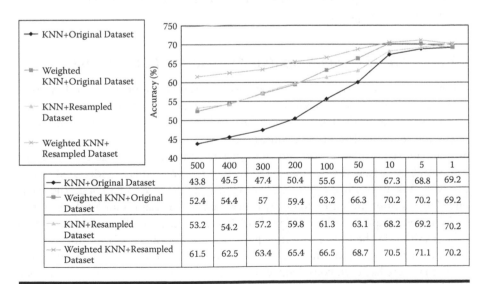

	500	400	300	200	100	50	10	5	1
KNN+Original Dataset	43.8	45.5	47.4	50.4	55.6	60	67.3	68.8	69.2
Weighted KNN+Original Dataset	52.4	54.4	57	59.4	63.2	66.3	70.2	70.2	69.2
KNN+Resampled Dataset	53.2	54.2	57.2	59.8	61.3	63.1	68.2	69.2	70.2
Weighted KNN+Resampled Dataset	61.5	62.5	63.4	65.4	66.5	68.7	70.5	71.1	70.2

Figure 16.11 Classification accuracy of KNN and distance weighted KNN with resampling.

16.6 Discussion

We have addressed a couple of fundamental research topics in the image semantic field, such as image annotation and image classification in the medical image domain. Our research addresses challenging problems of quantifying feature relevance for each individual class in the unsupervised learning process.

We describe several algorithms for estimating feature relevance in an unsupervised learning process, including an aggressive method, chi-square, and linear discriminant analysis. All these methods are embedded into our automatic image annotation framework, and evaluated in terms of precision and recall of image retrieval. Results show that the chi-square-based method has the best performance. In addition, the automatic image annotation framework is modified. During parameter estimations, instead of only considering correlations between blobs and keywords, correlations between blobs and correlations between words are considered. Performance of the whole framework is slightly improved.

We address the imbalanced data problem for medical image classification. A resampling method is presented to generate more data for small classes. Based on results, we believe our resampling method is effective for improving the accuracy of image classification. We modified the evidence-theory-based KNN algorithm, and compared it with various KNN algorithms. Performance was evaluated based on classification accuracy with ImageCLEFmed 2006 medical image dataset. Our density-based EKNN (DEKNN) algorithm outperforms other KNN algorithms.

We will discuss three directions of our future work. First, we will talk about the possibility of applying spatial association rule mining to image annotation; second, noise concept removal assisted by WordNet; and finally, potential usage of domain knowledge.

16.6.1 Enhancement: Spatial Association Rule Mining

It is possible that a particular blob token may correspond to more than one keyword, which causes ambiguity. Therefore, the disambiguation of blob token is required.

In text retrieval, the basic notion of disambiguation is that a set of keywords occurring together determine a context for one another, according to which the appropriate senses of the word (its appropriate concept) can be determined. For example, base, bat, and glove may have several interpretations as individual terms, but when taken together, the intent is obviously a reference to baseball. The reference follows from the ability to determine a context/correlation for all the terms.

What techniques can be employed to determine the correlation between blob tokens so that in the future we can exploit this correlation/association for the purposes of disambiguation? In order to develop implicit knowledge in transaction databases there has been considerable reliance upon data mining (see, for example, [13, 14]). Multimedia datasets pose a more difficult challenge because of the size and complexity of image and video data, but also because there are no image equivalents for the association rule components, such as itemsets and even the rules. Detecting items and item sets appropriate for discovering the implicit spatial knowledge contained in large collections of images is difficult and not a straightforward process. It is our purpose here to devise a framework for applying a specific set of traditional data mining techniques to the nontraditional domain of image datasets. In particular, we will propose spatial association rules as a novel, multimedia extension to traditional association rules that will be used for disambiguation purposes.

An association rule [13] is an expression of the form, A → B. This is to be taken as an indication of the presence of itemset A implying the presence of item set B. An algorithm, based on an association rule, discovers the rules that have support and confidence larger than a specified threshold. The bottom-up approach proposed by this work transforms the raw image data into a form suitable for such analysis in three steps. In step 1, image regions are labeled as blob tokens using a K-means algorithm. The blob tokens are analogous to items in transaction databases. In step 2, associations and rules are determined using an adaptation of the a priori association rule algorithm. At this stage, co-occurrences can be determined in various ways. On one hand, if two blob-tokens appear in an image, then they co-occur regardless of their spatial relationship in the image. On the other hand, co-occurrence of two blob tokens appear in an image will be based on spatial relationship such as adjacency, orientation, distance, or combinations thereof.

In step 3, irrelevant blob tokens will be subject to weighted correlation. Blob-tokens closely associated with each other will be given greater weight. Selected blob tokens, which correlate with each other, will have a higher score and a greater probability of being retained than noncorrelated blob tokens. If scores of a particularly ambiguous blob token fall below a certain threshold, which will be a minimum assigned to selected blob tokens for that particular object, these blob tokens will be pruned [15].

For example, using such association techniques, we observe that "sky" (v3) and "airplane" (v2) are more highly correlated than "water" (v1) and "airplane" (v2). Thus, we have the rule: v2 → v3. Let us assume that in an image, we have two objects. One is "airplane," which is correctly recognized; the other neighboring object in the image will be recognized as either "water" (v1) or "sky" (v2). In this case, we can exploit the spatial mining rule that "sky" (v3), and "airplane" (v2) are correlated, and it is likely that "water" will be discarded while "sky" will be recognized as the second object.

16.6.2 WordNet and Semantic Similarity

Most of the current image annotation models are based on statistical evaluation. For example, in TM, the value of parameter $P(w \mid b)$ will decide which keyword appears in the annotation. Because of lack of prior information, ambiguity can not be avoided completely. This will bring many noisy concepts/descriptions.

Therefore, it is quite difficult to get an accurate, meaningful understanding of images. We propose a novel approach that improves annotation accuracy by exploiting generic knowledge-based data, WordNet [16]. WordNet is a lexical reference system whose design is inspired by current psycholinguistic theories of human lexical memory. English nouns, verbs, adjectives and adverbs are organized into synonym sets, each representing one underlying lexical concept. WordNet 2.0 contains around 110,000 synsets; the noun group has 79,689 synsets. Each synset has a gloss that describes the concept and connects to another synset through explicit semantic relations. With the assistance of WordNet, we can quantify the semantic similarities between any two concepts.

Using semantic similarity, we can remove noisy concepts/descriptions for an image from annotated concepts generated by image annotation models and keep relevant concepts/descriptions at the same time. To do this, first we can find relevant concepts from annotated concepts in an image. Next, we will measure the similarity between these concepts. Finally, some concepts for which the total similarity measure with other concept falls below a certain threshold will be discarded. We will use the structure and content of WordNet for measuring the semantic similarity between two concepts. Current state-of-the-art approaches can be classified into three different categories: the node-based, distance-based, and gloss-based approach (see, for example, [17]). Based on these categories, various semantic similarities are defined, such as the Resnik measure (RIK), Leacock and Chodorow measure (LNC), Banerjee and Pedersen measure (BNP), and the LIN measure (LIN).

Besides applying WordNet after image annotation to remove noisy concepts, we can also embed WordNet into our image annotation framework. For example, in our current framework, correlations between keywords are estimated according to frequency of co-occurrence in the training dataset. It is not very accurate because of the bias of training dataset. We can apply WordNet to estimate correlations between semantic concepts (keywords). In addition, as we discussed before, most current image annotation models decide annotation keywords based on some parameter estimation such as $P(w|b)$ in TM. In many cases, for a given blob b, multiple keywords could have similar $P(w|b)$ and the keyword having the biggest $P(w|b)$ may not be the right one for the blob b because of lack of prior information. WordNet can be applied to break ambiguity. For example, for a given image, we are very sure word w_1 will appear in the annotation based on parameter estimation. However, we have low confidence about word w_2 and word w_3, and parameter estimation of w_2 is a little bit better than w_3. Normally, we will just pick w_2 and drop w_3. However, because parameter estimation is not totally accurate, w_3 could be the right one. We can apply WordNet to calculate semantic similarity between these keywords. If w_2 and w_3 have similar parameter estimations, we will pick the one having higher semantic similarity with w_1, because we are confident about w_1.

16.6.3 Domain Knowledge

Initially, we will provide domain-dependent knowledge to disambiguate blob tokens. For example, the blob tokens "window" and "building" are associated through the "part-of" relationship. When an image tentatively contains these two objects, we can easily disambiguate them from other possible objects based on this domain knowledge. Furthermore, we would like to propose a hybrid model in which domain knowledge initially will be given. Next, using spatial association rule mining, we will determine correlations among various blob tokens, and we will also refine domain knowledge if any inconsistency exists.

16.7 Summary and Directions

We studied different KNN classifiers and a modified EKNN algorithm. The modified algorithm (DEKNN) has the best performance based on classification accuracy. EKNN is second. Fuzzy KNN 1 is the worst compared to others. In addition, we tested our resampling approach by running KNN and distance weighted KNN with original ImageCLEFmed 2006 dataset and our resampled data. Results show that both algorithms generate better accuracy when we use resampled data. DEKNN solves the data imbalance problem in a better way. DEKNN improves the classification accuracy for both large classes and small class without increasing computational load.

In the future, we will generate a set of new features which are transition and rotation invariant. In addition, each feature is equally important in this chapter. We plan to apply our weighted feature selection algorithm to dynamically generate an optimal feature set. We believe that these enhancements will give improvements in medical image analysis.

References

1. Antonie, M., Zaiane, O.R., and Coman, A., Application of data mining techniques for medical image classification, in *Second International Workshop on Multimedia Data Mining (MDM/KDD)*, San Francisco, CA, 2001.
2. Brin, S., Near neighbor search in large metric spaces, *Proceedings of the 21st International Conference on Very Large Databases (VLDB-1995)*, Zurich Switzerland, Morgan Kaufmann, 1995, pp. 574–584.
3. Chapelle, O., Haffner, P., and Vapnik, V., SVMs for histogram-based image classification, *IEEE Transaction on Neural Networks*, 1999.
4. Chen, Y. and Wang, J.Z., Image categorization by learning and reasoning with regions, *Journal of Machine Learning Research*, 5, 913–939, 2004.
5. Denoeux, T., A k-nearest neighbor classification rule based on Dempster–Shafer theory, *IEEE Transaction on Systems, Man and Cybernetics*, 25, 804–813, 1995.

6. Hu, G., Bu, J., and Chen, C., Semantic image classification based on Bayesian framework and one-step relevance feedback, *IEEE International Conference on Systems, Man and Cybernetics*, Vol. 1, 268–273, 2003.
7. Dudani, S.A., The distance-weighted k nearest neighbor rule, *IEEE Transaction on Systems, Man and Cybernetics*, Vol. 6, 325–327, 1976.
8. Keller J.M., Gray, M.R., and Givens, J.A., A fuzzy k-nearest neighbor algorithm, *IEEE Transaction on Systems, Man and Cybernetics*, Vol. 15, No. 4, 580–585, 1985.
9. Denoeux, T., A k-nearest neighbor classification rule based on Dempster–Shafer theory, *IEEE Transaction on Systems, Man and Cybernetics*, Vol. 25, 804–813, 1995.
10. Wang, H. and Bell, D., Extended k-nearest neighbors based on evidence theory, *Computer Journal*, Vol. 47, No. 6, 662–672, 2004.
11. http://phobos.imib.rwth-aachen.de
12. http://www.cs.arizona.edu/people/kobus/research/data/eccv_2002
13. Agrawal, R. and Srikant, R., Fast algorithms for mining association rules in large databases, *VLDB*, 487–499, 1994.
14. Teredesai A.M., Ahmad, M.A., Kanodia, J., and Gaborski, R.S., CoMMA: A framework for integrated multimedia mining using multi-relational associations, *Journal of Knowledge and Information Systems (KAIS)*, November 2005.
15. Khan, L., McLeod, D., and Hovy, E., Retrieval Effectiveness of Ontology-based Model for Information Selection, *The VLDB Journal: The International Journal on Very Large Databases*, ACM/Springer-Publishing, Vol. 13(1): pp. 71–85, 2004.
16. Miller, G., WordNet: A lexical database for English, *Communications of the ACM*, Vol. 38, No. 11, November 1995.
17. Leacock, C. and Chodorow, M., Combining local context and WordNet similarity for word sense identification, in Fellbaum, C., Ed., *WordNet: An Electronic Lexical Database*, MIT Press, Cambridge, MA, 1998, pp. 265–283.

Chapter 17

Summary and Directions

17.1 Overview

This chapter brings us to the close of our survey of data mining tools. We discussed several aspects, including supporting technologies for data mining, data mining applications, and a detailed discussion of the tools we have developed. The applications we discussed were intrusion detection, Web page surfing prediction, and image classification. This chapter provides a summary of the book and gives directions for trustworthy semantic Webs.

The organization of this chapter is as follows. In Section 17.2, we give a summary of this book. We have taken the summaries from each chapter and formed a summary of this book. In Section 17.3, we discuss directions for trustworthy semantic Webs. In Section 17.4, we give suggestions as to where to go from here.

17.2 Summary of This Book

We summarize the contents of each chapter essentially taken from the summary and directions section of each chapter. Chapter 1 provided an introduction to the book. We first provided a brief overview of data mining techniques and applications and discussed various topics addressed in this book, including the data mining tools we have developed. Our framework is a three-layer framework, and each layer was addressed in one part of this book. This framework was illustrated in Chapter 1, Figure 1.10. We replicate this framework in Figure 17.1.

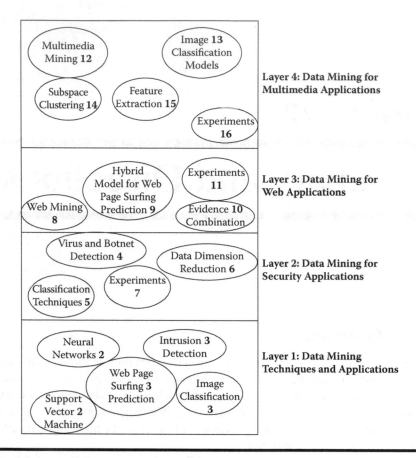

Figure 17.1 Components addressed in this book.

The book is divided into four parts. Part I, consisting of two chapters, Chapters 2 and 3, was on data mining techniques and applications relevant to the book. In Chapter 2, we first provided an overview of the various data mining tasks and techniques and then discussed some of the techniques that we will be discussing in this book. These include neural networks, support vector machines (SVMs), and association rule mining (ARM). In Chapter 3, we discussed three applications that we considered in this book. We have developed data mining tools for these three applications. They are intrusion detection, Web page prediction, and image classification. They are part of the broader class of applications: cyber security, Web information management, and multimedia or image information management, respectively.

Part II, consisting of four chapters, Chapters 4, 5, 6, and 7, described our tool for intrusion detection. Chapter 4 discussed data mining for security applications. We first started with a discussion of data mining for cyber security applications and then provided a brief overview of the tools we are developing. In Chapter 5, we described a particular technique called DGSOT that combined with SVM has significantly reduced training time, false positives, and false negatives. In Chapter 6, we discussed data reduction to enhance the data mining algorithms. We also described Rocchio bundling techniques that we have compared with our DGSOT algorithm. We combined this technique with SVM to enhance the training time of SVM. In Chapter 7, we described the dataset used and presented our experimental results. We have observed that SVM together with DGSOT outperformed the other approaches on average in terms of training time, false positives, false negatives, and accuracy. We used the same environment to test all the algorithms. It should be noted that our dataset is the MIT Lincoln dataset, which was obtained in 1998.

Part III, consisting of four chapters, Chapters 8, 9, 10, and 11, described the Web page surfing prediction tool that we developed. Chapter 8 provided a broad overview of Web data management and mining. In particular, we discussed digital libraries, including Web data management and search engine technologies, E-commerce technologies, semantic Web technologies, and aspects of Web data mining. As we have stated, Web data mining includes mining the databases on the Web, Web usage mining, and Web structure mining. Our Web page prediction tools are an example Web data mining tool. Chapter 9 described our tool for Web page surfing prediction. We use feature extraction and classification as our data mining technique. We also use domain knowledge to make the technique more efficient. Chapter 10 described how results from multiple classifiers can be combined for Web page prediction. Our approach is first to extract features of Web page surfing patterns and then train classifiers such as SVM, ANN, and the Markov models. We apply Sigmoid fitting to SVM and ANN outputs so that they can be in the appropriate format. We then combine the outputs from SVM + Sigmoid, ANN + Sigmoid, and the Markov model by applying the Dempster–Shafer theory of evidence. The combined result is significantly improved over the application of individual classifiers. In Chapter 11, we provided our results for Web page prediction. As mentioned in earlier chapters, we extract features of Web serving patterns and train various classifiers. We combine the results of the classifiers to produce the final result. We believe that combining multiple classifiers is better than using one classifier.

Part IV, consisting of five chapters, Chapters 12, 13, 14, 15, and 16, described the image classification tool that we developed. Chapter 12 provided an overview of approaches to managing and mining multimedia data. First, we discussed issues pertaining to handling multimedia data, and then we focused on initial data types such as text, images, audio, and video. The idea is to extract concepts from unstructured data and then mine them. Chapter 13 described various image classification models we have utilized in developing our image mining tool. In Chapter 14, we described a tool that we have developed which annotates the images. We also described the experimental results we have obtained and compared them with other approaches. In Chapter 15, we addressed the image annotation problem using enhanced feature weighting algorithms. We proposed aggressive and chi-square-based feature weighting mechanisms. In Chapter 16, we studied different KNN classifiers and modified EKNN algorithm and compared the performance results of these algorithms.

Chapter 17, which is this chapter, provides a summary of the book. In addition, Appendix A provides an overview of data management and discusses the relationships among the books we have written.

17.3   Directions for Data Mining Tools

There are many directions for data mining. We focus on directions for data mining applications in security, Web, and multimedia. Figure 17.2 illustrates the directions. In the following text we elaborate on the areas that need further work.

Data mining for security applications. Data mining has many applications in both national and cyber security. Our focus in this book is on cyber security. We need tools for various aspects, including intrusion detection, virus detection, and botnet detection. We also need to develop techniques for intrusion prevention. Finally, we need better tools that will improve accuracy and reduce the false positives and negatives.

Data mining for Web applications. Web mining includes Web data mining usage mining and structure mining. Web data mining essentially mines the data on the Web. We have focused on Web usage mining. We need better tools to predict Web page surfing patterns that will increase accuracy and reduce false negatives and positives. We also need tools for mining Web usage so that advice can be given to customers. Finally, Web structure mining needs a lot more work so that we can determine how the Web pages are organized.

Data Mining Techniques:

Enhanced versions of existing techniques, New techniques, Reduce false positives and Negatives, Improve accuracy, Reason under uncertainty

Security Applications	Web Applications	Multimedia Applications
Novel models and techniques for intrusion detection, botnet detection, worm detection, Firewall policy rule analysis. Also data mining techniques for National security and Bio security applications	New models and techniques for Web data mining, Web usage mining and Web structure Mining, Improved customer Relationship on the web, Better search engines, Semantic web mining	New models and techniques for Mining text, image, audio and video data, Mining combinations of data types, Detecting anomalies, Surveillance, Making correlations across documents

Figure 17.2   Directions for data mining tools.

Data mining for multimedia applications. We need better techniques for managing large multimedia databases and data mining tools to extract concepts from multimedia data (such as text, video, audio, and image) and mine the concepts and extract the nuggets. We also need to determine the most appropriate data mining outcome for particular applications. For example, do we classify images or do we detect anomalies in the images? With respect to text, do we associate words in the text or do we classify the documents? Furthermore, we need effective techniques for each outcome. We also need to focus on approaches to improve accuracy and reduce false positives and false negatives.

The directions relevant to Chapters 2 through 16 will be discussed in the following text:

Chapter 2: Data mining techniques. One of the major challenges today is to determine the appropriate techniques for various applications. We still need more benchmarks and performance studies. In addition, the techniques should result in fewer false positives and false negatives.

Chapter 3: Data mining applications. We need to expand on applying data mining for the broader classes of applications such as cyber security, multimedia information management, and Web information management.

Chapter 4: Data mining for security applications. We need better tools for different kinds of security applications, including tension detection and virus detection. We also need to focus on intrusion prevention.

Chapter 5: DGOST algorithms. As we make progress with data mining and understand the nature of the attacks, we need to incorporate more knowledge into the tools to reduce the false positives and false negatives and improve accuracy.

Chapter 6: Data reduction using hierarchical clustering and Rocchio bundling. We need efficient data reaction techniques so that the dimensions can be reduced without losing valuable information.

Chapter 7: Intrusion detection results. We need to determine which combinations of approaches would be good for a particular data mining problem.

Chapter 8: Web data management and mining. We need better tools for Web log, usage, and Web structure mining.

Chapter 9: Effective Web page prediction using hybrid model. We need to analyze the content of the Web pages and take this into consideration when giving advice to users. This means the Web pages that will be useful to a user will not only depend on his or her surfing patterns but also will depend on the content of the Web pages browsed.

Chapter 10: Multiple evidence combination for WWW prediction. Future work will include examining other classification techniques, including decision trees and nearest-neighbor algorithms.

Chapter 11: WWW prediction results. We need to conduct more experiments using other classifiers and different combinations of classifiers. We also need to test with multiple datasets.

Chapter 12: Multimedia data management and mining. There are many challenges in managing and mining multimedia data. Much of the work has focused on developing data modes for multimedia data. We need techniques to manage large multimedia databases. These include techniques for access methods and indexing. We also need techniques to extract concepts from the unstructured data.

Chapter 13: Image classification models. There are numerous challenges on mining image and geospatial data. First of all, we need appropriate feature extraction techniques. These techniques have to "understand" images and extract features. Next, we need appropriate classification models that will provide better accuracy and reduce false positives and false negatives. We need to develop ways to combine multiple models so that we can develop the most appropriate model for particular images.

Chapter 14: Subspace clustering and automatic image annotation. We need to examine different models based on different techniques. For example, what is the best approach to extract the blobs (binary large objects) from the images? What are the more appropriate approaches to correlate the blobs with the tokens?

Chapter 15: Enhanced weighted feature selection. We need to extend our work in the following directions. First, we need to study the impact of weighted feature selection on the continuous relevance model (CRM). Second, we need to extend this work to the video domain.

Chapter 16: Image classification and performance analysis. We need to generate a set of new features that are transition and rotation invariant. In addition, each feature is equally important in this chapter. We also need to apply our weighted feature selection algorithm to dynamically generate the optimal feature set.

17.4 Where Do We Go from Here?

This book has discussed a great deal about data mining tools. We have described many challenges in this field in Section 17.3. We need to continue with research and development efforts if we are to make progress in this very important area.

The question is where do we go from here? First of all, those who wish to work in this area must have a good knowledge of the supporting technologies, including data management, statistical remaining, and machine learning. In addition, knowledge of the application areas, such as severity, multimedia, and Web information management, is also needed. Next, because the field is expanding rapidly and there are many rapid developments, the reader has to keep up with them, including reading about the commercial products. Finally, we encourage the reader to experiment with the products and also develop security tools. This is the best way to become familiar with a particular field; that is, work on hands-on problems and provide solutions to get a better understanding.

We need research and development support from the government funding agencies. We also need commercial corporations to invest research and development dollars so that progress can be made in industrial research and applied to development of commercial products. We also need to collaborate with the international research community to solve problems and develop useful tools.

Conclusion to Part IV

In Part IV, we have described our tool for image classification. In particular, we discussed image classification models, our tool for automatic image annotation, and our approach to image classification. Our work has relied heavily on techniques such as SVM, KNN, and a combination of multiple techniques.

Although we have focused mainly on image classification, our work on multimedia mining is proceeding in many directions. We are conducting text mining on fault reports so that analysts can determine where fault has occurred in aircraft or spacecraft. We are conducting image mining to detect unusual patterns. We are working on geospatial data mining to form concepts. Finally, we are conducting video mining to detect suspicious behavior of individuals. We believe that although much progress has been made on image mining and multimedia data mining, there is much to be done to reduce false positives and false negatives and provide better accuracy of the results.

APPENDIX A

Data Management Systems: Developments and Trends

A.1 Overview

In this appendix, we provide an overview of the developments and trends in data management as discussed in our previous book, *Data Management Systems Evolution and Interoperation* [1]. Because database systems are an aspect of data management, and database security is an aspect of database systems, we need a good understanding of data management issues for data and application security.

As stated in Chapter 1, recent developments in information system technologies have resulted in computerizing many applications in various business areas. Data has become a critical resource in many organizations and, therefore, efficient access to data, sharing the data, extracting information from the data, and making use of the information have become urgent needs. As a result, there have been several efforts aimed at integrating the various data sources scattered across several sites. These data sources may be databases managed by database management systems, or they could simply be files. To provide the interoperability between the multiple data sources and systems, various tools are being developed. These tools enable users of one system to access other systems in an efficient and transparent manner.

We define data management systems to be systems that manage the data, extract meaningful information from the data, and make use of the information extracted. Therefore, data management systems include database systems, data warehouses, and data mining systems. The data could be structured data such as that found in relational databases, or it could be unstructured such as text, voice, imagery, and video. There have been numerous attempts in the past to distinguish between data, information, and knowledge. We do not attempt to clarify these terms. For our purposes, data could be just bits and bytes, or it could convey some meaningful information to the user. We will, however, distinguish between database systems and database management systems. A database management system is that

227

component which manages the database containing persistent data. A database system consists of both the database and the database management system.

A key component of the evolution and interoperation of data management systems is the interoperability of heterogeneous database systems. Efforts on the interoperability between database systems have been reported since the late 1970s. However, it is only recently that we are seeing commercial developments in heterogeneous database systems. Major database system vendors are now providing interoperability between their products and other systems. Furthermore, many of the database system vendors are migrating toward an architecture called the *client-server architecture*, which facilitates distributed data management capabilities. In addition to efforts on the interoperability between different database systems and client-server environments, work is also directed toward handling autonomous and federated environments.

The organization of this appendix is as follows. Because database systems are a key component of data management systems, we first provide an overview of the developments in database systems. These developments are discussed in Section A.2. Then we provide a vision for data management systems in Section A.3. Our framework for data management systems is discussed in Section A.4. Note that data mining, warehousing, and Web data management are components of this framework. Building information systems from our framework with special instantiations is discussed in Section A.5. The relationship between the various texts that we have written (or are writing) for CRC Press is discussed in Section A.6. This appendix is summarized in Section A.7. References are given in Section A.8.

A.2 Developments in Database Systems

Figure A.1 provides an overview of the developments in database systems technology. Although the early work in the 1960s focused on developing products based on the network and hierarchical data models, much of the developments in database systems took place after the seminal paper by Codd describing the relational model [2] (see also [3]). Research and development work on relational database systems was carried out during the early 1970s, and several prototypes were developed throughout the 1970s. Notable efforts include IBM's (International Business Machine Corporation) System R and University of California at Berkeley's INGRES. During the 1980s, many relational database system products were being marketed (notable among these products are those of Oracle Corporation, Sybase, Inc., Informix Corporation, INGRES Corporation, IBM, Digital Equipment Corporation, and Hewlett-Packard). During the 1990s, products from other vendors have emerged (e.g., Microsoft). In fact, to date, numerous relational database system products have been marketed. However, Codd has stated that many of the systems that are being marketed as relational systems are not really relational

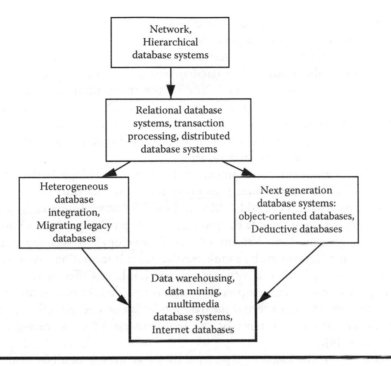

Figure A.1   Developments in database systems technology.

(see, for example, the discussion in [3]). He then discussed various criteria that a system must satisfy to be qualified as a relational database system. Although the early work focused on issues such as data model, normalization theory, query processing and optimization strategies, query languages, and access strategies and indexes, later the focus shifted toward supporting a multiuser environment. In particular, concurrency control and recovery techniques were developed. Support for transaction processing was also provided.

Research on relational database systems and transaction management was followed by research on distributed database systems around the mid-1970s. Several distributed database system prototype development efforts also began around the late 1970s. Notable among these efforts include IBM's System R*, DDTS (Distributed Database Testbed System) by Honeywell, Inc., SDD-I and multibase by CCA (Computer Corporation of America), and Mermaid by SDC (System Development Corporation). Furthermore, many of these systems (e.g., DDTS, Multibase, Mermaid) function in a heterogeneous environment. During the early 1990s, several database system vendors (such as Oracle Corporation, Sybase, Inc., Informix Corporation) provided data distribution capabilities for their systems. Most of the distributed relational database system products are based on client-server architectures. The idea is to have the client of vendor

A communicate with the server database system of vendor B. In other words, the client-server computing paradigm facilitates a heterogeneous computing environment. Interoperability between relational and nonrelational commercial database systems is also possible. The database systems community is also involved in standardization efforts. Notable among the standardization efforts are the ANSI/SPARC 3-level schema architecture, the IRDS (Information Resource Dictionary System) standard for Data Dictionary Systems, the relational query language SQL (Structured Query Language), and the RDA (Remote Database Access) protocol for remote database access.

Another significant development in database technology is the advent of object-oriented database management systems. Active work on developing such systems began in the mid-1980s, and they are now commercially available (notable among them include the products of Object Design, Inc., Ontos, Inc., Gemstone Systems, Inc., Versant Object Technology). It was felt that new-generation applications such as multimedia, office information systems, CAD/CAM, process control, and software engineering have different requirements. Such applications utilize complex data structures. Tighter integration between the programming language and the data model is also desired. Object-oriented database systems satisfy most of the requirements of these new-generation applications [4].

According to the Lagunita report published as a result of a National Science Foundation (NSF) workshop in 1990 (see [5] and [6]), relational database systems, transaction processing, and distributed (relational) database systems are stated to be mature technologies. Furthermore, vendors are marketing object-oriented database systems and demonstrating the interoperability between different database systems. The report goes on to make the point that as applications are getting increasingly complex, more sophisticated database systems are needed. Furthermore, because many organizations now use database systems, in many cases of different types, the database systems need to be integrated. Although work has begun to address these issues and commercial products are available, several issues still need to be resolved. Therefore, challenges faced by the database systems researchers in the early 1990s were in two areas. One was next-generation database systems, and the other was heterogeneous database systems.

Next-generation database systems include object-oriented database systems, functional database systems, special parallel architectures to enhance the performance of database system functions, high-performance database systems, real-time database systems, scientific database systems, temporal database systems, database systems that handle incomplete and uncertain information, and intelligent database systems (also sometimes called *logic* or *deductive database systems*). Ideally, a database system should provide the support for high-performance transaction processing, model complex applications, represent new kinds of data, and make intelligent deductions. Although significant progress has been made during the late

1980s and early 1990s, there is much to be done before such a database system can be developed.

Heterogeneous database systems have been receiving considerable attention during the past decade [7]. The major issues include handling different data models, different query processing strategies, different transaction processing algorithms, and different query languages. Should a uniform view be provided to the entire system or should the users of the individual systems maintain their own views of the entire system? These are questions that have yet to be answered satisfactorily. It is also envisaged that a complete solution to heterogeneous database management systems is a generation away. Although research should be directed toward finding such a solution, work should also be carried out to handle limited forms of heterogeneity to satisfy the customer needs. Another type of database system that has received some attention lately is a federated database system. Note that some have used the terms *heterogeneous database system* and *federated database system* interchangeably. Although heterogeneous database systems can be part of a federation, a federation can also include homogeneous database systems.

The explosion of users on the Web and developments in interface technologies have resulted in even more challenges for data management researchers. A second workshop was sponsored by NSF in 1995, and several emerging technologies have been identified to be important as we go into the 21st century [8]. These include digital libraries, managing very large databases, data administration issues, multimedia databases, data warehousing, data mining, data management for collaborative computing environments, and security and privacy. Another significant development in the 1990s was the development of object-relational systems. Such systems combine the advantages of both object-oriented database systems and relational database systems. Also, many corporations are now focusing on integrating their data management products with Web technologies. Finally, for many organizations, there is an increasing need to migrate some of the legacy databases and applications to newer architectures and systems such as client-server architectures and relational database systems. We believe that there is no end to data management systems. As new technologies are developed, there are new opportunities for data management research and development.

A comprehensive view of all data management technologies is illustrated in Figure A.2. As shown, traditional technologies include database design, transaction processing, and benchmarking. Then there are database systems based on data models such as relational and object-oriented. Database systems may depend on features they provide such as security and real-time. These database systems may be relational or object-oriented. There are also database systems based on multiple sites or processors such as distributed and heterogeneous database systems, parallel systems, and systems being migrated. Finally, there are the emerging technologies

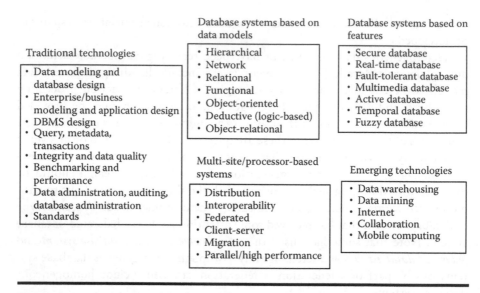

Figure A.2 Comprehensive view of data management systems.

such as data warehousing and mining, collaboration, and the Web. Any comprehensive text on data management systems should address all of these technologies. We have selected some of the relevant technologies and put them in a framework. This framework is described in Section A.5.

A.3 Status, Vision, and Issues

Significant progress has been made on data management systems. However, many of the technologies are still stand-alone technologies, as illustrated in Figure A.3. For example, multimedia systems are yet to be successfully integrated with warehousing and mining technologies. The ultimate goal is to integrate multiple technologies so that accurate data and information are produced at the right time and distributed to the user in a timely manner. Our vision for data and information management is illustrated in Figure A.4.

The work discussed in [1] addressed many of the challenges necessary to accomplish this vision. In particular, integration of heterogeneous databases, as well as the use of distributed object technology for interoperability, was discussed. Although much progress has been made on the system aspects of interoperability, semantic issues still remain a challenge. Different databases have different representations. Furthermore, the same data entity may be interpreted differently at different sites. Addressing these semantic differences and extracting useful information from the heterogeneous and possibly multimedia data sources are major challenges. This book has attempted to address some of the challenges through the use of data mining.

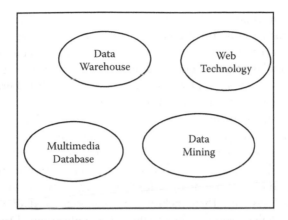

Figure A.3   Stand-alone systems.

A.4   Data Management Systems Framework

For the successful development of evolvable interoperable data management systems, heterogeneous database systems integration is a major component. However, there are other technologies that have to be successfully integrated with one another to develop techniques for efficient access and sharing of data as well as for the extraction of information from the data. To facilitate the development of data management systems to meet the requirements of various applications in fields such as medical, financial, manufacturing, and military, we have proposed a framework, which can be regarded as a reference model, for data management systems. Various components from this framework have to be integrated to develop data management systems to support the various applications.

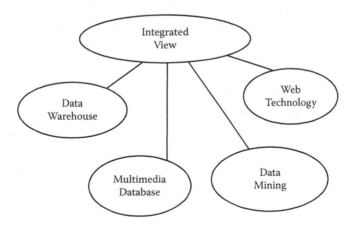

Figure A.4   Vision.

Figure A.5 illustrates our framework, which can be regarded as a model, for data management systems. This framework consists of three layers. One can think of the component technologies, which we will also refer to as components, belonging to a particular layer to be more or less built upon the technologies provided by the lower layer. Layer I is the Database Technology and Distribution Layer. This layer consists of database systems and distributed database systems technologies. Layer II is the Interoperability and Migration Layer. This layer consists of technologies such as heterogeneous database integration, client-server databases, and multimedia database systems to handle heterogeneous data types, and migrating legacy databases. Layer III is the Information Extraction and Sharing Layer. This layer essentially consists of technologies for some of the newer services supported by data management systems. These include data warehousing, data mining [9], Web databases, and database support for collaborative applications. Data management

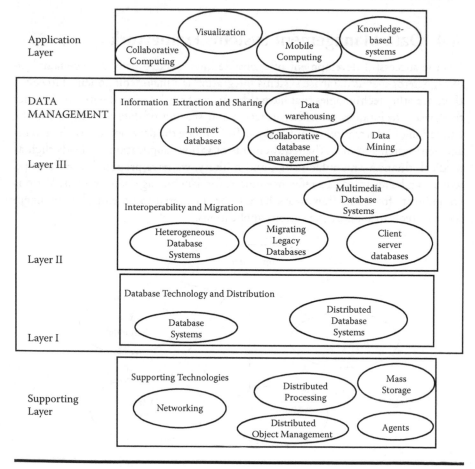

Figure A.5   Data management systems framework.

systems may utilize lower-level technologies such as networking, distributed processing, and mass storage. We have grouped these technologies into a layer called the *Supporting Technologies Layer*. This supporting layer does not belong to the data management systems framework. This supporting layer also consists of some higher-level technologies such as distributed object management and agents. Also shown in Figure A.5 is the Application Technologies Layer. Systems such as collaborative computing systems and knowledge-based systems, which belong to the Application Technologies Layer, may utilize data management systems. Note that the Application Technologies Layer is also outside of the data management systems framework.

The technologies that constitute the data management systems framework can be regarded as some of the core technologies in data management. However, features such as security, integrity, real-time processing, fault tolerance, and high-performance computing are needed for many applications utilizing data management technologies. Applications utilizing data management technologies may be medical, financial, or military, among others. We illustrate this in Figure A.6, where a three-dimensional view relating data management technologies with features and applications is given. For example, one could develop a secure distributed database management system for medical applications or a fault-tolerant multimedia database management system for financial applications.

Integrating the components belonging to the various layers is important to developing efficient data management systems. In addition, data management technologies have to be integrated with the application technologies to develop successful information systems. However, at present, there is limited integration between these various components. Our previous book *Data Management Systems Evolution and*

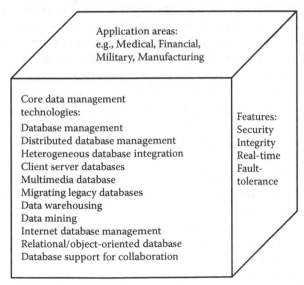

Figure A.6   A three-dimensional view of data management.

Interoperation focused mainly on the concepts, developments, and trends belonging to each of the components shown in the framework. Furthermore, our current book on Web data management, which we also refer to as Web data management, focuses on the Web database component of Layer 3 of the framework of Figure A.5.

Note that security cuts across all the layers. Security is needed for the supporting layers such as agents and distributed systems. Security is needed for all of the layers in the framework, including database security, distributed database security, warehousing security, Web database security, and collaborative data management security. This is the topic of this book. That is, we have covered all aspects of data and applications security, including database security and information management security.

A.5 Building Information Systems from the Framework

Figure A.5 illustrated a framework for data management systems. As shown in that figure, the technologies for data management include database systems, distributed database systems, heterogeneous database systems, migrating legacy databases, multimedia database systems, data warehousing, data mining, Web databases, and database support for collaboration. Furthermore, data management systems take advantage of supporting technologies such as distributed processing and agents. Similarly, application technologies such as collaborative computing, visualization, expert systems, and mobile computing take advantage of data management systems.

Many of us have heard of the term *information systems* on numerous occasions. These systems have sometimes been used interchangeably with data management systems. In our terminology, information systems are much broader in scope than data management systems, but they do include data management systems. In fact, a framework for information systems will include not only the data management system layers but also the supporting technologies layer and the application technologies layer. That is, information systems encompass all kinds of computing systems. It can be regarded as the finished product that can be used for various applications. That is, although hardware is at the lowest end of the spectrum, applications are at the highest end.

We can combine the technologies of Figure A.5 to put together information systems. For example, at the application technology level, one may need collaboration and visualization technologies so that analysts can collaboratively carry out some tasks. At the data management level, one may need both multimedia and distributed database technologies. At the supporting level, one may need mass storage and some distributed processing capability. This special framework is illustrated in Figure A.7. Another example is a special framework for interoperability. One may need some visualization technology to display the integrated information from the heterogeneous databases. At the data management level, we have heterogeneous database systems technology. At the supporting technology level, one may use distributed object management technology to encapsulate the heterogeneous databases. This special framework is illustrated in Figure A.8.

```
┌─────────────────────────┐
│      Collaboration,      │
│      Visualization       │
│                          │
└─────────────────────────┘

┌─────────────────────────┐
│   Multimedia database,   │
│   Distributed database   │
│         systems          │
└─────────────────────────┘

┌─────────────────────────┐
│      Mass storage,       │
│       Distributed        │
│        processing        │
└─────────────────────────┘
```

Figure A.7   Framework for multimedia data management for collaboration.

Finally, let us illustrate the concepts that we have described earlier by using a specific example. Suppose a group of physicians/surgeons want a system in which they can collaborate and make decisions about various patients. This could be a medical video teleconferencing application. That is, at the highest level, the application is a medical application and, more specifically, a medical video teleconferencing application. At the application technology level, one needs a variety of technologies, including collaboration and teleconferencing. These application technologies will make use of data management technologies such as distributed database systems and multimedia database systems. That is, one may need to support multimedia data such as audio and video. The data management technologies in turn draw upon lower-level technologies such as distributed processing and networking. We illustrate this in Figure A.9.

```
┌─────────────────────────┐
│      Visualization       │
│                          │
└─────────────────────────┘

┌─────────────────────────┐
│      Heterogeneous       │
│        database          │
│       integration        │
└─────────────────────────┘

┌─────────────────────────┐
│   Distributed object     │
│      management          │
└─────────────────────────┘
```

Figure A.8   Framework for heterogeneous database interoperability.

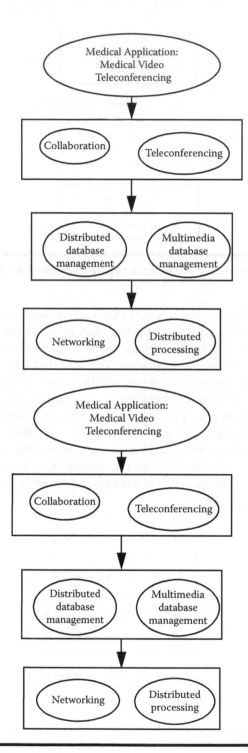

Figure A.9   Specific example.

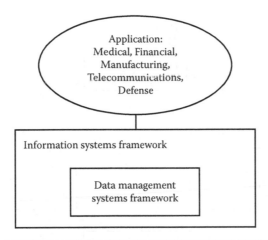

Figure A.10   Application–framework relationship.

In summary, information systems include data management systems and application-layer systems such as collaborative computing systems and supporting-layer systems such as distributed object management systems.

Although application technologies make use of data management technologies and data management technologies make use of supporting technologies, the ultimate user of the information system is the application itself. Today, numerous applications make use of information systems. These applications are from multiple domains such as medical, financial, manufacturing, telecommunications, and defense. Specific applications include signal processing, electronic commerce, patient monitoring, and situation assessment. Figure A.10 illustrates the relationship between the application and the information system.

A.6   Relationships among the Texts

We have published eight books on data management and mining. These books are *Data Management Systems Evolution and Interoperation* [1], *Data Mining: Technologies, Techniques, Tools and Trends* [9], *Web Data Management and Electronic Commerce* [10], *Managing and Mining Multimedia Databases* [11], *XML Databases and the Semantic Web* [12], *Web Data Mining Technologies and Their Applications in Business Intelligence and Counter-Terrorism* [13], *Database and Applications Security: Integrating Data Management and Information Security* [14], and *Building Trustworthy Semantic Webs* [15]. Our last book [15] has evolved from Chapter 25 of [14]. All of these books have evolved from the framework that we illustrated in this appendix and address different parts of the framework. The connection between these texts is illustrated in Figure A.11. Our current book

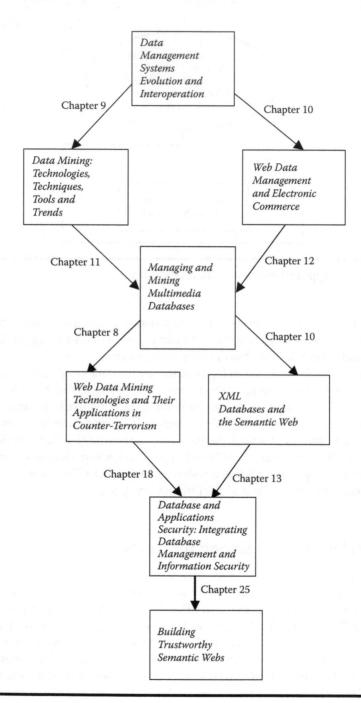

Figure A.11 Relationships between texts—Series I.

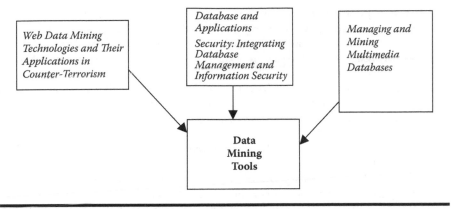

Figure A.12   Relationships between texts—Series II.

begins a new series and is illustrated in Figure A.12. This book has evolved from three of our books on multimedia data, Web data, and data security.

A.7   Summary and Directions

In this appendix, we have provided an overview of data management. We first discussed the developments in data management and then provided a vision for data management. Then we illustrated a framework for data management. This framework consists of three layers: database systems layer, interoperability layer, and information extraction layer. Web data management belongs to Layer 3. Finally, we showed how information systems could be built from the technologies of the framework.

We believe that data management is essential to many information technologies, including data mining, multimedia information processing, interoperability, and collaboration and knowledge management. This appendix stresses data management. Security is critical for all data management technologies.

References

1. Thuraisingham, B., *Data Management Systems Evolution and Interoperation*, CRC Press, Boca Raton, FL, 1997.
2. Codd, E.F., A relational model of data for large shared data banks, *Communications of the ACM*, Vol. 13, No. 6, June 1970.
3. Date, C.J., *An Introduction to Database Management Systems*, Addison-Wesley, Reading MA, 1990 (6th edition published in 1995 by Addison-Wesley).
4. Cattell, R., *Object Data Management Systems*, Addison-Wesley, Reading MA, 1991.

5. Proceedings of the Database Systems Workshop, Report published by the National Science Foundation, 1990 (also in ACM SIGMOD Record, December 1990).

6. Next Generation Database Systems, ACM SIGMOD Record, December 1990.

7. Special Issue on Heterogeneous Database Systems, *ACM Computing Surveys*, September 1990.

8. Proceedings of the Database Systems Workshop, Report published by the National Science Foundation, 1995 (also in ACM SIGMOD Record, March 1996).

9. Thuraisingham, B., *Data Mining: Technologies, Techniques, Tools and Trends*, CRC Press, Boca Raton, FL, 1998.

10. Thuraisingham, B., *Web Data Management and Electronic Commerce*, CRC Press, Boca Raton, FL, 2000.

11. Thuraisingham, B., *Managing and Mining Multimedia Databases for the Electronic Enterprise*, CRC Press, Boca Raton, FL, 2001.

12. Thuraisingham, B., *XML Databases and the Semantic Web*, CRC Press, Boca Raton, FL, 2002.

13. Thuraisingham, B., *Web Data Mining Technologies and Their Applications in Business Intelligence and Counter-Terrorism*, CRC Press, Boca Raton, FL, 2003.

14. Thuraisingham, B., *Database and Applications Security: Integrating Data Management and Information Security*, CRC Press, Boca Raton, FL, 2005.

15. Thuraisingham, B., *Building Trustworthy Semantic Webs*, CRC Press, Boca Raton, FL, 2007.

Index

243

Milton Keynes UK
Ingram Content Group UK Ltd.
UKHW040109071024
449327UK00019B/935